The Remaking of Republican Turkey

Between 1945 and 1960, the birth of a multi-party democracy and NATO membership radically transformed Turkey's foreign relations and domestic politics. As Turkish politicians, intellectuals and voters rethought their country's relationship with its past and its future to facilitate democratization, a new alliance with the United States was formed. In this book, Nicholas L. Danforth demonstrates how these transformations helped consolidate a consensus on the nature of Turkish modernity that continues to shape current political and cultural debates. He reveals the surprisingly nuanced and often paradoxical ways that both secular modernizers and their Islamist critics deployed Turkey's famous clichés about East and West, as well as tradition and modernity, to advance their agendas. By drawing on a diverse array of published and archival sources, Danforth offers a tour de force exploration of the relationship between democracy, diplomacy, modernity, Westernization, Ottoman historiography and religion in mid-century Turkey.

NICHOLAS L. DANFORTH has written widely about Turkey, US foreign policy, and the Middle East for publications including *The Atlantic, Foreign Affairs, Foreign Policy, The New York Times* and *The Washington Post*. He received his PhD in History from Georgetown University.

The Remaking of Republican Turkey

Memory and Modernity Since the Fall of the Ottoman Empire

NICHOLAS L. DANFORTH

CAMBRIDGE
UNIVERSITY PRESS

CAMBRIDGE
UNIVERSITY PRESS

University Printing House, Cambridge CB2 8BS, United Kingdom

One Liberty Plaza, 20th Floor, New York, NY 10006, USA

477 Williamstown Road, Port Melbourne, VIC 3207, Australia

314–321, 3rd Floor, Plot 3, Splendor Forum, Jasola District Centre, New Delhi – 110025, India

79 Anson Road, #06–04/06, Singapore 079906

Cambridge University Press is part of the University of Cambridge.

It furthers the University's mission by disseminating knowledge in the pursuit of education, learning, and research at the highest international levels of excellence.

www.cambridge.org
Information on this title: www.cambridge.org/9781108833240
DOI: 10.1017/9781108973779

© Nicholas Danforth 2021

First published 2021

A catalogue record for this publication is available from the British Library.

ISBN 978-1-108-83324-0 Hardback

Cambridge University Press has no responsibility for the persistence or accuracy of URLs for external or third-party internet websites referred to in this publication and does not guarantee that any content on such websites is, or will remain, accurate or appropriate.

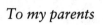

To my parents

Contents

Figures

Acknowledgments

It is a pleasure to acknowledge my deep gratitude to so many people who made writing this book not only possible but even, at moments, enjoyable: Aviel Roshwald and Mustafa Aksakal, who advised my research from the outset; David Painter and Nathan Citino, who offered further insight; Maria Marsh, who guided this work to completion as editor; Howard Eissenstat, Nora Fisher-Onar, Ryan Gingeras, Selim Koru, Daphne McCurdy, and Behlül Özkan, who took the time to comment so thoughtfully on my manuscript; an army of librarians, archivists, and secondhand booksellers, who kept so many sources alive through their efforts; the copy editors, who made me appear literate; Alan Makovsky and Amberin Zaman, who were consistently encouraging; Soha Sarkis, Graham Cornwell, Elçin Arabacı, James Ryan, Zachary Foster, Onur İşçi, Lale Can, Sam Dolbee, and the rest of my cohort at Georgetown, who all helped make graduate school that much better; Sarah-Neel Smith, who shared her enthusiasm for Ecevit as well as his archives; Joe and Laura Clinton, who fed and hosted me during my research; Sarah Dadouch, who asked to be acknowledged; Eric Gettig, Graham Pitts, and Daniel Singer, who were good friends throughout the process; Chris Gratien, who had his moments; Irina Levin, who survived the writing firsthand; Chris Trapani, who was always game to celebrate Fetih Günü; Merve Tahiroğlu, who is more excited about this book than I am; anyone else, who I might have forgotten; my sister Ann, who makes everything more entertaining; and of course my parents, who gave me my interest in the world.

Introduction

Turkey held its first democratic elections in 1950 and joined the North Atlantic Treaty Organization (NATO) in 1952. These dramatic domestic and international developments facilitated an equally dramatic reinterpretation of the country's imagined past and its anticipated future. Under the influence of electoral politics and Cold War competition, Turkish politicians, intellectuals, and voters articulated a distinct vision of mid-century modernity, at once aspirationally liberal, proudly nationalistic, rationally pious, and appropriately prosperous. They optimistically asserted, with the enthusiastic agreement of many foreign observers, that Turkey was on the verge of transcending its notorious clichés by finally reconciling religion and secularism, tradition and modernity, and, of course, East and West.

In exploring Turkey's transformation between 1945 and 1960, I argue that present-day thinkers intent on transcending these same purported binaries have misunderstood what was so unique about the country's mid-century politics. Moreover, recognizing the ease with which authors in this era reworked narratives about history and modernity in order to advance their rival agendas reveals the profound malleability of such narratives, and should make modern scholars more aware of how we politicize them in our own work today.

During the 1950s, Turkey's first democratically elected prime minister, Adnan Menderes, became perhaps the only twentieth-century leader to have both camels sacrificed in his honor and an affair with an opera singer. For critics, each was problematic. For some admirers, it was all part of a thoroughly modern persona. In these years, Turkish politicians sent troops to Korea to defend the liberal ideals of the Ottoman sultans and encouraged Arab leaders to emulate Atatürk's anti-imperial struggle. As future Prime Minister Bülent Ecevit told an American audience, "Turks are more conscious and prouder than ever

1

of their Asiatic heritage, now that they find themselves regarded as a European as well as an Asiatic nation."[1]

At the start of the Cold War, Turkish and American commentators shared a belief that Turkey had successfully progressed from the authoritarian modernization of Mustafa Kemal Atatürk to a superior form of democratic modernity. The country, they believed, had advanced to the point where pluralistic politics would replace one-party rule and the emergence of a more modern form of Islam would make heavy-handed secularism unnecessary. It was a time when even Bernard Lewis was cautiously optimistic about the resurgence of religious piety: "[T]he Turkish people," he declared "may yet find a workable compromise between Islam and modernism that will enable them, without conflict, to follow both their fathers' path to freedom and progress and their grandfathers' path to God."[2]

Current scholarship has often presented contemporary Turkish political debates as the continuation of those in the late Ottoman and early Republican eras. Where once scholars were inclined to see Republican history as the gradual realization of Atatürk's vision, recent work has instead described a mounting popular reaction against it. In this new narrative, the 1950s often appear as little more than an initial step toward the triumph of popular Islamism, as embodied today by the Justice and Development Party (AKP). Approaching mid-century Turkey on its own terms reveals a more complex story. The Democratic Party (DP) was both a realization and repudiation of Kemalist reforms, as well as something else entirely. Turkey's imperfect but very real democratization between 1945 and 1960 also facilitated a partial reassessment of the sweeping cultural changes the country experienced during the previous decades. In this context, some proposed reforms such as the Turkish language call to prayer were quietly abandoned, while others, such as the widespread translation of the Quran into Turkish, achieved unexpected success. Appreciating the specificity of mid-century cultural politics helps us understand how they shaped – and failed to shape – contemporary views on subjects as diverse as geography, art, sexuality, Ottoman history, urban planning, foreign policy, and Islamic piety.

---

[1] Draft speech for the Washington International Center, Personal Papers of Bülent and Rahşan Ecevit, Bülent Ecevit Bilim Kültür ve Sanat Vakfı.

[2] Bernard Lewis, "Islamic Revival in Turkey," *International Affairs* Vol. 28, No. 1 (January 1952), 48.

The early Cold War era also saw a surge of optimism about Turkey's ability to transcend its long-running identity debates. Rather than describe Turkey as torn between East and West or between tradition and modernity, mid-century politicians, artists, and intellectuals capitalized on a rich history of seizing the middle ground. Believing that the West had already abandoned positivist ideas of modernity as crude and outdated, figures from across the ideological spectrum proclaimed their unique ability to harmonize rival elements of Turkish identity. Through popular history magazines, diplomatic visits, architectural renovations, and religious travelogues, they sought to reconcile Turkey's contradictions in order to achieve some form of authentic civilizational synthesis. In claiming that Turkey could only be fully Western by becoming more Eastern or fully modern by embracing its traditions, individuals regularly used their rivals as foils, accusing them of being either reactionaries or blindly aping the West. These thinkers also made complex use of the United States as a model, identifying diverse aspects of America's political, economic, and cultural development that could justify their conflicting visions for Turkey. The intensity of their efforts was particular to the 1950s, but their rhetorical desire to privilege the often-paradoxical middle ground has proved enduring.

The debates of this period should make us more aware of how, throughout the twentieth century, Kemalist ideologues, American high-modernists, and Islamist reactionaries alike – the very people, that is, who supposedly embraced civilizational binaries – all claimed that Turkey's true destiny lay in overcoming them. Becoming modern, many insisted, meant rejecting oriental backwardness and hyper-Westernization alike. If we do not appreciate the caveats, contradictions, and criticism of the West that accompanied twentieth-century Westernization campaigns, we risk reducing a previous generation of often sophisticated thinkers to foils in our own critiques of hyper-Westernization. This book argues that almost every Turkish modernity was, to some extent, intended as an alternative one. Participants in Turkey's long-standing Westernization debates consistently claimed to be moving beyond them, and transcending Turkey's famous clichés has been a cliché for almost as long as they existed.

Mid-century geopolitical developments added an additional layer of complexity to these debates. In 1952, Turkey decisively ended several decades of foreign policy neutrality by joining NATO. This realignment was a pragmatic response to the strategic threat posed by the Soviet Union, but it has often been presented in more symbolic terms, as the foreign policy expression of Atatürk's commitment to Westernization. If joining NATO ratified Turkey's European identity, it also brought the country into an alliance with the very European powers against which Atatürk fought. Compounding the contradictions this raised, many Western diplomats were convinced that becoming a part of the anti-Communist West also required Turkey's renewed engagement with the Middle East. And as Turkish politicians unanimously decided to ally with America in order to preserve their country's independence, some began to worry that this new alliance might threaten their independence and national identity as well.

As a result, the foreign and domestic politics of mid-century Turkey prove a particularly poor fit for accounts of Republican history too caught up in criticizing Atatürk's excessive embrace of the West – what İlker Aytürk has called the "post-Kemalist paradigm."[3] In *Atatürk: An Intellectual Biography*, Şükrü Hanioğlu argues that Turkey's founder "rejected the very possibility of a non-Western modernity."[4] Erik Jan Zürcher offers a similar verdict: like other thinkers who advocated "blind submission to Western civilization," Atatürk believed that European modernity "had to be accepted lock, stock and barrel if Turkey was to survive in the modern world."[5] The result, according to Cemil Aydın, was that following decades of late-Ottoman experimentation with anti-Western, Pan-Asian, and Pan-Islamic ideologies, Turkey decided to "leave the Muslim World" after concluding that "Eastern-Islamic civilization was dead and could not be modern."[6]

Understanding the political, cultural, and international politics of the 1950s does not require completely rejecting this narrative, but it does require a renewed focus on the exceptions. A number of authors have recently taken a newfound interest in the conflicting attitudes toward the West that persisted in the Kemalist tradition. In discussing

[3] İlker Aytürk, "Post-Post-Kemalizm: Yeni Bir Paradigmayı Beklerken." *Birikim* (319), 2015, 34–48.
[4] M. Şükrü Hanioğlu, *Atatürk: An Intellectual Biography* (Princeton University Press: Princeton, 2013), 204.
[5] Erik Jan Zurcher and Taraj Atabaki, *Men of Order: Authoritarian Modernization under Atatürk and Reza Shah* (London: I. B. Tauris, 2003), 9.
[6] Cemil Aydın, *The Politics of Anti-Westernism in Asia* (New York: Columbia University Press, 2007), 201. Tellingly, one of the Pan-Asian thinkers Aydın discusses in his account of anti-Westernism is Rabindranath Tagore, whose poetry was first translated into Turkish by a young Bülent Ecevit.

how the early nationalist thinker Ziya Gökalp influenced Atatürk, for example, Orhan Koçak emphasizes his goal of synthesizing national essence [*has*] and global values [*medeniyet*] so Turks could "be like the West and still be [themselves]."[7] This ambition, Koçak writes, led Gökalp to criticize the "imitative nature of late Ottoman Westernizers," who sought to borrow too extensively from the West.[8] Subsequently, Perin Gürel has explored how early Kemalists deployed accusations of "hyper-westernization" and "westoxication" against their rivals.[9] Atatürk's attacks against the liberal feminist Halide Edip Adıvar, she argues, were echoed by Republican-era writers who condemned inappropriate Westernization through novels about "over-sexualized" and "treacherous" women engaged in illicit relationships with Western men. Mehmet Döşemeci, in turn, traces this legacy into the 1970s via Prime Minister Bülent Ecevit's left-wing nationalism. In opposing Turkey's membership in the European Economic Community, Döşemeci maintains, Ecevit sought "a return to Atatürk's original position," one he claimed had displayed "a profound ambivalence toward the West."[10]

Ideally, a more nuanced understanding of how Turkey articulated its relationship with Western modernity can help explain how so many observers misunderstood Turkish politics over the past two decades. For Turkish President Recep Tayyip Erdoğan, the meaning of the Menderes era was always clear. In Erdoğan's view, Turkey's initial decade-long experiment with democracy represented the first step in a long struggle against authoritarian modernization and hyper-

---

[7] Orhan Koçak, "1920'lerden 1970'lere Kültür Politikaları," in Ahmet İnsel's ed., *Modern Türkiye'de Siyasal Düşünce vol. 2, Kemalizm*. (Istanbul: İletişim, 2015).

[8] Ziya Gökalp, quoted in Koçak's "1920'lerden 1970'lere Kültür Politikaları." Gökalp specifically criticized the Servet-i Fünun literary movement, which he claimed borrowed not only styles and methods from Europe but also its "lyricism and taste," that is "things which should not be transferred from one society to another." Koçak argues that from the 1920s through the 1970s Gökalp's idea of a "synthesis of National Essence and Western Civilization" maintained its influence in cultural politics. This synthesis, he claims, proved far more popular among the Republican cultural elite than Ahmet Ağaoğlu's assertion, expressed in the 1927 *Üç Medeniyet*, that anything short of complete Westernization was impossible.

[9] Perin Gürel, *The Limits of Westernization: A Cultural History of America in Turkey* (New York: Columbia University Press, 2017).

[10] Mehmet Döşemeci, *Debating Turkish Modernity* (Cambridge: Cambridge University Press, 2013), 177, 188.

Westernization, one that he himself would ultimately bring to its triumphant conclusion. After carrying his party to victory in 2011, Erdoğan declared that the democracy for which Menderes had given his life was now secure. Then, after being elected president in 2014, he declared that the parenthesis opened by Turkey's 1960 coup had finally been closed.

By 2014, of course, very few Western or Turkish academics saw Erdoğan's victory as a triumph for democracy. But by this point, their work had already helped facilitate Erdoğan's rise to power. In response to Turkey's 1980 coup, a growing body of literature presented authoritarian modernization and hyper-Westernization as defining features of the Republican project, beginning under Atatürk and continuing up through the twenty-first century under the tutelage of Turkey's military and secular bureaucracy.[11] As a result, the AKP's Islamist ideology and politicized embrace of a pious Ottoman past were often presented as Turkey's authentic and perhaps predestined form of alternate modernity. Hyper-Westernized high modernism, associated with the Kemalist elite and American development experts, served as a perfect foil for the AKP's vision of Turkey at peace with its history, its faith, and its role in the Middle East.

Scholars of modern Middle Eastern history have been astute in demonstrating how their predecessors' work, beholden to outdated ideologies like modernization theory, served to justify authoritarianism and advance US geopolitical interests. And yet in the case of contemporary Turkey, these very scholarly critiques, while made with the best of intentions, served equally troubling ends. If reexamining the relationship between ideas and politics in early Cold War Turkey casts that era's thinkers and statesmen in a more complex light, the goal is not to absolve them but rather to become more self-critical about the politics of our own scholarship. Now that the AKP has so thoroughly appropriated scholarly critiques of Kemalism and high modernism, how will our understanding of Turkish history be recalibrated moving forward? We may well see a growing focus on the continuity of conservative or religious nationalism in Turkish politics. And perhaps with it, a renewed search for strands of liberal modernity in the late Ottoman

---

[11] For a pointed assessment of this trend and its political pitfalls, see Aytürk's "Post-Post-Kemalizm."

and Republican past, examples that can offer an alternative to both Kemalist and AKP authoritarianism.

Each chapter of this book examines an aspect of mid-century modernity that has been misunderstood: democracy, American influence, Westernization, Ottoman history, Orientalism, regional diplomacy, and religious reform. In each case, I argue that an overly simplistic or binary approach to these topics has blinded us to the creative and contradictory ways that people at the time approached them. As a result, recognizing the incoherence of mid-century discourses about history and modernity is a prerequisite for discussing any of them coherently. In working within prevailing narratives of history and modernization, politicians and writers consistently reached surprisingly diverse, and consistently self-interested, conclusions about Turkey's place in time and space – making the East West or the past modern as needed. Understanding how Turkish historians secularized and nationalized the Ottoman Empire, like understanding how American diplomats convinced themselves that successive Turkish regimes were all democratic, helps reveal how easily ideology can be made to accommodate more pressing practical needs.

Chapter 1 examines the immediate aftermath of Turkey's 1950 election, tracing the way both the country's major political parties incorporated democracy into their historical narratives and modernizing ambitions. The DP, for its part, sought to convince voters that democracy would enable them to more effectively realize the populist and materialist promise of Kemalist modernization. Finding itself in opposition for the first time since the country's founding, the Republican People's Party (CHP) sought to take credit for the advent of democracy, while also embracing democratic ideals in their criticism of the DP. In the process, both parties opened an ongoing debate about which of the many Kemalist-era reforms Turkish voters had truly accepted.

Chapter 2 addresses the diverse ways American diplomats employed their ideas of modernization when crafting policy and propaganda for Turkey. While Americans' general understanding of what it meant to be modern remained consistently democratic, it was sufficiently malleable that it could accommodate contradictory conclusions about Turkish democracy as US interests shifted. State Department documents also reveal how American ideas about modernity were, with the cooperation of the Turkish government, consciously transformed into propaganda aimed both at encouraging Turkish modernization and advertising America's modernity.

Chapter 3 explores the ways mid-century writers used art, history, travel, and gender to articulate a vision of Turkish identity that claimed to synthesize Western modernity and Eastern tradition or transcend this division entirely. While writers from rival ideological backgrounds promoted different versions of Turkish modernity, they nonetheless shared the belief that this modernity should be a synthetic one, combining the best of East and West. In citing American examples to critique European modernity or putting a modern imprimatur on radically different ideas about women's role in society, these authors demonstrated how creatively Turkey's clichés could be employed.

Chapter 4 traces the Kemalist appropriation of Ottoman history, beginning at the moment the empire itself ceased to exist and building up to the 1953 quincentennial of the Ottoman conquest of Istanbul. From the 1930s, Turkish historians used a narrative of fatal decline to not only justify Kemalist reforms but also facilitate the selective incorporation of the empire's triumphs into Turkish nationalist history. By 1953, the Kemalist appropriation of the Ottoman past had reached a point where it was possible to celebrate Fatih Sultan Mehmet II as a secular, pro-Western sultan who laid the groundwork for Turkey's membership in NATO.

Chapter 5 analyzes the visual and rhetorical styles through which Ottoman history was modernized. Faced with enduring Western Orientalism, Turkish authors, architects, and illustrators took a number of distinct stylistic steps to celebrate their history while presenting their relationship to it as an unequivocally modern one. The explosion of popular history magazines and historical novels during the 1950s provided a forum in which the act of reading about the past could itself become a performance of modernity. Whether blending popular history with pulp fiction or encouraging Turkish citizens to approach their country from the perspective of Western tourists, Turkish authors pioneered approaches to reappropriating their own past that remain popular today.

Chapter 6 examines how ideas about history and geography shaped Turkey's relations with NATO and the Arab world. After joining NATO by de-emphasizing the alliance's geographic character, Turkey went on to embrace NATO membership as proof of its European identity. Subsequently, Turkish and American officials clashed over what it meant for Turkey to be a "bridge between East and West." During the 1950s, Turkey's initial sympathy toward the Arab world quickly transformed into hostility as Arab nationalism took a pro-Soviet turn. As a result, Arabs who were previously seen as victims of British imperialism suddenly, in a Cold War context, became agents of Soviet imperialism instead.

Chapter 7 addresses the self-consciously modern religious revival of the 1940s and 1950s. It investigates the way government officials and conservative magazine editors promoted this revival as a part of a broader return to faith that encompassed the Christian West and offered a necessary corrective to the limits of positivist modernity. Across the ideological spectrum, they insisted Islam was fully compatible with modern thought and science, while holding very different ideas of what this meant. Their reform efforts won praise from many Western observers, who saw in the advent of modern religiosity proof that Turkey no longer needed the rigid secularism of the Kemalist era.

All of these chapters draw on a range of published and archival sources. The complexity of 1950s modernity can be seen in the print culture of the period. Following World War II, a combination of press freedom, foreign aid, and increased prosperity led to an explosion of publishing in Turkey. Colorful, abundant, and diverse magazines spanned topics from popular history to politics and religion, employing many of the period's best-known writers and artists and attracting the attention of many influential readers.[12] There was also a vibrant newspaper industry at the time, with papers representing both political parties and a number of more or less independent outlets as well. Finally, several scholarly journals begun in the Republican period continued and expanded their activities during these years. Many of the contributors to Turkey's mid-century magazines remain famous for their enduring literary and artistic talents. Other contributors, in their eccentricity or earnestness, still contributed something remarkable to the country's cultural history. If the beauty of their images does not always come through in reproduction or the eloquence of their writing

---

[12] Even in this era, many publications still fared poorly. Searching in libraries and used bookstores, it is often possible to trace the fortunes of a magazine or its owner as, issue by issue, page tallies shrink, paper grows courser, black-and-white photos replace color, and then, finally, publication ceases altogether, after perhaps a few last-minute appeals for readers to pay their outstanding subscription fees.

in my translation, this book nonetheless seeks to convey the richness of their work alongside its historical significance.

The early Cold War era is uniquely well represented in US government archives. The material in Turkey's Republican Archive (*Başbakanlık Cumhuriyet Arşivi*) is sparse by comparison, and, while occasionally fascinating, offers only intermittent glimpses into official Turkish thinking during this period. However, close contact between the Turkish and American governments has at times created the odd situation where confidential Turkish documents unavailable in Ankara appear in translation in the United States instead. Conspiracy theories abound about the many ways Washington supposedly influenced Turkish politics during the Cold War. Largely declassified US records offer an excellent source for disproving most of them – and confirming a few as well.

In bringing together intellectual, cultural, political, and diplomatic history, this book explores the relationship between ideas and politics in twentieth-century Turkey. Ideas about modernization theory or the Ottoman legacy were intimately bound up in foreign and domestic policymaking, but consistently proved too malleable to play the causal role historians sometimes assign them. Diplomats, politicians, and writers were adept at interpreting dominant discourses in remarkably creative ways in order to accommodate their immediate interests. This book tells the story of individuals exploiting ideologies, creating and deploying both democratic and authoritarian versions of modernity just as they created secular and pious versions of the Ottoman past.

Moreover, though all these arguments are specific to Turkey, they can help us better appreciate how nations and states across the world position themselves within space and time. Among the many countries that have been described as the meeting point of East and West, Turkey certainly has a unique relationship with this cliché. But every identity is, to an extent, built from paradoxical and flexible components in accordance with the confines and possibilities of the world around it. This book, then, seeks to create a synthesis of its own, reconciling the near-infinite malleability of ideas with the reality of the past, of technological advancement, and of physical location.

In highlighting this malleability, I argue that we have always been too clever to let ideas influence our thinking. For better or worse, agile minds can draw pragmatic conclusions from within the most inhospitable ideological paradigms. On rare occasions, we may prove clear-headed enough to recognize an inescapable choice between our ideals and our interests. More often, the world is complicated enough that we can convince ourselves they are one and the same. Any attempt to treat ideology as a causal factor in history must at least reckon with this malleability. Admittedly, the possibility that academics and policy-makers alike share a capacity for sophisticated rationalization is not terribly radical. Yet we sometimes struggle to acknowledge just how pervasive this phenomenon is. Without completely dismissing our ability to craft meaningful and politically relevant narratives about history or modernity, I hope the accumulated evidence will at least lead us to pursue these efforts with a better awareness of how readily they can be co-opted.

1 | A Nation Votes
Democratic Modernity for the Masses

On the morning of May 14, 1950, with rain falling across much of the country, millions of Turkish citizens went to polls for what they did not yet know would be the country's first free election. Yet the votes they cast that day ultimately left them, winners and losers alike, convinced that their future was, and had always been, democratic.

Newspaper reports from the election conveyed both the novelty and solemnity of the occasion (see Figure 1.1). In Kayseri, at the City Club, a heartfelt handshake between government and opposition candidates left fellow diners in tears.[1] In Eskişehir, men and women, some in full veils, formed separate lines and alternated voting.[2] In Izmir, care was taken to allow women with children to vote first.[3] At a ballot box in Balıkesir, members of the government provoked involuntary laughter when they complained, after twenty-seven years of one-party rule, that the opposition was intimidating them.[4] In Adana, elderly voters were brought to the polls with stretchers and wheelchairs to "taste the joy of casting a free ballot in their final years."[5] Even voters who remembered the "fevered elections" of the late Ottoman period were "awed" by their experience.[6] One opposition journalist in Ankara spotted the Speaker of Parliament waiting to vote.[7] Just as he was about to say "I bet this is the first time you've ever stood in line" an impatient citizen told the Speaker to hurry up. Later, as

---

[1] Kadri Kayabal, "İşini Bilen Köylüler," *Cumhuriyet*, May 15, 1950.
[2] Hüsameddin Polat, "Sandık Başında Kuyruk Olan Kadın Seçmenler," *Cumhuriyet*, May 15, 1950.
[3] "İzmirde Seçim 1946"dan Bambaşka Şekilde Geçti," *Cumhuriyet*, May 15, 1950.
[4] Necmi Erkmen, "Balikesirde İştirak Yer Yer Yüzde 90," *Cumhuriyet*, May 15, 1950.
[5] Çoban Yurtçu, "Rey Veren Nineler, Dedeler ve Aileler . . .," *Cumhuriyet*, May 15, 1950.
[6] Ibid.
[7] Faruk Fenik, "Seçimde Neler Gördüm," *Zafer*, May 15, 1950. Fenik claimed on the day of the 1946 election he had been summoned in front of Izmir's chief prosecutor eight times. By chance, he wrote, he had run into the same man on election day in Ankara, but this time simply as a citizen who greeted him, not as a prosecutor holding him to account.

Figure 1.1 Banner from *Ulus* on the morning of Turkey's first free election, May 14, 1950.

the sun went down, the Democratic Party (DP) distributed food to ballot box observers, as well as candles in case the electricity went out.[8] The "election marathon" continued throughout the night, with eager listeners staying up next to their radios and bringing news to impatient neighbors.[9]

At the end of World War II, President İsmet İnönü and his Republican People's Party (CHP) held a firm monopoly on power in Turkey.[10] They had inherited this monopoly from Mustafa Kemal Atatürk, who created the party to help institutionalize his revolutionary agenda in the early years of the Republic. After serving as his prime minister for much of the 1920s and 1930s, İnönü took over from Atatürk as president with little opposition after his death in 1938. Stripped of Atatürk's charisma, one-party rule in the following decade became more nakedly authoritarian.[11] Though İnönü carefully maintained

[8] "Seçim Tam Bir Sükun İçinde Geçti," *Cumhuriyet*, May 15, 1950.
[9] Adnan Aktan, "Karadeniz Bölgesinde Seçim Mücadelesi," *Cumhuriyet*, May 16, 1950.
[10] For a comprehensive English-language account of Turkey's transition to multiparty democracy, see John VanderLippe, *The Politics of Turkish Democracy: İsmet İnönü and The Formation of the Multi-Party System, 1938–1950* (Albany, NY: State University of New York Press, 2005).
[11] For an unflinching examination of the violent nature of CHP rule, see Uğur Ümit Üngör, *The Making of Modern Turkey* (Oxford: Oxford University Press, 2011). On ideological trends specifically during the İnönü period, see Cemil Koçak, *Türkiye'de Milli Şef Dönemi (1938–1945)* (Istanbul: İletişim Yayınları, 2018). On Turkish foreign policy during the Second World War, see Selim Deringil, *Turkish Foreign Policy during the Second World War* (Cambridge: Cambridge University Press, 1989).

Turkey's neutrality through World War II, his governing ideology displayed the influence of fascist thought. As İnönü styled himself *National Chief,* Turkish nationalism grew more explicitly racialized and an extortionary wealth tax targeted religious minorities.

Turkey's democratic transition began in 1945 when a small group of politicians from within İnönü's party split off, founding their own party and demanding competitive elections. After ensuring the new party would remain loyal to Atatürk's revolution and defend Turkey's independence against the Soviet Union, İnönü allowed them to proceed. Explicitly naming themselves the Democratic Party [*Demokrat Parti*], these breakaway politicians repeatedly restated their commitment to secularism, while making it clear they would take a more permissive approach to the role of religion in public life. Despite accusations to the contrary, the party appeared more aggressively anti-Communist than the CHP, making free-market policies central to their platform. Celal Bayar, the DP's most prominent founder, had promoted a less statist approach to the economy during his years in the CHP. In addition to being prime minister for two years under Atatürk, he had served as Minister of the Economy and headed one of the Republic's leading banks. The DP's cofounder Adnan Menderes, in turn, was born to a wealthy provincial landowning family and entered the opposition through his active objection to land reform. In its founding years, however, the DP drew members and support from diverse quarters, including liberals, religious conservatives, businessmen, and those who had fallen afoul of the CHP for any number of ideological or personal reasons.

If Bayar, in his background and demeanor, represented the DP's continuity with the CHP, Menderes represented what appeared to be new about it.[12] Many members of Atatürk's political generation had been officers in World War I and leaders in Turkey's War for Independence. Menderes, by contrast, had been stricken with malaria on his way to the front in 1917, then played a more minor role in the subsequent fighting. He only entered the CHP almost

---

[12] For a concise English-language overview of Menderes and the DP, see Metin Heper and Sabri Sayarı, *Political Leaders and Democracy in Turkey* (Lanham, MD: Lexington Books, 2002). For a detailed retelling of Menderes's political life that combines history, anecdote, and literary tragedy, Şevket Süreyya Aydemir's *Menderes'in Dramı* (Istanbul: Yükselen Matbaası, 1969) remains unequalled.

a decade later, after impressing Atatürk with his practical and enthusiastic knowledge of agricultural issues. His early career in the CHP
had been without distinction, and there was little indication of the
vehemence with which he would subsequently take on his party.
After 1945, Menderes's rising prominence within the DP and the
country reflected a charisma somewhat at odds with what companions described as an intensely private nature. Contemporary
accounts emphasized his hunger for popular approval and deep
empathy for ordinary voters, as well as his romantic, even mystical
attachment to farming and the land. By 1950, Menderes had secured
his role as a leader in the DP, but it would still be several more years
before he became its personification.

Whereas in 1930 Atatürk allowed the formation of an opposition
party that he quickly closed, Inönü instead allowed the Democrats to
grow. In 1946 he oversaw a heavily manipulated election where
truncheon-wielding police at the ballot box helped him secure victory. Despite this, fifty-eight DP parliamentarians were elected.
Some opposition figures pushed for a boycott, but the leadership
declined, continuing to criticize the CHP's authoritarianism from
the floor of parliament. Over the subsequent four years, Inönü
fended off resistance from other factions within his party in order
to introduce a reformed electoral law and keep the country's transition toward pluralistic politics on track. His party also took
a newfound, if still limited, interest in accommodating popular
opinion on subjects like religion, thereby beginning some of the
cultural changes that would come to fruition in the 1950s.
Through this approach, Inönü believed the CHP would legitimate
its hold on power, continuing to dominate the electoral landscape in
the face of a real but hobbled opposition. Then, in 1950, he promised the country fair elections. But until the results were in, no
one – in the government, in the opposition, or abroad – quite
believed a democratic transfer of power to be possible.

And so, as it became clear on the morning of May 15 that the DP
would both win and be allowed to win, the country experienced the
quiet shock of things turning out exactly the way they were supposed
to.

In the following week, Turkish papers sought to articulate the historic meaning of what had just happened. "After this great war, Turkey
has taken its place among the Western democratic states," the editor of

one paper declared.[13] "Among the Eastern nations," added another, "it was perhaps the first show of this maturity."[14] Credit belonged to the Turkish nation itself. In the words of one columnist: "Our nation, which throughout history founded strong states and mighty empires, which remained unbowed by the fierce blows of fate, has embraced the advanced methods of contemporary civilization and taken charge of our government with our own hands."[15] Indeed, cast in these grand terms, it was a "happy coincidence" that Turkey's "Democracy Holiday" had fallen on the same month as two other equally fortunate events: Fatih's May 29 conquest of Istanbul and Atatürk's May 19 journey to Anatolia to launch Turkey's War of Independence.[16]

Zafer, the semiofficial newspaper of the DP, proudly proclaimed the election results a victory for Republican ideals. Participation rates, it declared, exceeded those in many Western countries, and at many polling stations women exceeded men.[17] With this election, the paper announced, "national sovereignty perfected the principles and institutions established by Atatürk."[18] "May 19th was the start of our war of independence," one *Zafer* columnist declared: "Since that date, we built a free homeland and independent country. But with May 14 we now feel we live as free citizens with independent consciences upon this free and independent land."[19] Another added: "with our final democracy revolution, the Turkish nation has proven itself qualified to achieve all of Atatürk's revolutionary expectations."[20] More pointedly, one of the paper's writers argued that, among its most significant mistakes, the CHP had "appropriated the revolutionary achievements that belong to the nation as a whole" and "exploited them for partisan purposes."[21]

The CHP-aligned newspaper *Ulus*, by contrast, tried to put the best historic spin on its defeat. The CHP had given Turkey's citizens "the world's greatest election laws," which allowed for the birth and victory

[13] Mümtaz Faik Fenik, "Halk Niçin D.P.yi Tercih Etti," *Zafer*, May 19, 1950.
[14] Falih Rıfkı Atay, "İktidar," *Cumhuriyet*, May 21, 1950.
[15] Nadir Nadi, "O Günün Manası," *Cumhuriyet*, May 16, 1950.
[16] "19 Mayıs Gençlik Bayramından İlhamlar," *Cumhuriyet*, May 20, 1950.
[17] Turkey's *Women's Newspaper* went as far as to declare the election a "women's victory," as female voters had disproportionately supported the Democrats. İffet Halim Oruz, "Kadınların Zaferi," *Kadın Gazetesi*, May 22, 1950.
[18] Sarıçizmeli, "19 Mayıs," *Zafer*, May 20, 1950.   [19] Ibid.
[20] "19 Mayıs Gençlik Bayramı," *Zafer*, May 19, 1950.
[21] Adviye Fenik, "Zafer Sarhoşluğuna Düşmeyeceğiz," *Zafer*, May 17, 1950.

of the opposition.[22] For its part, the DP had emerged from within the CHP's ranks and largely "copied" its policies.[23] With the Democrats accusing İnönü of being a dictator, an *Ulus* editorial argued the election results definitively proved otherwise. Turkey "was not a dictatorship and had not been."[24] To the contrary, "Atatürk laid the foundation for this democratic revolution. He raised the statue. İsmet İnönü gave life to the statue."[25] The world had "never encountered a statesman of İnönü's stature who encouraged the wishes of the nation and gave up power in deference to them .... That this lofty gesture had been engraved into the history of civilization by a Turkish leader was an honor to the nation." Moreover, many CHP members believed that this setback, while embarrassing, would likely prove temporary when their party, chastened by its defeat, returned to power in the next election.

Meanwhile, the independent paper *Cumhuriyet* published a series of interviews with ordinary voters, presenting them as motivated by both mundane concerns and a deeper democratic spirit.[26] Asked what he expected from the new government, a tailor told a reporter he hoped the number of people who could afford suits would increase. A chauffer expressed his anger at state officials who drove fancier cars than individuals in the United States or Britain. A restaurateur wanted an end to strict rules about prices and portion weights. A vegetable seller expressed a similar concern: "The mayor comes and lowers the price of spinach to 5 cents. What good does that do? I couldn't say it then but if he comes again it seems we have democracy now so I'll have a lot to say to him." Crucially, if the country's new leaders did not meet these expectations, voters believed they would be held accountable. As one villager said, "[a]fter throwing out a government that's been planted in power for 25 years, we'll throw out the new one whenever we like."[27]

Turkish papers eagerly reprinted foreign coverage of the elections as well. American, French, and British praise received the most interest, but positive responses from countries such as Greece, Brazil, and Russia were also featured. From Paris, *Le Monde* declared that above all, the significance of the moment lay in the "appearance of political

---

[22] "Son ve Kati Neticeler Bugün Anlaşılacak," *Ulus*, May 16, 1950.
[23] Feridun Osman Menteşeoğlu "Millet Böyle İstedi, Vazifemiz Ona Hürmettir," *Ulus*, May 16, 1950.
[24] Hüseyin Cahit Yalçın, "Büyük İsmet İnönü," *Ulus*, May 16, 1950. [25] Ibid.
[26] "Halk İktidara Getirdiği DP'den Neler Bekliyor," *Cumhuriyet*, May 19, 1950.
[27] A. Adnan Adıvar, "Yeni Hükümeti Beklerken," *Cumhuriyet*, May 18, 1950.

will in a nation that had at no point ever been invited to seriously proclaim its views."[28] Another French paper concluded that "if the simple Turkish peasant has found his self-respect, we must conclude that this noble nation realized a four-century achievement in four years."[29] For their part, British papers were eager to give both Atatürk and the Turkish people their due. The elections were "Atatürk's greatest victory" wrote the *Daily Mail*. "He appreciated what the Turkish nation needed to learn before they were thrown into Western-style democracy and he taught it to them himself."[30] Under the headline "In a Country Used to Earthquakes, an Election Landslide!" the *Glasgow Herald* noted that while "[d]ictatorship in Turkey was never of the worst sort .... These elections proved that modern people won't support dictatorship of any sort."[31]

American observers were no less grand in their assessments. The *New York Times* declared it "the first transfer of power in accordance with the freely-stated popular will in six centuries of Turkish history."[32] "The astonishing upset in the Turkish elections," another article announced "is a result of which not only Turkey but Western democracy can be proud. That ancient country, once known as the 'Sick Man of Europe' looks today like a vigorous young recruit to the sort of world we believe in and want to see."[33] With similar optimism, a spokesman for the US State Department described the elections as a sign of democracy's healthy development in the Near East.[34]

Two weeks after the election, the Turkish Parliament started its new term with Prime Minister Adnan Menderes reading his party's program and the opposition offering its response.[35] Menderes began his speech

[28] Quoted in "Dünya Basını DP Zaferile Meşkül," *Zafer*, May 20, 1950.
[29] Quoted in "Dünya Basınında Seçimin Akisleri," *Zafer*, May 17, 1950.
[30] Quoted in "Dış Memleketlerde Seçimlerin Akisleri," *Cumhuriyet*, May 19, 1950.
[31] Quoted in "'Türkiyede Seçim Heyelanı'," *Cumhuriyet*, May 19, 1950.
[32] "Bayar Takes Oath as Turkey's Chief," *New York Times*, May 23, 1950.
[33] "Turkey Votes for Democracy," *New York Times*, May 15, 1950. The article also said of the election: "Islam is democratic in the sense of genuine individual equality before God and man's law, but not in the newer modes of constitutional government. This [election] is the culmination of a process that began with the spread of ideas from the French Revolution. Constitutionalism was a gradual but steady growth, and now we see the fine fruits of it."
[34] "Seçimlerin Neticesi ve Türkiye ile Amerika," *Cumhuriyet*, May 16, 1950.
[35] Türkiye Büyük Millet Meclisi (T. B. M. M.) Tutanak Dergisi, 3 Birleşim 29. V. 1950.

by discussing the subject of historical periodization and offering a deterministic or normative model of modernization. "For the first time in our history," he announced, "this august body has taken charge of the fate of our nation through the full and free manifestation of the national will." As a result, "[a]fter five years of fierce struggle under unnatural conditions, normal political life has finally begun in our country." "There is no doubt," he continued, "that the 14th of May will always be remembered as a historic day of unrivaled importance which ended one era and began a new one."

Segueing into a discussion of the government's economic program, which would be the main focus of his speech, Menderes explained that "in bringing a country that remains centuries behind up to the level of today's advanced nations" the DP faced enormous challenges. As leader of a government that had been brought to power by the national will, he felt compelled to refute the CHP's rosy picture of the country's condition and tell the people the true state of affairs: "After even the most worthless government had been in charge of a country for a long period of time, it could be praised for having realized a few achievements here or there." But the CHP must be judged in light of the enormous national resources at its disposal. As a result, he deemed it necessary to conclude that "they in fact blocked the country's natural course of development with their mistaken and deficient policies."

The CHP's Faik Ahmed Barutçu began his response by offering an alternate narrative of the country's history and progress.[36] First, he explained that representing the will of the people in a more "full and perfect" form had been an ongoing and unchanging goal of the Turkish Parliament since its formation on April 23, 1920. Each parliament had been an improvement over the last, he explained, and no country in the world could boast a perfect system of representation. Then, he moved on to the question of periodization. "The new era in Turkey began with the Republic," he insisted. "If May 14 normalized today's governing party, and began a new era for them in terms of appreciating the importance of behaving according to their governing responsibilities" the nation would be all too pleased. After implying that the government's criticism still reflected the irresponsibility of its opposition years, he went on to refute it. Menderes's words, he claimed "were clearly intended to disparage the entire period that lasted from 1920 to

[36] Ibid.

1950." But "it was clearly laid out in Atatürk's great speech what a wretched state this country was in when the Republic began." He continued to elaborate the numerous economic, political, and global challenges the young Republic had faced, as well as its success in bringing Turkey into the family of Northern and Western European nations. "To hear it formally stated," he declared, "that this achievement of the 20th century which inspired awe around the world, that is, that the Turkish Republic, amounts to nothing is sad." "Unfortunately," interrupted a DP representative from Istanbul, "it's the truth."[37]

Democracy Means Progress

The DP came to power by condemning the authoritarianism and failed economic policies of the CHP. Once in power, the leaders of the party, as well as individual party members and their allies in the media, went to the masses with a new model of democratic modernity that promised both freedom and wealth. Appreciating the logic and appeal of this democratic rhetoric is important to understanding not only the DP's electoral success but also the nature of the CHP's response, and the way ordinary citizens continued to view democracy and modernity in the ensuing decades.

Where the CHP had emphasized industrializing the country by building factories and modernizing the countryside through education, the DP sought to bring modernity to the countryside with mechanized agriculture, while continuing to build even more factories. Contemporary praise for the party often revolved around its provision of tractors to farmers, as well as the construction of factories, roads, dams, and other material markers of progress. Indeed, alongside

---

[37] A similar debate erupted when the Turkish Parliament voted to ratify Turkey's membership in NATO. One DP deputy from Erzurum announced: "the truth is, the People's Party government did nothing to prepare Turkey for joining the Atlantic Pact; this is a splendid achievement realized entirely by the skill and persistence of the new government." Then, another deputy told the assembled body: "None of your deeds have been as worthy and honorable as the historic deed you will perform today." At this, there were "Ooos" from the crowd. "A slip of the tongue," said the deputy. The Speaker intervened, repeating that it had indeed been a slip of the tongue: "What he meant to say was that, like your many great achievements, this will be among them." T. B. M. M. Tutanak Dergisi, 41 Birleşim, 18.II, 1952.

statistics charting the country's increased agricultural and industrial output, pictures of Bayar or Menderes opening a new factory or dam became a defining feature of press coverage from the era.

This chapter examines the arguments that accompanied the tractors and the photo ops. Touring the country in his first years in office, Menderes explained to crowd after crowd of supporters why freedom and material progress went hand in hand. The CHP, he insisted, had promised them prosperity but the DP would actually deliver it. And they would do so with the people's help. Modernity, Menders and his colleagues argued, was democratic by necessity, and only a representative government could achieve truly revolutionary progress and realize Atatürk's vision.

According to the Democrats' narrative, the country's democratic revolution, and ensuing change in mentality, had for the first time brought to power a government that represented the national will. As a result, party leaders explained, this government existed to serve the people. It prioritized their interests and was responsive to their concerns. Democracy, therefore, made the government more efficient and able to work systematically instead of being diverted by its own self-interest. An elected administration also trusted the people, giving them the freedom to help themselves. More importantly, with their new-found freedom of speech, the Turkish people could air their grievances for the first time in history. With their votes, they could then punish any party that did not provide solutions.

"With your struggle, you opened the road to progress, to national sovereignty, to well-being," Menderes told an audience in the city of Kocaeli.[38] Refik Koraltan, the new Speaker of Parliament, praised the residents of the Black Sea town of Giresun by saying: "You are the ones who secure the country's march toward progress."[39] "With the full representation of the national will, a new era opened after 14 May, 1950," explained another parliamentarian. In this era, the DP took on the "national responsibility" to "hear the appeals from the nation's collective conscious and to succeed in fulfilling their wishes."[40] The result was a newfound national prosperity "aris[ing] from the Turkish homeland having found the atmosphere of freedom it needs."[41]

[38] "Başbakanın Bolululara Hitabı," *Zafer*, December 14, 1952.
[39] "Koraltan Girsunda," *Zafer*, November 18, 1952.
[40] Ali Rıza İncealemdaroğlu, "14 Mayıs'in Milli ve Siyasi Manası," *Zafer*, December 30, 1950.
[41] "Başbakanın Kocaelililere Dünkü Hitabı," *Zafer*, September 13, 1952.

According to DP rhetoric, this was not just Turkey's experience but a law of history: "If other nations of the world have progressed," observed Koraltan, "if they have already taken their places in the caravan of civilization, the reason for this is nothing but the work of governments formed by the will of the people."[42] Authoritarian regimes, he went on, "have, in every era, been unproductive." Without popular oversight, they would inevitably "fall into error." But, DP leaders insisted, they were not the ones telling voters all of this. Rather, it was "a conclusion reached, with an unshakable understanding, by the Turkish nation."[43]

Building on this logic, DP leaders regularly emphasized their commitment to serving the public, presenting it not only as a virtue of their party but also as a requirement of democratic governance. Where President Bayar told listeners of his desire to "be in your service" and "work to be as helpful to you as I can be," his colleagues put the matter in loftier terms. On the anniversary of the party's founding, one parliamentarian wrote in *Zafer*: "Understanding the nation's desires and spirit, the Democratic Party has worked with excitement for four years without tiring or stopping to serve the nation and win its satisfaction through beneficial and worthy labors."[44] In this vein, Koraltan told voters that "I call the democracy revolution a happiness revolution . . . " because it "achieved a brand new mentality and administration in every field."[45] In fact, under the present system, this new mentality was a matter of necessity. To ignore the public's needs was "not possible for a government that came to power through the will of the people."[46] Even if the party wanted to behave otherwise, Menderes told the people of Adana, "you wouldn't let us, you'd throw us out."[47]

In addition to consistently highlighting the role of elections in ensuring accountability, DP rhetoric also emphasized the role of free speech. Party leaders pointed out the practical benefits that came with ending the repression of the one-party era. "In this country for many years the silence of death reigned," Menderes declared. "We lived as a nation awaiting the next curse from the capital with fear, with the resignation

---

[42] "Kırklarelide Koraltanın Dünkü Nutku," *Zafer*, October 13, 1952.   [43] Ibid.
[44] Ali Rıza İncealemdaroğlu, "14 Mayıs'ın Milli ve Siyasi Manası," *Zafer*, December 30, 1950.
[45] "Yeni Bir Türkiye Doğdu," *Zafer*, September 4, 1952.
[46] "Çukurovanın bütün meseleleri görüşüldü," *Zafer*, January 9, 1952.
[47] "Başbakanın Bolululara Hitabı," *Zafer*, December 14, 1952.

shown to divine calamities."[48] Without the right to "criticize and complain," "warnings and guidance were wasted," as the Turkish nation "writhed in agony" while "the disrepair and disorder of our economic and social life" "led thousands of our citizens to ruin."[49] Under democratic rule, by contrast, "troubles which once merely passed from ear to ear or at most to a friend on the condition they went no further, now, via political institutions, reach those in charge as matters to be solved."[50] After "twenty-seven years" of "no one listening to our voice nor hearing our local needs," Menderes claimed, "we now have a state that listens to our troubles, that offers us all kinds of aid."[51]

The DP's theory of modernization attached particular importance to the people's ability to express their wants and troubles. Menderes, for example, announced his "pride and satisfaction" when "citizens expressed their desires."[52] In doing so, they showed that his party had created "tens of thousands of children of the homeland who follow the country's affairs closely and know how to discuss them."[53] Bayar, in turn, declared that a "country or nation's needs never end. To not feel a new need each day is to abandon that purpose called progress." Rather than remain indifferent, the government's responsibility was "to work as possible, beyond what is possible," to address such needs and "in this way return the confidence and affection granted us by the nation."[54] The alternative, in a country with free speech, was that an angry citizenry would speak out. According to Menderes, if the party's leaders prioritized their own interests over the people's, "citizens would say it, the press would write it, the parliament would discuss it."[55] If the party had not fulfilled its promises, Menderes told the people of Bolu, "[Y]our criticism would have burned us like flames from the mouth of an oven."[56]

---

[48] "Başbakanın Boludaki Nutku," *Zafer*, December 15, 1952.
[49] Ali Rıza İncealemdaroğlu, "14 Mayıs'ın Milli ve Siyasi Manası," *Zafer*, December 30, 1950.
[50] Kemal Cündübeyoğlu, "Yol Davamızın bir Veçhesi: il yolları," *Zafer*, February 5, 1951.
[51] "Başbakanın Kocalililere Dünku Hitabı," *Zafer*, September 13, 1952.
[52] "Başbakanın Nutku," *Zafer*, April 30, 1951. [53] Ibid.
[54] Cumhurbaşkanı Celal Bayarın Hitabesi," *Zafer*, September 14, 1952.
[55] "Menderes Malatyada," November 23, 1952.
[56] "Basbankanın Bolululara Hitabı," *Zafer*, December 14, 1952.

In this context, the party members' constant travels around the country were presented not merely as an opportunity to campaign or give speeches but rather as a way of maintaining close contact between the citizens and their government. It was an opportunity for politicians to listen to the people's concerns and to provide evidence of their service as well. "To visit every corner of the country is one of the principles of your government," Refik Koraltan told one audience.[57] Samet Ağaoğlu, the Deputy Prime Minister, explained in Çukurova, "Right now in your presence I am doing my duty just as I would be at my desk in Ankara."[58] Addressing a crowd in Eastern Anatolia in August, one DP minister announced that "[b]efore our administration, neither a minister nor a parliamentarian passed along these roads nor called on these places."[59] The DP, by contrast, had promised to do things differently and "said that the villager was our master."

And look. By coming to his feet, by listening to his complaints and troubles, by crossing mountains and valleys in the heat and hard days of this season, we have shared his plight. We are bringing roads, water, schools, lighting, and a land office . . . to the villages. We are fulfilling our promises . . . not with empty words but with work, with results, with numbers.[60]

In the course of visiting their constituents, parliamentarians would have "performed inspections" and "identified needs," while "taking notes as necessary" in order to return to Ankara with "inspiration and fresh strength" to "meet the people's needs."[61] But maintaining "unconditional and unrestricted contact" between the people and their leaders also required the leaders to report back to their voters.[62] Menderes explained that "[o]ur duty clearly requires us to give evidence by displaying in front of your eyes the work which has been done."[63] Or, as Bayar told the people of Bursa, "I have a debt that I must pay to you – I will have paid it when I answer the question 'how are you and your friends serving the nation?'"[64]

Not surprisingly, the DP also articulated its model of democratic modernity with more explicit references to the failures of the one-party era. In

[57] "Koraltanın Çubuk Konuşması," *Zafer*, October 24, 1952.
[58] "S. Ağaoğlunun Konuşması," *Zafer*, January 9, 1952.
[59] "Doğu İllerin Kalkınması," *Zafer*, August 14, 1952.   [60] Ibid.
[61] "Meclisin Yeni Çalışma Yılı," *Zafer*, November 1, 1952; "Celal Bayar Karsta," *Zafer*, September 30, 1952.
[62] "S. Ağaoğlunun Konuşması," *Zafer*, January 9, 1952.
[63] "Koraltan Girsunda," *Zafer*, November 18, 1952.
[64] "Bayar Bursada," November 13, 1952.

condemning the CHP's mentality [*zihniyet*], party members pointed out the practical drawbacks of authoritarian rule and made the case for why democracy would bring improved economic development through greater efficiency and more rational planning. As one op-ed writer summarized it: "Thankfully the era when donkeys led has been left behind. The long-eared ones are history. Now let's look toward those with long propellers."[65] In addition to explaining how the CHP's intolerance of criticism compromised its efficiency, DP politicians argued that its administration suffered on account of maintaining "a mentality which protects its own party and cares little for others."[66] CHP governors did not concern themselves with the "practical work of building roads," one columnist wrote, because it would not "earn them praise from men of importance making brief inspections from their private train cars."[67] Menderes was particularly emphatic in describing how the party's arrogance and distance from the people led to misplaced priorities. The party spent an outrageous amount to "build a parliament building like the pyramids of Egypt" while villagers were without sandals. It built stadiums and giant statues while villages were without roads. "That era's architecture was like a shop window. We weren't building a country, it was as if we were staging a fair."[68] Were someone to do this in a democratic era, Menderes declared, they would be called crazy. "We all thought [this was crazy] before too, but we couldn't say anything."

Alleviating the CHP's authoritarian mentality, then, would enable more systematic and better planned government work. When thousands of employees at state-controlled industries "worked under threat and under pressure with their futures uncertain" then "the mentality of rational work was not dominant" and "there could be no talk of a sense of profit motive."[69] When these industries were run with an "exploitative mentality" and as a "tool" for "political profits," rather than with "recourse to technique and organization," they could never yield satisfactory results.

---

[65] Kemal Cündübeyoğlu, "Kalkınan Doğu," *Zafer*, September 7, 1952.

[66] Ali Rıza İncealemdaroğlu, "14 Mayıs'ın Milli ve Siyasi Manası," *Zafer*, December 30, 1950.

[67] Kemal Cündübeyoğlu, "Yol Davamızın bir Veçhesi: il yolları," *Zafer*, February 5, 1951.

[68] He went on to note: "We're not saying these things shouldn't be done. We know these are civilizational needs." But the people's needs, he insisted, should have been met first. "Başbakanın Malatyadaki Mühim Nutku," *Zafer*, November 25, 1952.

[69] Ali Rıza İncealemdaroğlu, "14 Mayıs'ın Milli ve Siaysi Manası," *Zafer*, December 30, 1950.

Similarly, in the Ministry of Public Works, when "the mentality of defer-
ring responsibility reigned" ordinary people were stifled by the resulting
bureaucracy.[70] Making the Ministry's work "more programmatic" by
"establishing the authority and responsibility of every official" would
therefore benefit the voters directly.

   Particularly when making the case that free-market economic principles
would fuel Turkey's modernization, the DP also linked criticism of the
CHP's authoritarian mentality with its supposed lack of faith in the
ordinary Turkey villager. Rejecting the "bankrupt" "nonsense" that
"this nation cannot govern itself," the party's leaders praised the nation's
"skill, its advanced thinking and spirit."[71] Where the CHP saw the villager
as "unconscious or dishonest," the DP trusted the villager's "centuries of
wisdom."[72] In Menderes's words, "[CHP] policies rested on a foundation
of not trusting the economic wisdom, capability and strength of the
Turkish farmer," whereas the DP believed that "[i]ncreasing his purchasing power increases his productivity."[73] Dismissing CHP criticism of one
financial decision, he asked, "Did we throw this money as food for the
fish? No, we gave it to the Turkish villager."[74]

   In the CHP era, Menderes argued, "[E]veryone went about their
work without effort or enthusiasm." They ignored politics "because
they knew it was not subject to their will." But when they "learned that
they are citizens," they "embraced public affairs with four hands" and,
"because they know they will not be interfered with," began "looking
toward [their] own affairs with enthusiasm."[75] In short, the country's
rapid progress after 1950 showed that the government's faith in the
farmer was being rewarded:

As the Turkish farmer becomes richer his enthusiasm grows as well. He wasn't
a medieval man. The scene in front of us, all of you, demonstrates this. On every
side the farmers are enthusiastic. He wasn't lazy the way they thought.[76]

As a result, Menderes concluded, the DP's faith in the Turkish farmer
was not just a matter of "social justice" but rather a "realist" economic

---

[70] "Bayındırlıkta 1951 Program," *Zafer*, March 15, 1951.
[71] "Yeni Bir Türkiye Doğdu," *Zafer*, September 4, 1952.
[72] "Basbankanın Bolululara Hitabı," *Zafer*, December 14, 1952.
[73] "Başbakanın Malatyadaki Mühim Nutku," *Zafer*, November 25, 1952.
[74] Ibid.   [75] "Basbankanın Bolululara Hitabı," *Zafer*, December 14, 1952.
[76] "Muğlada Başbakanın Verdiği Mühim Nutuk," *Zafer*, May 4, 1951.

policy: "If such a policy had been put in place before, our country would have long ago become prosperous."[77]

Strikingly, the DP's criticism of the CHP and its mentality consistently conflated the CHP's mistreatment of the Turkish villager with the neglect and abuse the villager suffered at the hands of the Ottoman Empire during its centuries of decline. "What would happen," Menderes asked an audience in Malatya, "if we returned to the Turkish villager one percent of what we stole from him for years, under the Ottomans, under the Republic?" These governments, Menderes explained, had forced the peasant to sell his crops at a minimal price, all in return for "not building him schools, not building him roads, and not bringing him water."[78] In this spirit, newspaper columnists declared that with the arrival of roads, Eastern Turkey was "joining the civilized world after fulfilling its centuries of suffering."[79] Because of the government's efforts "villages that have been without water for hundreds of years will receive water and fountains."[80] In his speeches to rural audiences, Refik Koraltan was particularly insistent in condemning the Republic and late Ottoman eras alike for their neglect. "The villager, who makes up the majority of this great nation, has been neglected by a mentality that sees him as a herd," Koraltan declared, and "over the centuries he has become a skeleton.[81] While the country "always progressed in eras when the state served the prosperity, happiness, and development of our nation," over "the last three centuries" these goals were abandoned. As a result, the country fell into decline and in that time "not even another nail was added."[82]

Against this backdrop, the DP's historical narrative suggested that Turkey's political transformation began with the Tanzimat and continued through the revolutions of the Kemalist era, but only came to fruition with the party's election in 1950. As Samet Ağaoğlu explained, "the struggle for freedom, rule of law and popular sovereignty that began a century ago ended in victory on May 14, 1950."[83] Discussing

---

[77] "Başbakanın Malatyadaki Mühim Nutku," *Zafer*, November 25, 1952.
[78] Ibid. [79] Kemal Cündübeyoğlu, "Kalkınan Doğu," *Zafer*, October 19, 1952.
[80] Mümtaz Faik Fenik, "Kervan Yürüyor," *Zafer*, August 5, 1952.
[81] "Kırıkkale'de Koraltanın Dünkü Nutku," *Zafer*, October 13, 1952
[82] "Yeni Bir Türkiye Doğdu," *Zafer*, September 4, 1952.
[83] "14 Mayıs Yurtta Törenle Kutlandı," *Zafer*, May 15, 1951. Writing in 1967, after Menderes's death, Ağaoğlu described Menderes as a victim of the breakdown of the moral hierarchy undergirding the state that had survived through the Tanzimat but not into the Republic. Samet Ağaoğlu, *Arkadaşım Menderes* (Istanbul: Yapı Kredi Yayınları, 2011), 101.

nineteenth-century reforms helped expand the story of Turkey's modernization beyond the foundation of the Republic, while also suggesting that it had always been marked by a struggle between democratic and authoritarian impulses. In 1951, for example, the government repatriated the remains of Mithat Pasha, the Ottoman statesmen who helped craft the empire's first constitution before being killed on Sultan Abdülhamid's orders in the Hejaz. *Zafer* announced that crowds lined the Istanbul docks waiting for the bones of Turkey's heroic "martyr for freedom" to arrive from Saudi Arabia.[84] The paper's editor then joined the president for an elaborate funeral at which Mithat was eulogized as a "man of the people," who "began the struggle against personal and unaccountable government."[85] Bayar then told reporters that when this "brave and patriotic statesman" who "gave his head" for "liberty and independence" was laid to rest, justice for Abulhamid's crime had been served.[86]

In its treatment of history, the DP also built on a line of Kemalist rhetoric that, as will be discussed in a subsequent chapter, sought to blame bad governance for the country's underdevelopment while absolving the nation itself. Koraltan explained this in terms that echoed Kemalist critiques of Ottoman misadministration:

For centuries Turkish history has had its bright and dark days. The Turkish nation is not responsible for its dark days, its disastrous years, its period of decline. Because in those times governments cast a shadow over this country ... by walking down the wrong road away from the nation. Later, if this nation ... became separated from the caravan of civilization ... the responsibility belonged to those at the nation's head.[87]

While Atatürk was held above reproach, the DP was happy to suggest, implicitly or explicitly, that İsmet İnönü's reign had been no different from the tyrannical despotism of Abdülhamid: there were those leaders who moved the country forward by respecting the will of the people and those who thwarted progress by stifling it.

In describing their commitment to the Turkish villager, DP officials regularly invoked Atatürk's saying that "the villager is the master of the nation." In doing so, they insisted that only in 1950 did the saying

---

[84] "Mithat Paşanın Kemikleri dün İstanbula getirildi," *Zafer*, June 25, 1951.
[85] "Hürriyet Şehidi," *Zafer*, June 27, 1951.
[86] "Hürriyet Davası İçin Başını Veren Mücahit," *Zafer*, June 27, 1951.
[87] "Başbakanın Kocaelililere Dünkü Hitabı," *Zafer*, September 13, 1952.

finally become true.[88] Their appropriation of this slogan reflected their broader appropriation of Atatürk's legacy. The Democrats embraced the goals, rhetoric, and deeper narrative of the Kemalist modernizing project. Moreover, they explicitly embraced Atatürk: Among other efforts to claim his mantle, they passed a law against insulting his memory in 1951 and used every national holiday as an opportunity to print pictures of Atatürk together with Celal Bayar. But they removed the CHP from the story and insisted that only with the added element of democracy could this project be realized.

In subsequent decades, the DP was both praised for offering the country a new democratic spirit and condemned for abandoning Atatürk's modernizing mission. But what stands out in the Democrats' rhetoric is how readily basic tenets of Kemalist moderniza-tion could be reconfigured for a democratic era. The nationalism, the focus on material prosperity, the emphasis on rationality, and the need to "catch up" with more advanced countries all served a democratic vision of modernization as well as they did an authoritarian one. Tellingly, in the DP's articulation, these were not ideas or objectives that had been imposed on the nation in a top-down manner. Rather, the Democrats stressed that this modernity was something the people had long craved and which their party was now at long last delivering.

Democratic Modernity in Opposition

As the DP – rhetorically at least – embraced a new spirit of democratic modernity, the CHP was forced to respond. From the outset, CHP leaders condemned the new government for behaving undemocratically, whether on account of its hiring practices, taxation policies, or efforts to investigate critics. These charges inevitably led the DP to respond with accusations of hypocrisy, pointing out that the CHP had done far worse when it was in power (see Figure 1.2). These debates only intensified after 1954 when the DP increased its vote share in parliamentary elections and subsequently increased its use of legal measures against the opposition. As partisan hostility mounted and the CHP's hopes of an immediate electoral come-back were dashed, the party was forced to wrestle with the question of how to make its ideals viable in a democratic era.

---

[88] "Menderesin 35 Bin Adanalıya Hitabı," *Zafer*, December 7, 1952; "Şahlanan Adanadan Bazı İntibalar," ibid.

Figure 1.2 İsmet İnönü watching democracy sail away, with Bülent Ecevit to his right. *Zafer*, 1957

One of the most politically relevant responses to the DP's democratic discourse came from Bülent Ecevit. As a young journalist and art critic who had studied poetry in London and interned at a newspaper in North Carolina, Ecevit engaged with the CHP's future during the 1950s from a largely intellectual perspective. Yet in the following decade he would rise to prominence in the party and become, during the 1970s and again briefly in 1999, the only CHP politician to win power democratically. Thus Ecevit's early efforts to reconcile his party's high-modernist history with the requirements of democracy played a defining role in the mid-century reconceptualization of Turkish modernity.

In his writing from the mid-1950s, Ecevit tackled the question of how to make the basic tenets of Kemalism popular to an electorate that had just dealt Atatürk's party multiple electoral defeats. In many of his columns, Ecevit sought to reclaim Atatürk on more liberal terms, showing Atatürk's commitment to democracy and portraying his secularism as a form of religious tolerance. Then, while insisting the CHP must remain true to its secular principles, Ecevit increasingly sought to shift emphasis and appeal to voters by emphasizing left-wing critiques of the Democrats' economic policies. Paradoxically, though, with the CHP out of power, Ecevit was increasingly attuned to the need for private initiative in the social realm, suggesting, for example, that an entrepreneurial spirit could free artists from their dependence on state patronage. In this manner, Ecevit addressed the question of who besides the government could promote a more liberal mindset in the population. He argued that Turkey's intellectuals, or *aydınlar*, should recommit themselves to enlightening the masses. Their leadership, he hoped, could bypass the state and thus overcome the paradoxical challenge of instilling an independent spirit in people whose flaw was an overreliance on traditional state authority.

Where the DP, upon coming to power, claimed credit for finally allowing citizens to embrace their initiative, Ecevit argued that encouraging this spirit was all the more important from the position of the political opposition. On the subject of roads, art, or industry, Ecevit attached particular importance to individual initiative precisely because his party was out of power. On vacation in the small seaside town of Akçakoca, for example, Ecevit could not resist chastising his fellow citizens for their lack of motivation. Though he admitted he could understand the appeal of doing nothing in life but sitting by the window, watching the sea, and getting a shave, he felt that the villagers had the time and money to make better roads and houses, that is, to "develop" their lives and their village.[89] It was not just that villagers were too lazy to improve their own villages, he argued, but that they "waited for the state to open parks, schools, and libraries. Even most of our charitable foundations depend on the government."[90]

While this might not be dangerous, Ecevit claimed, in countries with established democracies, Turkey's developing democratic culture made such dependence on the state uniquely risky. Since the DP could not be trusted to patronize the right sort of art, for example, Ecevit emphasized the importance of freeing Turkish artists from government patronage. In describing why he and his wife opened one of Turkey's first art galleries, he stressed that enabling artists to support themselves through the private sale of their paintings was crucial. While he hoped for an impartial mechanism to distribute state funding, in the end only the establishment of an independent art market could truly liberate Turkish artists.[91]

---

[89] Bülent Ecevit, "Deniz," *Ulus*, August 8, 1955.
[90] Bülent Ecevit, "Merkeziyetçilikten kurtulma yolları," *Ulus*, July 16, 1956.
[91] Bülent Ecevit, "Londra Notları," *Ulus*, November 7, 1951.

All the more important, Ecevit argued, was for Turkey's cultural and intellectual elite to take initiative and fulfill their transformational social role independent of the government. In doing so, they would lead voters to embrace his party's views on democratic terms. Indeed, Ecevit believed that if Turkey's elite truly understood the essence of Western modernity, they would persevere in their democratic efforts despite the manifest shortcomings of the Turkish people. Importing European civilization, Ecevit explained, was not like importing a refrigerator or a car; it was like planting a tree.[92] The responsibility of Turkish intellectuals was to help this tree take root. Ecevit repeatedly returned to the idea that elitist Turks who thought their countrymen were too uneducated for democracy were only Western in their clothing and appearance: "Intellectuals who give in to the impulse to say our society isn't ready for democracy aren't doing their job as intellectuals, which is to lead society to a better place."[93] In trying to reconcile his faith in democracy and his frustration with the voters themselves, Ecevit even appealed to the West's own shortcomings[94]. Criticizing the DP for restricting workers' right to strike, for example, he dismissed the argument that Turkish workers were too ignorant to use it responsibly by asking "when Western workers received the right to strike were they educated? Are they even educated now?"

But while the DP repeatedly told voters, before and after 1950, that they had already demonstrated their maturity, Ecevit argued that a more engaged, populist form of elitism was still needed to help the population mature. Ecevit insisted that a successful democracy required intellectuals who were focused on the problems of the people,

---

[92] Bülent Ecevit, "Siyaset ve fikir hürriyeti," *Ulus*, August 19, 1955.

[93] Bülent Ecevit, "Kötü bir hastalık: aydın karamsarlığı," *Ulus*, July 9, 1955.

[94] Bülent Ecevit, "Grev," *Ulus*, July 19, 1955. Indeed the idea that American democracy succeeded in spite of the shortcomings of the American people had previously served as evidence that Turkey was ready for democracy despite its uneducated population. In 1948, for example, when the subject of Russian veto rights in the newly founded UN was the subject of international debate, a Gallup poll revealed that 42 percent of Americans did not understand the term "veto right." "These are the very people who founded and preserve American democracy," a Turkish author declared. If democratic government required a thoroughly educated population "it would be natural to think that America must wait years longer before it could achieve democracy." The implication, of course, was that it would be equally absurd to suggest Turkey had any reason to wait. Hıfzı Oğuz Bekata, "Demokrasiye 'veto' denilemez," *İşte Türkiye*, Volume 1, Issue 1, January 1948, p. 63.

suggesting that they must form a relationship with ordinary citizens akin to what DP rhetoric demanded of politicians. Ecevit argued that just as wealthy individuals should develop a "social conscience" and "spirit of service" in order to help fight the society's dependence on state patronage,[95] intellectuals must similarly interest themselves in the nation's political affairs: "[A]n intellectual who reads English papers and French magazines must endure the sacrifice of buying a Turkish newspaper for his home every day and, whether with wonder or hate, reading it."[96] In short, before the Turkish people could be expected to become modern, Ecevit believed Turkish intellectuals had to become more modern in their own views and thus become more effective instruments of democratic modernization:

In truth democracy is not, as we assume, a regime where the votes of the enlightened don't count and their words are ignored. Democracy is a regime that teaches intellectuals the humility they need to pay attention to the problems of the majority and take an interest in them.[97]

Ecevit's belief that Turkey's intellectual elite could play this role in Turkish society endured in the face of successive electoral defeats, thereby perpetuating his faith that the democratic model of modernity would one day bring his party victory.

It was, in fact, Ecevit's commitment to a remarkably deterministic vision of modernization that let him make the case for democracy even as political developments led other modernizers to give up hope. While the DP leaders argued that democracy would finally allow them to realize Atatürk's revolutionary vision of modernity, Ecevit offered an alternative reading where modernity itself would eventually bring the masses back to the CHP democratically:

In Turkey, every person who learns to read and write, every person who becomes accustomed to understanding matters of state as something more than just personal or local profits, is a new hope for the CHP and a new threat to the Democratic Party .... In Turkey time is on the side of the political parties who embrace revolution .... The CHP must wait for this preordained [*mukadder*] time's arrival without changing course. In the one-party era, the Six Arrows [a symbolic representation of Atatürk's principles] were imposed

---

[95] Bülent Ecevit, "Merkeziyetçilikten kurtulma yolları," *Ulus*, July 16, 1956.
[96] Bülent Ecevit, "Kültürsüz politika," *Ulus*, July 17, 1955.   [97] Ibid.

on the people. In the multi-party era, the Six Arrows must originate from the people![98]

Ecevit, in other words, used his faith in the idea of democratic modernity to explain why he felt Kemalist ideals would triumph even without resort to the authoritarian methods used by Mustafa Kemal himself.

Alongside the DP's rhetoric, Ecevit's views on the relationship between democracy and modernity can help shed light on the nature of Turkey's postwar transition. In the late 1930s, it was not at all clear that throughout the second half of the twentieth century a majority of Turkish politicians and voters would remain convinced that the national will should be expressed through competitive multiparty elections. And yet in the 1950s, members of both parties insisted on the fundamental harmony of democracy and Kemalist ideals. The DP could present its political agenda as an extension of Turkey's historic modernization process while the CHP, in response, could present its long-standing ideological goals as the inevitable end point of democratic rule.

In the following half century, Turkey experienced a number of coups whose leaders defended their violent intervention in democratic politics with reference to Ataturk's modernizing vision. This, like Turkey's democratic transition, naturally led to a reassessment of Atatürk's rule. Where a decade of democratic elections had helped consolidate a belief, among Turkish citizens and foreign observers alike, that democracy was the natural end point of Kemalist modernization, Turkey's successive coups have now led to a newfound focus on the authoritarian nature of Kemalism. In the 1950s, when Bülent Ecevit declared Atatürk's rule "a dictatorship to end dictatorship," he did so in the belief that the era of dictatorship had ended.[99] When this proved false, it brought the enduring and undemocratic aspects of Ataturk's ideology to the fore.

A Democratic Legacy?

In his first address to parliament as prime minister, Menderes restated the promise made in his party's election platform: the DP would

---

[98] Bülent Ecevit, "Halktan Doğacak Altı Ok," *Ulus*, May 5, 1954.
[99] Bülent Ecevit, "Atatürk: He Defied an Empire in the Name of Freedom," *Winston-Salem Journal*, November 14, 1954.

preserve and uphold all of the Kemalist revolutions that had been "internalized by the nation"[100] [*millete mal olmuş inkılâpları*]. Today, seven decades, four coups, and dozens of elections later, scholars and citizens are still debating which exactly those reforms are. In these debates, Turkey's democratic experience during the 1950s represents an imperfect, perhaps misleading, reference point. Surely the views expressed by Turkish voters in these years can tell us something about their attitudes toward the Kemalist reform program at the time. And yet we should resist the temptation to treat the era as offering some fundamental and enduring insight into where the Turkish nation stands vis-à-vis secularism or the West.

Consider the case of the Turkish-language *ezan* or call to prayer. As part of Atatürk's nationalist secularization program, the traditional Arabic call to prayer was replaced in 1932 with a Turkish-language translation that was recited from the country's minarets for the rest of the one-party era. Religious conservatives viewed the ban on the Arabic *ezan* as a defining example of Kemalist oppression they expected the DP to reverse. Arguing that this would be both a moral and electoral triumph, one Islamist writer explained: "If the cry of *Allahuekber* rises from 65 thousand minarets, 18 million Turkish men, women, and children will hear it and know religious freedom has arrived."[101]

Shortly after assuming power, the DP prepared to lift the ban on the Arabic *ezan*. The responses reflected a wide range of opinions about which reforms the people had internalized and what, by extension, the people would do with their newfound freedom. Some citizens worried that because "Atatürk's revolutions are a totality" undoing one would quickly undo the others.[102] They feared, in other words, that even the most basic reforms had not been internalized, and the nation, if left to

---

[100] T. B. M. M. Tutanaklar, 3 Birleşim 29. V. 1950. He then renewed the party's promise to remove all undemocratic laws remaining from the one-party era and modify the constitution to secure citizens' rights and freedoms. The DP, he announced, would never allow extreme leftists – and, indirectly, religious fundamentalists or ultra-nationalists – to hide behind these freedoms in order to destroy them: "We will not hesitate in taking all legal measures against left-wing extremist movements which often exploit and hide behind the mask of disruptive agendas like reaction or racism. [*irticai ve ırkçılık*]."

[101] Eşref Edip, "Yeni Gelen Milletvekilleriyle Mülakat," *Şebilürresad*, May 1950, Volume IV, No. 79.

[102] Ethem İzzet Benice, quoted in Eşref Edip, "Hükümetin Program ve Ezan Meselesi," *Sebilürreşad*, May 1950, Volume IV, No. 80.

its own devices, would reject almost all of them. A writer at the paper *Son Telegraf*, for example, worried the Arabic *ezan* would bring the return of the Arabic alphabet, while the editor of the *Women's Newspaper* feared the return of mandatory veiling.[103] At the other extreme, Ahmet Emin Yalman, a journalist who initially championed the DP before growing more skeptical, believed that permitting the Arabic ezan would not make much of a difference. The reform in question, he suspected, had already been largely accepted: "When the ban is lifted those who want to will use Arabic. But we assume that in spite of this freedom there will still be many who prefer to use their mother tongue."[104]

When the DP, with the support of a number of CHP deputies, lifted the ban, it seemed both Yalman's hopes and others' fears were misplaced. Very few people sought to preserve the Turkish ezan voluntarily, but there was also no immediate push to bring back forced veiling or Arabic letters. A decade later, it became clear that even a coup would not bring the Turkish ezan back. The military-appointed court that sentenced Menderes to death cited the legalization of the Arabic ezan as part of the case against him, while some prominent figures such as İsmet İnönü suggested the country's new military rulers might reinstate the Turkish ezan. And yet neither the junta, nor any subsequent government, ever did. Nor, to date, have any tried to reintroduce Arabic letters or mandatory veiling.

As a result of this experience, the Turkish ezan remains widely seen as an example of Kemalist overreach democratically rejected by popular opinion. But the violent, undemocratic end of the DP left open, in many people's minds, the question of where, or whether, voters would draw a line in the other direction if they were truly free to choose. Perhaps the Turkish people were happy with the level of religiosity the DP offered them? After all, they definitively preferred the DP to the much more overtly religious Nation Party, which got a mere 3 percent of the vote in 1950. Moreover, even as the DP turned more emphatically toward religion as the decade went on, voters nonetheless shifted toward the CHP in the country's 1957 election. But in the aftermath of the 1960 coup it was impossible for scholars, citizens, or foreign observers to be sure. As a result, many continued to fear that the masses

---

[103] Ibid, İffet Oruz, "Softalar Canlanıyor," *Kadın Gazetesi*, February 21, 1949.
[104] Yalman, quoted in "Hükümetin Programı ve Ezan Meselesi," ibid.

would have kept cheering the DP on as it became more and more religious.

When the Justice and Development Party (AKP) came to power in 2002, it provoked renewed debate over whether, in the absence of military interference, the Turkish people would seek to overturn the Republic or preserve it of their own accord. In this context, alarm about the return of sharia coexisted with confident predictions that Turkish voters would finally make a more liberal form of secular modernity work. Pessimists could justify their position with reference to sweeping claims about the irreconcilability of Islam and democracy or, more specifically, by citing the 1950s as evidence of voters' unreliability. Optimists, by contrast, could bolster their sweeping assumptions about the triumph of liberal democracy by noting that the 1960 coup denied Turkish voters the chance to embrace modernity on their own terms.

History, of course, cannot answer to these expectations. No account of the 1950s will predict just how far Erdoğan might push his religious politics or how the Turkish people might respond. If nothing else, the evidence in this book demonstrates why we would do well not to think of the Menderes era, in all its complexity, as prefiguring the rise of the AKP. But it does not prefigure any other path either. No historical account will unearth Turkey's true views on democracy, secularism, modernity, or the West.

This book, then, explores the historic legacy of the 1945–1960 period in more modest terms. I argue that the debates of this era helped consolidate the idea of democratic modernity in Turkish political discourse. But these debates also revealed how flexible this idea could be. Paradoxically, by the end of the 1950s, democratic modernity had become so well entrenched that even the 1960 coup was justified as a restoration of democratic rule. The following chapters seek to show how, alongside democracy, new attitudes toward subjects such as Ottoman history, the Arab world, and the West were articulated between 1945 and 1960. I argue that the manner in which these attitudes emerged, whether as the result of long-standing trends or in response to new political circumstances, can reveal how little influence they actually had. That is to say, recognizing how easily Turkish thinkers reworked their relationship to all facets of Western modernity in the middle of the twentieth century remains crucial to understanding how so many people continue to do so today.

2 | Turkey Attends the American Classroom

US Modernity as Policy and Propaganda

Turks, being semi-Oriental, have certain similarities and dissimilarities to Americans.

> – General William Arnold, head of the Joint American
> Military Mission for Aid to Turkey, 1952[1]

In the early Cold War period, American diplomats, soldiers, and economists working in Turkey had a very clear idea of what it meant to be modern and, more specifically, what it meant to be modern in an American way. They appealed to this idea of modernity – which required societies to be democratic, participatory, literate, and mobile – in crafting all of their policies, aid programs, and propaganda. Yet a closer examination reveals this broad rhetorical coherence belied a profound but necessary incoherence in the way they applied their thinking. That is, while the qualities identified as "modern" were consistent and explicitly democratic, intelligent people could apply this vision of modernity to concrete situations in quite different ways. As seen in the opening quotation, even crudely stereotypical American assessments of the Turkish character were consistently contradictory enough to allow for rival conclusions. Americans could appeal to the Turkish nation's oriental or non-oriental characteristics as needed to defend either democracy or authoritarianism. As a result, in the course of two decades, arguments couched in the logic of modernization explained why US support for İnönü's one-party regime, Menderes's increasingly authoritarian government, and the coup that removed Menderes from power were all in the best interest of Turkish democracy. With successive Turkish governments broadly supportive of US foreign policy goals, Washington was happy to work with all of them.

---

[1] General William Arnold, "Briefing for New Arrivals," undated, 1952, Joint American Military Mission for Aid to Turkey, Adjutant General Section Decimal File, Classified, Box 2, RG 334, NARA.

Modernization was not the reason, but it repeatedly served as the explanation.

There has been a growing body of literature over the past two decades examining how American views on modernity – which reflected long-standing cultural prejudices and were codified into the discipline of modernization theory by social scientists – drove US support for authoritarian regimes during the Cold War.[2] Building on Salim Yaqub's argument that US policy was pragmatic *in spite of* American prejudices, I argue that modernization as an ideology proved durable precisely because of how readily it served to justify pragmatic decisions.[3] In short, the Turkish and American experience of the early Cold War period reveals that both the power and persistence of modernization discourse depended upon its flexibility.

This chapter also explores how America's modernization discourse resonated with mid-century Turkish views on the subject. During this period, Washington launched a number of projects that were intended to modernize Turkey and advance shared US and Turkish geopolitical interests. Turkish politicians were partners in these projects, but also used modernization discourse to challenge American policies, as well as their own domestic rivals. Meanwhile, American diplomats sought to build on a common understanding of modernity to craft propaganda that would showcase America's modernity and win Turkish support in the Cold War.

Modernization as Politics

In 1947, President Truman called on Congress to provide aid to Turkey and Greece in order to help both countries resist the threat of Soviet expansion. In his speech, which became the basis of the Truman Doctrine, he described Greece, with several caveats, as an imperfect democracy. Turkey, by contrast, was "an independent and

---

[2] See, for example: Nils Gilman, *Mandarins of the Future: Modernization Theory in Cold War America* (Baltimore, MD: Johns Hopkins University Press, 2003), Bradley Simpson, *Economists with Guns: Authoritarian Development and U.S.-Indonesian Relations, 1960–68* (Palo Alto: Stanford University Press, 2008), Michael Latham, *Modernization as Ideology in American Social Science and Nation Building in the Kennedy Era* (Chapel Hill: University of North Carolina Press, 2000).

[3] Salim Yaqub, *Containing Arab Nationalism: The Eisenhower Doctrine and the Middle East* (Chapel Hill, NC: University of North Carolina Press, 2004), 13.

economically sound state" whose future was "important to the freedom-loving peoples of the world."[4] Indeed, at the end of World War II, the reigning US attitude toward Turkish President İsmet İnönü was perhaps best characterized by the description of Atatürk in a contemporary guide for US soldiers: "Many accused him of being a dictator. If so, he was a strong man of the right sort."[5] When the US-Turkish relationship began, this was the status quo US officials assumed would continue indefinitely, and they did not seem unduly perturbed by it. Moreover, when Portugal, under the quasi-fascist Salazar regime, became a founding member of NATO in 1948, İnönü had every reason to believe his government was democratic enough for the Western alliance as well.

Over the past half-century, it has been widely suggested that US pressure prompted İnönü's decision to hold multiparty elections in 1946 and then step down after losing in 1950.[6] At the time, the Democratic Party (DP) also argued that real democracy was needed to secure US support.[7] But even assuming İnönü would have been susceptible to such pressure, Washington never gave him a chance to feel it. Finding evidence of absence is difficult, but US State Department records from 1945 to 1950 have not, so far, divulged any examples of US officials actually trying to convince their Turkish counterparts that free or fair elections were necessary to secure American backing. To the contrary, on one of the few occasions the subject came up, CHP officials appeared remarkably confident in their position. In December 1948, a member of the US military mission discussed with Naci Perkel, head of the Turkish National Security Service, rumors that the United States had abandoned Chiang Kai-shek because of his undemocratic

---

[4] President Truman's Message to Congress; March 12, 1947; Document 171; 80th Congress, 1st Session; Records of the United States House of Representatives; Record Group 233; NARA. Accessed via archives.gov.

[5] Guide to Turkey, Research and Analysis Branch Detachment "C" 2799 Prov OPR & TNG Unit APO 787, U.S. Army.

[6] For the first example of this claim in English, citing newspaper reports from the time, see Kemal Karpat, *Turkey's Politics: The Transition to a Multi-Party System* (Princeton: Princeton University Press, 1959). For a further discussion of this subject, see Barın Kayaoğlu, "Strategic Imperatives, Democratic Rhetoric: The United States and Turkey, 1945–52," in Cold War History, Volume 9, Issue 3, 2009.

[7] Memorandum to John Evarts Horne from G. H. Damon, November 14, Unclassified General Records, U.S. Embassy, Ankara, Box 91, RG 84, NARA.

behavior.[8] The American colonel drew Perkel's attention to "remarks by some of the Turkish opposition members that the United States would realize that Turkey is also not democratic and would take similar action here to withdraw U.S. Aid." "Naci's response," he reported, "was to laugh and say that since aid is still coming in, the U.S. evidently is convinced that Turkey is democratic."

Perkel then went on to explain that "Turkey could not be democratic until the level of education is much higher, and such a condition is many, many years away."[9] Reporting his conversation, the colonel concluded, parenthetically:

Naci does not even bother to give lip service to democracy, which he considers, I believe, unsuitable for Turkey. As a loyal, patriotic Turk, he does his best for his country by the means he knows best – a good police system which helps the Turks vote the straight PRP [CHP] ticket.

When Turkey's parliamentary elections were scheduled for 1950, State Department officials and CIA analysts largely expected İnönü to once again use his "good police system" to achieve victory. Tellingly, in private conversations with İnönü about US-Turkish cooperation in the months before Turkey went to the polls, US participants made it clear they expected relations to continue apace.[10] Publicly, US descriptions of İnönü's rule were sufficiently ambiguous that pro-government papers could interpret them as praise for İnönü's modest reforms while opposition papers could read them as a critique of his authoritarianism. When a congressional delegation visited Turkey in April 1947, for example, coverage in the CHP party paper *Ulus* reported Congressman Carl Hatch as saying, "All my life I have been a supporter of democracy and government by the people. I must express my admiration for the speedy development which democratic life has shown in Turkey." *Kuvvet*, by contrast, quoted Congressman Brewster as saying, of the same democratic progress, "I hope that this development will expand."[11]

---

[8] Memorandum to the Ambassador, from Colonel GSC J. S. Robinson. Ankara, December 16, 1948. Top Secret General Records, Box 1, RG 84, NARA.
[9] Ibid
[10] Despatch No. 38, American Embassy Ankara to SecState, February 3, 1950. Top Secret Records, Box 1, RG 84, NARA.
[11] *Ulus*, April 14, 1947; *Kuvvet*, April 14, 1947.

Such ambiguity was not just a product of US officials trying to be polite. Rather, it reflected a profound ambiguity in private assessments of Turkey's political maturity. This ambiguity, in turn, stemmed from the fact that while everyone agreed being a modern country ultimately required being democratic, people could disagree on what it meant for a country whose level of modernity was up for debate. According to an April 1950 CIA assessment about the upcoming election:

Although the Turk has been accustomed to being pushed around (provided it is done by duly constituted authorities in what he accepts as a proper and customary manner) he has now been told by both government and opposition that mishandling of his electoral privileges this time would be most improper. If it happens, he will object most strenuously.[12]

Here, as in other similar statements, the ordinary Turk's traditional mentality appears as the foundation for a contradictory conclusion: He is used to being pushed around but will no longer accept being pushed around because those pushing him around have told him not to accept it. More striking, though, is the parenthetical caveat that renders the initial statement about the Turk's passivity almost meaningless. Caveats like this in fact played an important role in giving modernization its flexibility as an ideology. Government officials whose opinions did not fit neatly within the prevailing rhetoric could easily find exceptions or qualifications that would enable seemingly irreconcilable ideas to coexist.

When Turkish voters, of their own free will, elected a party that enthusiastically supported an American alliance and free-market capitalism, State Department observers were excited to have an example of modernity working the way they always thought it should. US officials were quick to praise Turkey for having taken a vital step on the road toward modernity and also worked to understand what had made this step possible. Thus subsequent years brought a newfound American interest in the factors that enabled Turkey's villagers, often seen as too "traditional" to even have opinions on matters of high politics, to reach such an enlightened decision. Like DP politicians, US officials saw a harmonious logic in the interplay of democracy and modernity, one in which they played a starring role. In US assessments, the newly

[12] CIA Near/East Africa Intelligence Summary, April 12, 1950. NARA, Electronic Reading Room.

elected DP's commitment to rural development and agricultural modernization improved the villager's life, making him both grateful and more modern in the process. For the Turkish peasant, who held "no conviction that the passage of time connotes progress," and had been "born and raised in an environment where the material things of life are sparse at best," improved living standards challenged his fatalism and made him demand even more improvements.[13] This newly modern attitude made the peasant grateful to the DP, but also to the country which supplied the tractors, built the roads, and engineered the irrigation projects that made life better.

American observers consistently sided with the DP in its preference for agricultural development. While the CHP saw industrialization as necessary to make Turkey more like modern Western countries, Americans justified the DP's program through a historical reading of America's own modernization process. Saying that "agricultural development was the basic requirement of a country," US Ambassador and proud Texan George McGhee explained:

[T]he United States had started off as an agricultural country and as the farmers began to accumulate money they started investing in various industries, leading to the development of industry.[14]

Indeed, while Turkish accounts of American modernity focused on the dynamism of cities like New York, Americans often envisioned Turkey emulating the dynamism they associated with romanticized mid-century depictions of more rural regions. A US consul visiting Bursa, for example, was impressed when eating with a group of city notables

---

[13] "Evaluation of the 1954 Turkish General Election," May 6, 1954, Department of State. Classified General Records, 1938–1958, Box 72, RG 84, NARA.

[14] "Memorandum of Conversation between the Ambassador and İsmet İnönü, Former President of the Republic of Turkey and Current President of the Republican People's Party, the Principle Party in Opposition," undated. *George C. McGhee Papers*, Georgetown University Library Special Collections. Series XXIV, Box 1. Yet here too, the logic of modernization could justify the opposite conclusion. As McGhee explained elsewhere: "I, myself, had not been as critical of the policy of etatism in Turkey during the 1930's as some observers, because it appeared evident that if the State had not taken the initiative at that time nothing would have happened. It was better that something happen … than that nothing happen." "Memorandum of Conversation between Ambassador McGhee and Foreign Minister Köprülü on February 1, 1952." *George C. McGhee Papers*, Georgetown University Library Special Collections. Series XXIV, Box 1.

to find "the atmosphere had much of the informality of a mid-Western businessmen's lunch at home."[15]

With these ideas in mind, lower-ranking members of the embassy staff frequently went out into rural Turkey to evaluate the success of the DP's modernization efforts. Their subsequent reports were consistently contradictory. Returning from a partridge-hunting expedition in 1951, for example, Izmir Consul Edward Rivinus declared: "I have seen nothing during my journey to cause me to dissent from the generally accepted thesis that the old Turkish cultural pattern is still dominant in Anatolia." He then went on to note that "the Anatolian peasant adapts himself to the tractor with remarkable facility."[16] A year later, his successor drew a similar conclusion in Thrace: "Mechanization of agricultural has clearly taken hold," he reported, "and has had a leavening effect on the spirit and outlook of the whole countryside." Yet the population nonetheless lacked initiative, this passivity being "presumably ... a Turkish trait."[17] In Adana, a visiting diplomat declared himself "elated" at the "Turkish awakening" he discovered. He echoed DP rhetoric in describing the "signs of wealth" he saw in the countryside – "wide, straight, paved roads," farms and villages which gave the appearance of "cleanliness and efficiency," "expensive automobiles," and "even women drivers." Still, this enthusiasm only went so far. The cities in the region, he was shocked to find, "have maintained their cramped and backward Anatolian appearance."

Crucially, all of these assessments revealed just enough cause for optimism to justify further American support, but never so much optimism as to obviate the need for it. In some cases, observers declared themselves quite pleased with how modern the Turkish people appeared. In other cases, observers found diverse ways to reconcile pessimistic assessments of the citizens themselves with their enduring belief in democracy or the DP.

After Turkey's 1954 elections, the virtuous cycle Americans had identified between the DP's support for the peasants and the peasants' freely given support for the DP began to break down on two fronts. The

---

[15] "[A] far cry," he noted, "from Oriental formality."
[16] "Partridges and Politics in Muğla and Aydin Vilayets." September 7, 1951. Records of the Izmir Consular Post, Box 69, RG 84, NARA.
[17] "Turkish Thrace: A Frontier Area, a Preliminary Economic and Political Survey," May 23, 1952. Records of the Izmir Consular Post, Box 71, RG 84, NARA.

high-profile arrest of several journalists, coupled with violent anti-Greek riots in 1955, inspired public criticism of Menderes's democratic credentials in the US press. Meanwhile, the failure of Turkey's wheat crop after three profitable seasons led to a budget crisis that made Menderes's high-profile rural development projects seem more like wasteful pandering than inspired modernizing. Yet here the evolutionary aspects of the modernization model came to Menderes's defense: After accepting İnönü's democratic credentials, it was relatively easy for US officials to explain why supporting a democratically elected leader who was behaving undemocratically could serve the long-term interests of Turkish democracy. In one typical assessment, an ultimately positive evaluation of the Turkish people's democratic development is used to explain why a recently manifest lack of political maturity in other realms should be overlooked:

Turkey is far from being an operating democracy in our sense of the word. It never has been and is not likely to be for many years to come, for it takes time to develop the psychological attitudes among both leaders and people and the institutions and traditions which are essential to the democratic system. It is true that the really revolutionary step was taken in 1950 when the Turkish people discovered that they could be the masters, via the ballot box, and throw out a repressive government. They are not likely to forget this basic lesson ... On the whole, Emb[assy] is satisfied Turkey is headed and will continue in right direction despite our feeling there has been some retrogression or at least slackening of evolutionary pace in past year.[18]

In other words, because Turkey was not a democracy, but had taken a key step toward becoming one, the fact that it had become less democratic did not mean it was not moving forward on the long and difficult path toward democracy.

On the economic front, embassy officials argued that Menderes's enthusiasm for projects like big-budget dams revealed that he was simply "over-eager" for modernization – "all steamed up" in the words of one memo.[19] Such overeagerness, in turn, was often seen as a common symptom of incompletely modernized elites within traditional societies and could be grounds for criticism or praise as

---

[18] Deptel No. 693 from Ankara to the Department of State, January 3, 1955. Department of State. Classified General Records, 1938–1958, Box 72, RG 84, NARA.
[19] *Foreign Relations of the United States, 1955–57*. Volume XXIV, 617.

circumstances necessitated.[20] When US officials supported Menderes, overeagerness was seen as preferable to reticence. After he was toppled by a coup, some Americans would argue that perhaps leaders from the even more modernized military would be more mature, and thus more measured, in their pursuit of modernization.

Among Menderes's political opponents in Turkey, it was the DP's changing attitude toward secularism that most frequently called its modernist credentials into question. However, the State Department's faith in the party's vision for Turkey was such that US officials routinely justified the revival of public religious practice that occurred after 1950. Though embassy reports frequently contained a section for "Religious Reaction," quite often the ensuing analysis merely explained why a recent incident was not as bad as it initially appeared or why CHP charges against the government were exaggerated. At first, alarming developments were written off as manifestations of the country's new democratic spirit. After visiting a city near Izmir, for example, Rivinus quoted approvingly the reassurances of the governor or *vali*:

He insisted that there is no difference in the number or extent of reactionaries in the Turkish social picture since the coming to power of the new regime, and that the only difference lies in the healthy fact that these and all elements feel free to speak their desires openly . . . . The Turkish nation today is in the hands of such men as the Vali and his generation to whom a return to religious law or similarly reactionary tendency is so repugnant as to be inconceivable.[21]

Even when, at a later stop, he learned that citizens had been petitioning the government to be allowed multiple wives, Rivinus remained

---

[20] Introducing the translation of a Turkish teacher's description of traditional village life, anthropologist Paul Stirling excused the author's excessive desire to "fill the vacuum of ignorance with the blessing of modern knowledge" by saying he was one of those men "deliberately indoctrinated with modern ideas and ideals," who have not had "the opportunity to witness the kind of society which had invented [them], and to which they were adapted." Thus with "these notions," the author, "a lad of seventeen, was sent back to a totally different type of society with the naive goal of altering it to suit his inevitably half-understood ideas of progress." Mahmut Makal, (Wyndham Deedes Trans.) *A Village in Anatolia* (London: Valentine, Mitchell & Co., 1954).

[21] "Observations made on an inspection trip in the Izmir Consular District," from Izmir Consulate to Ankara Embassy, May 16, 1951, Records of the Izmir Consular Post, Box 69, RG 84, NARA.

nonplussed. "Naturally the social habits of a people cannot be completely eradicated in 25 years," he stated, before again repeating that all the rural leaders he met were "children of the Republic."[22] In addition, he noted that there had, after all, been a large number of unmarried women in the village relative to the number of eligible men.

Moreover, in some accounts, even the traditional Turk's lack of initiative would help keep him on the path to modernity:

[T]he Turkish people are by nature and background disciplined and will follow their appointed or elected leaders unless the latter are grossly unsatisfactory. Certainly at the present time, there are no reactionary leaders ... who have even passing appeal to the people.[23]

Other voices in the embassy reinforced this logic. A report from the State Department's in-house Turkish advisor Ali Nur Bozcalı, for example, acknowledged that "religion continues to exert a hold on the thinking of the majority of the rural population" but then states that "counteracting such menace is the dominant political influence of the educated class and the majority of the urban population." The role of the DP is made explicit when he concludes, "If no serious mistake is committed by those holding the reins of government, the safeguards in question, without undue coercion, serve to preserve the essentials of the reforms."[24] Throughout the 1950s, the embassy remained convinced that on the religious question at least, the DP was not committing any serious mistakes.

This faith persisted until the very end of Menderes's time in power. As opposition criticism of the regime's "exploitation of religion" grew, State Department officials dismissed these concerns as "name calling."[25] Prominent displays of religious sentiment (see Figure 2.1) were "isolated incidents," "in line with worldwide trends," and "hardly a threat to the secular foundation of the regime."[26] In 1959,

---

[22] Ibid.   [23] Ibid.

[24] Letter from Ali Nur Bozcalı to Bartel E. Kuniholm, April 16, 1951, Department of State. Classified General Records, 1938–1958, Box 72, RG 84, NARA. Bozcalı's sister, Sabiha, was a prominent illustrator at the time, most famous for her work on Reşat Ekrem Koçu's *Istanbul Encyclopedia*.

[25] "Religion in Turkey – Spring 1959," April 24, 1959, Central Decimal File, Box 3734, RG 59, NARA.

[26] Despatch No. 563, Ankara to Department of State, June 4, 1958; "Religion in Turkey – Spring 1959," April 24, 1959; "Exploitation of Religious Sentiment for Political Ends," March 18, 1957. Ibid.

Figure 2.1 "Recent Developments in Turkish Islam." US Embassy cable, 1959.

Menderes, having survived a plane crash in London that killed a number of his companions, returned to Istanbul where "literally thousands of animals were sacrificed" as his motorcade passed through the city. "So much sacrificial blood was thrown upon the car that the driver had difficulty seeing the road," wrote the US Consul, before again concluding that there was nothing to worry about.

The State Department's calm acceptance of such displays reveals the extent to which the political implications of modernization as an ideology lay in its application. In the face of religious activities that could easily have been used to brand Menderes a reactionary, the embassy continued to confidently assert that these made it more important than ever to have a thoroughly modern man like Menderes at the nation's helm.[27] This was not a case of ideology shaping politics or

[27] Daniel Newberry echoed the complaints of other junior embassy staff (for example, George Harris, interview with the author, November 17, 2010) in saying "[Fletcher Warren]'s idea of being an effective ambassador was to give Prime Minister Menderes whatever he wanted ... Ambassador Fletcher Warren

politics shaping ideology. It was a case of officials maintaining both their policies and principles by rationalizing away any evidence that they might be in conflict with one another.

As domestic opposition to the DP grew, US officials grew increasingly concerned about the possibility of a coup, particularly after a group of radical officers in the Iraqi army ousted pro-Western Prime Minister Nuri al-Said in a bloody putsch in 1958. The rhetoric of modernity, in turn, served to both calm and exacerbate these fears. Turkish soldiers were by nature obedient, meaning they were less likely to initiate a coup, but also less likely to resist one once initiated. The country's Byzantine-Ottoman inheritance was an obstacle to a functioning democracy, but after making the "hard break" with Ottoman authoritarianism, the people were now even more committed not to return to it. One State Department memo written in 1958 takes the contradictory possibilities of this style of reasoning to an extreme:

There is general agreement [among foreign observers] that the stolid Turk very seldom blows up but when he does there is a major explosion. Certainly no other Mediterranean would have so long endured without vociferous protest the inconveniences, discomfort, privations and outright hardship that have been the lot of Istanbul citizens for nearly two years .... The fact remains that a Turkish society so long static and dormant is now in movement and it would be unwise to take for granted that the superficial political stability rests on any rock-like base of economic and social stability .... On the whole I believe that the Turkish Army is in most ways typical of the faults and virtues of the Turkish people .... The tradition of respect for and obedience to elders and superiors, characteristic in all Turkish life, seems to retain a firm hold among the military.[28]

To summarize, the Turks were stolid, which made a coup less likely, but also meant that, once some unspecified threshold was crossed, it would be more likely. The Turk's stolidity also trumped the passionate Mediterranean aspect of his character, which might have made him more likely to rise up in revolt. At the same time, Turkey's recent experience with modernity made instability more likely, though the

did not want his 'constituent posts' reporting things that reflected against Prime Minister Adnan Menderes." Frontline Diplomacy interview with Daniel Newberry, December 1, 1997.

[28] Embassy Despatch No. 89, Ankara to Department of State, August 5, 1958. Department of State, Classified General Records, 1938–1958, Box 77, RG 84, NARA.

military was still too traditional to move against civilian authority. On top of all this, the memo ends with a quote from a Turkish officer who explains that there will not be a coup in Turkey because "this is not Syria." In his eyes, the military's respect for authority marked Turkey not as traditional but as more modern than its backward, coup-prone neighbor.

When a coup ultimately toppled the Menderes regime in 1960 and the new military government immediately declared itself loyal to NATO, the meaning of modernization had to be recalibrated once more.[29] The new attitude was perhaps best encapsulated by a 1962 United States Information Agency (USIA) exhibition that began with its title, "The Birth of American Democracy," facing a large drawing of a musket-bearing minuteman. Even in America, it seemed, the armed forces had sometimes been needed to play the role of democracy's midwife. Academic literature evaluating the coup from this period seldom praised the military, but still at times sought to find a silver lining. Richard Robinson, for example, who had worked for American Universities Field Staff before becoming professor of history at Harvard, did not hide his sympathy for the DP. Nonetheless, he concluded that "the lesson to be derived from the failure of civilian leadership in Turkey is that such leadership can survive only as long as it continues to lead."[30] While faulting Menderes for corrupt mismanagement and admitting there was an "appeal and validity to the idea of temporarily setting aside popular government" Robinson argued that the solution was not military rule but better civilian government.[31] Writing about the coup for the Brookings Institution in 1963, fellow historian Walter Weiker concluded by saying that though the United States "cannot look with benign approval on military usurpation of

---

[29] Where contemporary prejudice often cast Middle Easterners as unduly susceptible to economic inducements, the British Ambassador offered a diametrically opposed explanation of why attempting to use economic pressure to prevent Menderes's execution would be counterproductive: "The Turks are oriental enough to enjoy standing on their honour against sordid economic considerations." Fo-371/153037, RK 1018/1, Burrows to FO (Ross), Ankara, October 21, 1960, as quoted by Cihat Göktepe's "1960 'Revolution' in Turkey and the British Policy towards Turkey," *The Turkish Yearbook*, Volume XXX, pp. 139–189, p. 183.

[30] Richard D. Robinson, *The First Turkish Republic: A Case Study in Development* (Cambridge: Harvard University Press, 1965), 272.

[31] Ibid., 273.

power," "[t]he questions whether and to what extent the United States might encourage continuation of military or one-party governments . . . are extremely difficult ones."[32]

Modernization as Policy

The politically convenient ways US policymakers and scholars applied the tenets of modernization theory inevitably raise the question of whether they sincerely believed in their rhetoric or if they deliberately used this discourse in order to advance their interests. The best evidence of their sincerity comes from the importance they placed on modernization in programs designed to directly serve US political and military goals. Even as Americans conveniently adjusted their ideas about what modernization meant, or deployed the rhetoric of modernization in their propaganda, they remained genuinely convinced that it was a vital process that would advance vital US interests.

The discourse of modernization has been heavily criticized by authors such as Timothy Mitchell for the ways in which it served to justify exploitative imperial or neo-imperial relationships with third world peoples. This critique sometimes seems to imply that modernization discourse existed purely for local consumption while in private canny "experts" knew better than to fully believe their own schemes.[33] Yet in examining US discussions of modernization in mid-century Turkey, what stands out is the striking similarity between language Americans used in what was openly described as propaganda and their language in classified correspondence about crucial military and economic projects. Only when these two aspects of modernization discourse are viewed side by side does it become clear that the distinction between belief and rhetoric is often an unnecessary one.

The Turkish military was the target of the United States' most extensive modernization effort in the 1950s. At a moment when many American military planners believed that a war with the Soviet Union was a real possibility, they set about trying to modernize Turkey's military because they were convinced that, were such a war to erupt, Western access to Middle Eastern oil would hinge on Turkey's

[32] Walter Weiker, *The Turkish Revolution, 1960–1961* (Washington: Brookings Institution, 1963), 161–162.
[33] Timothy Mitchell, *Rule of Experts: Egypt, Techno-Politics, Modernity* (Berkeley: University of California Press, 2002).

ability to successfully stand against Soviet forces. For US officials, "modernizing the Turkish military" meant making it as strong as possible so it could hold its own for as long as possible. It meant providing Turkey with modern equipment, training soldiers to use this equipment and instilling the modern psychological attitudes that, Americans believed, were necessary for winning modern wars. As the United States Information Service (after 1953 the United States Information Agency) explained in language which mirrored the military's internal reports:

The courage of the Turkish soldier is well-known. But there is more than courage needed in modern warfare ... because the nature of war has changed. Weapons of the past are obsolete. The soldier of today must be well-equipped, well-trained and well-organized to survive and be an effective fighting unit.[34]

Complicated as it proved to be, delivering vehicles and weaponry was still the most straightforward aspect of US military aid efforts. JAMMAT (the Joint American Military Mission for Aid to Turkey, subsequently JUSMMAT, the Joint United States Military Mission for Aid to Turkey) monthly reports from the early 1950s provided regular, detailed breakdowns of equipment delivered and discussed whether it was effectively utilized. These reports devoted considerably greater space, though, to detailing the number of Turkish soldiers and officers entering, enrolled in and graduating from various training programs. The United States Army established a series of specialized training centers, including an engineering school in Istanbul; a commando training school in Izmir; an armored school in Ankara; and artillery, anti-aircraft, and ordnance schools in smaller cities. While ordinary recruits were sent to these schools to learn specific skills, a smaller number of English-speaking officers were sent for more advanced study at US or NATO bases in America or Germany. The US military worked to ensure that Turkish soldiers who graduated from these courses were given positions in which they could teach the skills they had learned to other soldiers. JAMMAT also tried to ensure that the classes Turkish soldiers took deviated as little as possible from those of their American counterparts. The training manuals provided for

---

[34] "Modern Turkish Army," VOA Turkish Production, February 3, 1954, Movie Scripts 1942–1965, Box 25, RG 306, NARA.

Turkish courses were translations of those used in the equivalent US schools, and JAMMAT officials sometimes became worried when they feared a "Turkish twist" had been introduced into the translations.[35]

In addition to teaching a wide range of technical skills, US military advisors also sought to impart a new ethos, at once more American and more modern, to the Turkish military. "The tradition of a Turkish enlisted boy" they feared "is not that of the Janissaries but of the patient mute immemorial Oriental infantry, the uncomprehending serf of an inflexible fate."[36] The US military wanted to replace what they saw as a culture of blind obedience and slavish devotion to authority with a new spirit of initiative in which responsibility would be delegated to younger officers who would in turn be more assertive in exercising it. The JAMMAT leadership also worked to encourage greater meritocracy with promotions based on ability rather than seniority. Not only did JAMMAT officials believe that greater initiative and meritocratic promotions had strategic benefits in their own right, but they were also aware that the methods advanced by younger, lower-ranking officers were more likely to be those taught by JAMMAT.[37]

In 1952, JAMMAT identified several methods for the "indoctrination of the Turkish Forces in the principles of leadership and the exercise of initiative."[38] At the most basic level, these included holding special classes for Turkish units, emphasizing leadership and initiative at military schools, using "on-the-spot correction" during officers' field visits and providing a "good example" through the conduct of

---

[35] "Report of Ad Hoc Committee on Turkish Infantry," January 2, 1951, Joint American Military Mission for Aid to Turkey, Adjutant General Section Decimal File, Classified, Box 7, RG 334, NARA.

[36] Memorandum from Betty Carp to Ambassador, "Morale of the Turkish Armed Forces," June 18, 1946. Classified General Records, Box 17, RG 84, NARA. This quote, too, included a pragmatic acknowledgment that, alongside cultural factors, "poverty" remained one of the major reasons for Turkey's failure to adopt to modern warfare.

[37] In the words of a JAMMAT evaluation: "In many units where senior officers are non-graduates of American supervised schools or of Stateside schools, there is a marked tendency to side track or disregard any advice which might be forthcoming from junior officers who have had such schooling. The tendency on the part of such senior commanders is to adhere to the old methods with which they are familiar." "Reassessment of results of training efforts of TU.S.AG in advice of Turkish Ground Forces, Appendix X," November 24, 1952, JAMMAT Army Group Adjutant General's section, Box 116, RG 334, NARA.

[38] Ibid.

American advisors. The memo also suggests giving "public credit and recognition to outstanding officers who exhibit qualities of initiative and leadership," along with eliminating "those officers, young or old, who prove themselves to be obstructionists or reactionaries." On several occasions during the 1950s JAMMAT leaders, in coordination with the State Department, worked to secure the replacement of members of the Turkish General Staff who they felt fit this description. Meeting with Prime Minister Menderes shortly before leaving Turkey, General Arnold praised him for deciding to retire all but one of Turkey's four-star generals, saying that this would "bring into leadership of the Turkish army a new and more flexible mentality."[39] Arnold went on to say that "one of the principle deterrents to the development of initiative on the part of the younger officers in the Turkish army was the fact that at the present time no man could be promoted without the unanimous concurrence of the heads of the army, navy and air force." This, Arnold felt, led junior officers to "keep their mouths shut" instead of making suggestions or questioning their superiors. The prime minister agreed and "indicated he would do something about this situation." Later in the decade, the one general Menderes retained in 1953 was also retired with the support of the United States when he too began to appear as an obstacle to reform. Ironically, the democratic aspects of mid-century modernization discourse sometimes seemed most pronounced in a military context, where there were fewer competing political interests to interfere with the US goal of winning wars.

An emphasis on participation, mobility, and initiative also informed aid programs in other realms that Washington saw as crucial for its Cold War aims.[40] Alongside trying to modernize Turkey's military,

---

[39] "Memorandum of Conversation of the Ambassador and General Arnold with the Prime Minister and Foreign Minister on March 19, 1953." McGhee Papers, Series XXIV, Box 1. See also "On the Military Resignations. Members of Cabinet, the Ministry of Defense and Military Establishment in Turkey," February 6, 1953. Department of State, Classified General Records, 1938–1958, Box 77, RG 84, NARA.

[40] Interestingly, discussions of Turkey's highway program frequently reflected the United States hope that increasing the physical mobility of the Turkish villager would also increase his "psychic mobility" thereby giving him a more modern outlook. This goal, however, could be equally well served by any configuration of roads. As a result, the main debates concerning road construction at the time were over the relative importance of military versus economic goals. In the brief period that a Soviet attack seemed potentially imminent after World War II, the

State Department officials also felt that freeing the Turkish bureaucracy from its overly centralized, authoritarian character would facilitate more efficient economic management, thereby decreasing Turkey's dependence on US aid. While Americans fervently encouraged free-market reforms, they also reasoned that as long as Turkey's economy remained largely state-run, the bureaucracy running the economy should at least be as modern as possible. Ambassador George McGhee, like his counterparts in the DP, believed that America must "encourage Turks to revise the present rigid civil service system to provide greater incentive to civil servants to take initiative and responsibility, particularly in state economic enterprises."[41]

Americans also felt increasing initiative was necessary to improve Turkish education and bring about broader social reform. The Turkish government seemed so intent on maintaining tight control over Turkish schools – the US military even had to obtain special authorization to run a private school for the children of enlisted men – that American officials concluded the field of education was too sensitive for major reforms efforts. However the first time that the Turkish Ministry of Education allowed the Ford Foundation to implement an experimental curriculum in a girls elementary school, the result was a program emphasizing individual initiative, parental participation, and practical training. Students were allowed to choose their own electives, and courses were "remodeled to suit the needs of young women going out into the world of Turkey today." Parents, too, were invited to the

---

Turkish General Staff had anticipated a rapid effort to link Istanbul, Ankara, Erzurum, and Iskenderun through three major highways that could transport men and material from the country's capital and major port directly to the front. In the early 1950s, though, US military planners felt the short-term threat of war had sufficiently receded to prioritize more systematic, long-term economic growth. Thus the JAMMAT development program built a road network that slowly but methodically expanded out from Turkey's major cities with the result that it was over a decade before an unbroken paved road linked even such major cities as Istanbul and Ankara. In the process, Turkish political and economic factors seem to have led the government to prioritize building roads in the Western part of the country, rendering national security concerns secondary to the partisan interests and personal profits of the country's elite. Confidential Memorandum Conference on Roads, Ministry of National Defense, April 14, 1946. Classified General Records, Box 17, RG 84, NARA.

[41] Untitled speech of George McGhee. *George C. McGhee Papers*, Georgetown University Library Special Collections, Series XVII, Box 2.

schools and "asked to comment on the school program" for "perhaps the first time."[42]

In even more varied, if less vital, areas of Turkey's cultural life US rhetoric remained the same. From basketball to beekeeping, American advisors recommended rationality, meritocracy, and innovation. After arranging for an American to serve as temporary coach of the Turkish national basketball team, the State Department concluded that in addition to teaching the fast-break game, the coach had "done a great deal toward instilling American concepts [of] fair play and sportsmanship."[43] He also apparently convinced Turks of the American idea that "[the] selection of any national team should be based solely on ability and performance [instead of seniority, as was the case before]." In an entirely different context, a Voice of America (VOA) radio skit reminded farmers that modern American agricultural techniques could also help them better deal with bees. The dialogue opened with a village chief asking a farmer named Ahmet why his face and eyes were swollen. "Don't ask, Chief," Ahmed replies, before explaining his bee-trouble. The Chief suggests Ahmet apply to the "Agricultural Center" for help, where he could learn about "scientific bee-culture and how to extract honey and what to do about enemies of bees." Ahmet worries, though, that the center's advice would conflict with "what we have learned from our fathers." The Chief reassures him, stating that when the "number of scientific bee farmers" grew, "these hornets won't have a chance." In the end, Ahmet is convinced. "You gave me courage, Chief," he declares, "I feel as if I can forget the pain caused by the hornets stinging."[44]

Even further afield, American officials were equally convinced that the version of modernity that worked for Turkey's bureaucracy and beehives could also bring benefits to Greek monks. After visiting the

[42] "Ambassador Warren's speech to the Propeller Club," an attachment to Department Circular Telegram 153, August 28, 1954, General Records of the State Department 1955–1959, Central Decimal File, Box 2213, RG 59, NARA.

[43] Embassy Telegram, Ankara to Department of State, August 4, 1956, U.S. Consulate General, Istanbul Classified General Records, 1950–1955, Box 2, RG 84, NARA. In the words of a 1956 *New York Times* article, "To participate in sports results in much more than just recreation and fun. Sports develop better citizens because they teach cooperation, courtesy, discipline and democracy" ("Former Football Giant Now Pleases the Turks," February 4, 1956).

[44] Voice of America Daily Broadcast Content Reports and Script Translations, 1950–1955, Box 44, RG 306, NARA.

Greek Orthodox monastic community on Mount Athos, George McGhee declared:

> The Mount does not appear to have ... any positive mission .... The Mount, by its very nature cannot be related to the modern world at large, except as a curiosity for tourists .... If it is to survive it will require strengthening internally – and increased outside support .... Additional education facilities for the monks on Athos are believed to be required if there is to be developed an intellectual approach to the mission of the Mount. Also, it is believed that the caliber of the monks must be improved. Vigorous young men with qualities of leadership must be attracted to The Mount.[45]

An official who accompanied him added, "I too was depressed by what might best be described as the futility of purpose and selfishness of the monks' life ... [and] the apparent mechanical method in which the liturgies are practiced." Another concluded, more optimistically, that Mount Athos "could become a center of valuable research and creative thinking – if the proper stimulus were present."[46]

Modernization as Propaganda

Alongside the push to instill "American concepts" and provide the "proper stimulus" in diverse aspects of Turkish life, there was an equally important effort, largely orchestrated by the USIA, to advertise the extent of America's modernity and highlight American generosity in sharing this modernity with Turkey. The State Department consciously distinguished between its modernization programs and its "propaganda" campaigns, though they saw both as complementing each other. US officials believed that wanting to be modern was the first step toward being modern and that being modern meant appreciating modernity. As a result, showing off how modern America was would inspire Turks to be more modern themselves, and as they became more modern, they would develop an even greater appreciation for America, the most modern country of all.

---

[45] "My Visit to Mount Athos, Greece, From October 18 to 22, 1952" Report prepared by George McGhee, December 11, 1952. *George C. McGhee Papers*, Georgetown University Library Special Collections, Series XXIV, Box 1.

[46] "General Records of the Patriarchate 1947–1953," Istanbul Consulate General, Box 1, RG 84, NARA.

Among many programs that aired on VOA in Turkey during this period, *Here Are the Answers* was among the most paradigmatic in showing just how much modern knowledge America had to share. Called "Hazırcevap Adam," or literally, "the ready-answer man" in Turkish, the show featured a pair of Turkish hosts answering questions submitted by Turkish listeners. The questions selected sometimes touched on social or political topics, but the general focus was American science and industry. Fairly typical were questions like: "When was Nylon invented and who invented it?" "Where are the longest bridge and tunnels in America?" "How many tons of tobacco are grown in America annually?" "How old is the invention of bells?" and "Which cars were invented in America and at what dates?" For every two or three of these, though, the hosts would bring their earnest attention to more general questions: "Among the weapons invented until now are there any that are useful to human beings or nations?" "How long will the Cold War last?" "Will it be possible to form a world nation?" "Where in America are the redskins located?" "Is there a remedy against snoring?" "Do they make Turkish movies in Hollywood?" "Are there men or women who have more than one spouse in America?" "What kind of flowers are exhibited at American flower shows?" and "How can a seventeen-year-old man become a woman?"[47]

The answers to all of these questions varied between the overtly politicized and the relatively objective. Bells, listeners learned, were actually first made in Moscow. Nylons were discovered by accident, but the process still involved "a deep farsightedness" and "thousands of experiments." Of course military weapons could have useful benefits; throughout history they "helped people to progress in the field of learning." "Redskins" lived mainly in the Southwest and enjoyed many rights. In fact, in 1952, "all the Redskins in America" would vote for the first time in the country's history. And "no, no cure has been found for the disease of snoring, which has given rise to a number of psychological crises, complaints and even divorces in America." Likewise,

---

[47] "Here Are the Answers," November 11, 1951, Voice of America Daily Broadcast Content Reports and Script Translations, 1950–1955, Box 29, RG 306, NARA; January 10, 1952, Box 34; March 22, 1953, Box 67; March 6, 1955, Box 78; Ibid; November 11, 1952, Box 29; January 10, 1952, Box 34; Ibid; January 10, 1952, Box 34; September 4, 1952, Box 51; October 19, 1952, Box 51; Ibid; March 22, 1953, Box 67; Ibid.

Hollywood made no Turkish movies, but did you know Turkish was spoken in such films as *Terrible Journey* and *Background to Danger?* Polygamy was not only illegal in America but "people who do not obey this law are punished." Finally, "a male can to a certain extent become a female and a female can become a male. Our listener can obtain more detailed information on this subject through physicians, medical journals and books." Even when the questions themselves were not about America, VOA implied that there was an answer to every question and that more often than not America could provide it.

Whenever Turkish citizens came to America on educational exchange programs, the USIA took it as an opportunity to show that America was eager to transfer this vast store of knowledge to Turkey. Press releases written for VOA interviews with dozens of Turkish visitors followed a similar pattern: First, the visitor was introduced, along with the subject they came to study.[48] Then there was a quote reflecting the visitor's impressions of America or their excitement over their visit. Finally, the press releases would often end with either a quote from the visitor about how they hoped to share what they learned when they returned to Turkey or a third-person statement to that effect. All of these interviews reflected the idea that in almost every conceivable field America possessed modern knowledge and techniques that it was giving to Turks for their benefit. Indeed, VOA closed with almost identical sentences when promoting interviews with a delegation of engineers, a boxer, and a playwright:

"On their return, the men plan to put the technical knowledge gained in the United States to practical use in the construction of public power projects throughout Turkey."[49]

---

[48] Records of the USIA VOA radio news press releases, Boxes 4 and 5, RG 306, NARA. Marked-up drafts of these announcements reveal that these quotes were occasionally altered for effect. Thus a visiting Turkish radio journalist went from saying "we're busy learning ... all we can about how America lives," to "we're busy ... absorbing as much as we can of the fascinating kaleidoscope that is known as 'The American way of life'." A Turkish woman who said "I was amazed to see how many women work here .... It's wonderful to see how many important positions women hold in the United States, but sometimes I wonder if it gives them enough time to dream" had the final part of her thought removed by an editor. Likewise, when a visiting Turkish journalist wrote that the Turkish immigrants he met in Detroit "cling tenaciously to their Turkish traditions and speech," this observation disappeared in the final draft. "Bingul Gulsever," "Interview with Nazli Tlabar," "Naci Serez." Records of the USIA VOA radio news press releases, Boxes 4 and 5, ibid.

[49] "Public Power Discussion," ibid.

"The young boxer intends to demonstrate American techniques to Turkish fighters upon his return to Turkey."[50]

"After Ozdogru finishes his remaining three study semesters, he plans to return to Turkey, where he hopes to add modern American theatre techniques to his country's expanding dramatic outlets."[51]

If this message was not explicit enough, VOA made it more clear in the title of a later program, "Turkey attends the American Classroom." This show, which featured profiles of Turkish exchange students funded by the Fulbright Commission, emphasized both American hospitality and American learning, all part of the flow of knowledge from America to grateful Turkish recipients.[52]

Modernity in Translation

Turkish citizens did not merely consume US modernization rhetoric, however. They also critiqued it, reappropriated it and helped produce it. Much more so than other parts of the US mission in Turkey, the USIA relied on the Turkish elite to help in crafting its propaganda. Unlike the US military and its fears about the "Turkish twist," VOA asked that translators be "chosen on the basis, and constantly reminded of the fact, that their jobs are as much creative writing as translating."[53] In addition to seeking advice from the staff of Turkey's state radio, VOA hired Turkish journalists to listen to broadcasts and give feedback on their quality and content. VOA staff told these "monitors" to be "critical" but not "hyper-critical" and asked them a series of questions such as "[w]as there ever a program that infuriated

---

[50] "Turkish Fighter Necmi Karahan," ibid.

[51] "Nuvit Ozodgru: [*sic*] Student," ibid.

[52] When Turks came to America to teach Americans, however, they were generally described as "helping Americans understand Turkish culture" or "explaining Turkish problems to America." On occasion, VOA quoted Turkish visitors speaking about Americans and Turks jointly addressing shared problems, but they seldom used this language themselves. "Mayor of Istanbul Fahrettin Kerim Gokay," ibid.

[53] Embassy Despatch No. 696, June 27, 1951, General Records of the State Department 1955–1959, Central Decimal File, Box 2213, RG 59, NARA. The USIA welcomed the work of Turkish censors who screened all USIA films before they could be shown in Turkey. Censorship was "considered helpful in eliminating films which might be offensive to the local population on the basis of custom or religious faith." "Filmstrips – Cooperation with Turkish Ministry," January 8, 1953. Ibid.

you as a Turk or had the potential for doing that to other Turks."[54] Most of the feedback VOA received concerned the accent and word choice of their Turkish broadcasters. Comments on the programming itself, though, often veered into the hyper-critical, with entire shows frequently written off as "useless" or "a waste of time."[55] Turkish monitors helped push the VOA toward creating separate programming tracks for listeners of different social classes. Faced with complaints that "broadcasts were not directed at either the well-educated … or to the peasant class," VOA decided early on to "eliminate the fruitless quest for a non-existent common denominator."[56] As time went on, VOA staff continued to find it "an agreeable surprise to note that monitors broke down their suggestions for programs into categories designed for the well-educated and the peasant."[57]

Furthermore, Turkish broadcasters and monitors suggested a number of the ideas that eventually found their way into VOA programming, including almost all of those discussed in this chapter. According to VOA staff, Turks wanted more anti-Communist material and more classical music. Turkish broadcasters also proposed a program featuring interviews with Turkish visitors to America and a question-and-answer show. A publisher and farmer from Adana encouraged VOA to broadcast "talks to farmers on how to improve their crops by modern American methods." The director of the Radio Section of the Press Bureau, meanwhile, suggested "more news on UNESCO, the World Bank, and 'culture news' such as items on new American inventions, science, education, research, medicine and industry."[58] When US officials assumed that Turks shared their vision of modernity, they found ample reinforcement from their Turkish partners.

There were other issues, however, on which Turkish feedback was much more divided. Monitors criticized some VOA broadcasts as too condescending toward listeners, others as not condescending enough. One anonymous monitor gave Radio Moscow grudging praise for the

[54] Radio Broadcast Records. Ibid.   [55] Ibid.
[56] Embassy Despatch No. 696, June 27, 1951. Ibid.
[57] The recommendations themselves were not surprising. "For the well-educated, better designed music programs were suggested, as well as more thorough investigations into political and economic questions. For the peasant, more Turkish music was prescribed augmented by simple agricultural talks, lengthier news bulletins and informal chats about American community life." Ibid.
[58] Ibid.

fact that it presented material "in language the peasant can understand." Another added, "Sure Radio Moscow pounds in its propaganda, but the VOA is <u>too subtle</u>."[59] Haughtiness, however, was
worse. The Turkish host of a show called "A Widely Traveled Turk"
earned almost universal criticism from VOA's paid monitors, as well as
from the Turkish friends and colleagues of the VOA staff.[60] Regretting
that the widely traveled Turk had given the impression that "he and the
people of the country about which he reports are snobs," the VOA
Ankara staff recommended that the show be "revamped" with a new
announcer and material that presented "a reasonable rather than an
eulogistic picture of America."

When the US sponsored an underwhelming pavilion at the 1956
Izmir Fair, the city's political and intellectual elite were quick to criticize what they saw as a missed opportunity to propagandize rural fair-
goers. Throughout the decade, US participation in the fair had been
a source of conflict between the USIA officers on the ground in Turkey
and higher-ranking State Department officials in Washington.[61]
Washington insisted that, as the fair was nominally a commercial
one, it should be up to US companies to participate or not as they
saw fit. USIA officials, by contrast, argued that this was an important
opportunity to demonstrate the depth of America's commitment to
Turkey and show off American industry. They wanted Washington
to provide the money and leadership in organizing a US pavilion, saying
that US companies could not be trusted to adequately demonstrate the
superiority of private enterprise in the face of slick, government-
organized exhibits put on by Eastern Bloc countries. Fearing that a sub-
par exhibit would be worse than no exhibit at all, USIA officials sat out
the 1953, 1954, and 1955 fairs when Washington did not provide the
resources they requested. In 1956, however, strains in US-Turkish
relations and increasing fears over Soviet propaganda victories came
together to convince USIA staff that they had no choice but to enter the
fair with whatever resources they could muster. These proved to be
meager. Washington said no to the double-decker Greyhound bus and
emphatically rejected their suggestion to build a brand-new six-story

[59] Ibid.
[60] Deptel 48, July 24, 1951, General Records of the State Department 1955–1959,
Central Decimal File, Box 2213, RG 59, NARA.
[61] Department of State. Classified General Records, 1938–1958, Box 77, RG 84,
NARA.

hotel as part of the exhibit. Instead of a model cigarette machine whose output could be given away to visitors, they got a nail machine. In other rooms of the pavilion they were forced to make do with pictures instead of models.[62]

After the conclusion of the fair, the USIA commissioned a survey to gauge the Turkish response. It was harsh. Of the twenty-five members of Izmir's economic, political, and intellectual elite who were interviewed, most were critical, some emphatically so. One mechanical engineer went as far as to compare the US pavilion to "the studying of a lazy student for an examination a few days prior to it." Another businessmen said the exhibits "meant nothing" to him.[63] A more moderate critic claimed it was "not smart enough for intellectuals and not practical enough for ordinary people."[64] "Turks do not understand statistics," opined one government official, while another explained, "[T]he logic of our people lies in their eyes."[65] Tellingly, many comments displayed a sense of betrayal. Turkey, specifically the Turkish elite, had thrown in its lot with the Americans and now they expected the Americans to do their part in showing Turkish voters this had been a wise choice. As one critic said, "[b]ecause our fates are linked we want a better pavilion. [This one] did not show the strength of the American Nation."[66] Ultimately, the one aspect of the fair participants praised was the one they had not seen. Asked about the USIA film series at the American Pavilion, a large number of participants responded that while they themselves did not go to watch any of the films, such things were undoubtedly "useful" for less-educated fair-goers.

DP members were particularly invested in the success of America's military and economic modernization programs, both because they thought these programs were good for Turkey and because they thought these programs were good for their party. Menderes spoke to his

---

[62] Sezgi Durgun notes that when General Gürsel visited the Izmir fair in 1961, the Americans gave him a cup of Coke out of a vending machine while the Soviets gave him a model of Sputnik and a shot of vodka. Sezgi Durgun, "Cultural Cold War at the Izmir International Fair: 1950s–60s," in Örnek, Üngör et al. (ed.), *Turkey in the Cold War Ideology and Culture* (London: Palgrave Macmillan, 2013), 67–86.

[63] "Survey of Visitor Reactions to the U.S. Exhibitions and the Izmir Fair 1956." Prepared by Professor Dr. Hıfzı Timur. (Istanbul: İsmail Akgün Printing Establishment, 1956). Office of Research and Evaluation International Survey and Research Reports 1950–1964, Box 99, RG 306, NARA. Pages 79, 93.

[64] Ibid., 131. [65] Ibid., 104, 135. [66] Ibid., 148.

constituents in the language of modernization and, for most of the 1950s, his constituents responded enthusiastically.[67] The synergy between American and Turkish visions of democratic modernity and the fierce criticism directed at "inadequate" US propaganda efforts offer additional evidence for Odd Arne Westad's argument that "modernization" was not a discourse imposed on the third world countries by their superpower patrons. Rather, it was one that third world leaders expected any power seeking their support to engage in, and engage in convincingly.[68]

Where the DP's response to the Izmir fair demonstrated how support for America could provoke criticism of its modernization rhetoric, the writing of Bülent Ecevit shows how the same rhetoric could also be used to criticize both the DP and America's support for it. This is all the more striking because Ecevit was an early participant in a State Department program intended to demonstrate American modernity to Turkish journalists firsthand. In 1954 he spent four months at the *Winston-Salem Journal* in North Carolina (see Figure 2.2). At the end, the State Department, Ecevit, and paper's staff were all effusive about the experience. "The Journal has been most lavish in its praise of Mr. Ecevit, who appears to have made a very excellent impression both as an individual and as a newspaperman," a State Department report concluded, adding in a letter to the paper's editor that Ecevit had "described in glowing terms his most enjoyable and informative time in Winston-Salem."[69] Explaining the benefits that would accrue to the United States from Ecevit's visit, the letter went on:

By providing Mr. Ecevit with an insight into two leading American newspapers, and by allowing him to witness at firsthand the functions of the American press in our democratic society, you have contributed greatly toward the accomplishment of our aims. Your help in making the United States better known to this foreign journalist, and through him to his reading

---

[67] DP rhetoric frequently downplayed the role of religion and culture in explaining Turkey's economic underdevelopment and instead emphasized the crippling effect of the military expenses Turkey had incurred as a result of World War II and the Cold War. The CHP, by contrast, was usually quicker to join American observers in identifying ideological factors.

[68] Odd Arne Westad, *Global Cold War: Third World Interventions and the Making of Our Times* (Cambridge: Cambridge University Press, 2005).

[69] Central Files, 511.823/2–1 455 SCBM, Letter to Mr. Wallace Carroll, February 14, 1955. NARA.

Figure 2.2 Bülent Ecevit photographing a football game in North Carolina, 1954.

public in Turkey, has been a real service to the cause of international understanding.[70]

Ecevit found much to admire about America and American democracy. The vast majority of the articles he wrote on his return were exactly the sort that the State Department officials hoped for. But Ecevit also used his experience, as well as the rhetoric of American modernity, to criticize both the DP and US policy.[71]

In his final guest column for the *Winston-Salem Journal's* Sunday edition, Ecevit wrote at length about the injustice of segregation and the cruelty of racism. Accompanying his criticism with a Charlie Brown cartoon and the polite title "Even Angels Can Go Wrong," Ecevit

[70] Ibid.
[71] Like many other foreign leaders, however, Ecevit's positive experiences in America did not lead him to adopt pro-American policies when in office. His terms as prime minister was marked by conflicts with Washington over Cyprus, opium production, and other issues.

couched his argument in American Cold War rhetoric. Not unlike the attendees at the Izmir fair, Ecevit argued that Turkey's alliance with America gave him the right to criticize America for failing to live up to its own ideals:

This so-called "segregation" or "color-bar" business is not merely America's own business. It is my business, too, and the business of hundreds of millions of other people like me all over the world who are looking up to America today as their only hope. But an America with the "color bar" cannot fulfill their hopes. That is why I regard myself entitled to poke my nose into an affair which many a racist would regard as solely his own.[72]

Ecevit applied the same logic with reference to the Menderes government when he called on NATO to hold its members to a higher standard of democratic behavior. In one 1956 article, he asked if NATO merely expected members to honor their military commitments or "stay loyal to the democratic principles laid out in the preamble and second article [of its charter]." To win the support of "nations fighting for freedom" against Communism, he argued, NATO should "boldly warn" its members on this subject, even at the risk of angering them.[73] In another article he called more concretely for NATO to investigate and report on the experiences of individuals in member states who had their freedoms and rights violated.[74]

Ecevit also made regular use of his firsthand observations of American and British democracy when criticizing the DP for restricting political freedoms. For example, when a pro-government paper asked rhetorically if US reporters had the right to violate the privacy of the White House, Ecevit responded emphatically that they did. After noting that the paper had mistranslated "white house [*beyaz ev*]" as "white palace [*beyaz saray*]," he continued:

In America, the president has no privacy, so there can be no talk of violating his privacy .... American newspapers have special correspondents whose assignment is to monitor the White House. If President Eisenhower gets tired of work and goes to play golf for two days, the papers argue about whether the President has time to play that much golf. No one considers this

---

[72] Bülent Ecevit, "Visiting Turk says of Americans: Even Angels Can Go Wrong," *Sunday Journal and Sentinel*, January 9, 1955.
[73] Bülent Ecevit, "Üç akıllı adam ne yapacak?," *Ulus*, October 25, 1956.
[74] Bülent Ecevit, "NATO'nun düştüğü çıkmaz," *Ulus*, November 8, 1956.

argument an affront to his dignity. No one accuses the papers of violating the President's privacy because they are against him playing golf.[75]

In another article, Ecevit quoted a North Carolina policeman explaining that while his town would drop everything to honor a foreign dignitary, if Mamie Eisenhower came they would throw eggs at her.[76] Not because they disliked her, of course. Quite the contrary she was well-liked. "Her only fault was that she was the President's wife." Americans, the policeman explained, "seized every opportunity to be able to display rudeness [*istiskal*] toward their leaders. So that they know their place. So that they don't become full of themselves and cause trouble for us." In fact, Ecevit often cited the demeanor of the American and English police to demonstrate the appropriate relationship between a government and its people. "England," he explained, "is a country where mothers don't frighten their children by saying 'I'll give you to the police' ... because English children only know the police as smiling, polite individuals who will stop traffic, hold their hand and guide them across a busy street."[77]

Where Washington sought to use democratic modernization to justify US support for Menderes and win Turkish support for US goals, Ecevit, a product of American modernization programs, appealed to the same ideology to insist that US support for Menderes was a betrayal of US values. Meanwhile, the Menderes government, in order to counter such domestic criticism, continued to ask America to more effectively promote its own modernization efforts.

Conclusion

Paradoxically, the ideology of modernization and the stereotypes that informed it were so central to the worldview of US policymakers during the early Cold War that they have only limited use in explaining US policy during this period. Turkey in the 1950s was exceptional in the degree to which democratization seemed to coincide with US interests. And yet even here, the US government's application of modernization theory frequently depended on its malleability. Subsequently, in other countries and decades, when American policymakers found that their

---

[75] Bülent Ecevit, "Hususi hayatlar ve isbat hakkı," *Ulus*, July 25, 1955.
[76] Bülent Ecevit, "Makyavelli ve Demokrasi," *Ulus*, June 8, 1955.
[77] Bülent Ecevit, "Polis ve Halk," *Ulus*, May 2, 1956.

interests were better served by supporting dictatorial regimes, they quickly articulated a version of modernization theory that recognized the benefits of autocracy. In short, wherever US diplomats' interests lay, modernization theory could conveniently take them there.

The deeper irony of this period is that Atatürk's authoritarian modernization never looked better to foreign observers than the moment Turkey appeared most democratic. Over the past several decades, at a time when Turkey's democratization seemed to lag behind global trends and optimistic expectations, scholarship naturally focused on explaining the persistent failure of liberal democracy in Turkey. This framework created a justifiable cynicism toward academics who had once hailed Atatürk for laying Turkey's democratic foundations or government officials who promoted Turkey's imperfect democracy as a "model" for Middle Eastern countries. But in the early Cold War period, when work by scholars like Bernard Lewis helped promote Turkey as a modernization success story, the country appeared to have undergone a remarkable transformation. By 1950s standards, Turkey's democracy was not just "bon pour l'orient" but for much of Southern and Eastern Europe as well. If modernization theory was malleable enough to justify authoritarianism, it could also serve to articulate people's sincere hopes about democratization as well.

Moreover, just as the US government did not pressure İnönü to hold free elections, the US model of democratic modernity was not so clear or coherent as to determine Turkish thinking on the subject. After May 1950, the DP government eagerly insisted that Turkey had finally and fully joined the free, democratic, and Western world. Then, even as its behavior grew steadily more autocratic, it continued to cite Western backing as evidence of its democratic status, even in the face of critics using the Western model against it.[78] If the American model could mean so many different things to Americans, then it is no surprise Turkish politicians and voters showed even greater flexibility in deciding what it meant to them.

---

[78] And, as seen in the previous chapter, Menderes also justified his model of democratic modernity to voters with reference to their own needs and experiences.

3 | Asia in Europe, Europe in Asia
The Possibilities of Synthesis

Saved from that fanaticism of the East, which is drowned in its fixation
with all things Arab and Persian; rejecting that crude mimicry of the West,
which succumbs to a fixation with all things Frankish; Pure, clean, and
naked in spirit, toward the grand ideal, toward the grand tomorrow!

– Behçet Kemal Çağlar in *The East*, a publication from the Zonguldak
People's House dedicated to maintaining "the most Western mentality
possible."[1]

In the early Cold War period, thinkers from a wide variety of backgrounds insisted that moving beyond the overly rigid aspects of
Kemalist Westernization represented the final stage of Turkey's modernization. This chapter explores their visions for a synthetic modernity
that would reconcile Turkey's Eastern and Western identities while
rejecting the worst of both. In articulating these visions, some writers
invoked the Democratic Party's promise of material prosperity, while
others looked to the creativity of Turkish artists. Some found
a template in the non-European form of American modernity they
discovered in New York; others used the Hajj to demonstrate their
cosmopolitan sophistication. Men found evidence of Turkey's synthetic identity in the appearance of Turkish women while Turkish
women argued that in doing so they were misunderstanding the essence
of Western modernity.

Taken together, these examples suggest that not only could modernity mean everything to everyone, but that a specifically synthetic
modernity could as well. That is to say, a widespread rhetorical

---

[1] Behçet Kemal Çağlar, "Kurultay'da Türkçülük Ülkümuz," *Doğu*, Volume 11,
Year 6, Issue 61–63, 1947. The journal *Doğu* appeared in 1942 and claimed its
title was inspired by Ziya Gökalp's "Doğu'dan gelmişiz Batı'ya doğru." *Doğu*
embraced a conservative nationalist line that later won it praise in these circles as
a "rising voice of Turkishness." Doğu Karaoğuz, "Türkçülüğün Zonguldak'tan
Yükselen Sesi: 1940'lı Yılların 'Doğu' Dergisi," *Türk Yurdu*, October 2006, Year
95, Issue 230.

consensus around the idea that Turkey's identity should transcend simplistic binary debates about East and West or tradition and modernity still left room for plenty of debate over what this transcendent identity should look like. The very ambiguity of Western modernity itself allowed writers to use "hyper-Westernization" as a foil to promote diverse interpretations of their preferred alternative modernity.

To illustrate the breadth of this mid-century synthetic discourse, the examples in this chapter highlight its appearance at various points across Turkey's political and ideological spectrum. While previous scholars have sought to identify rival, contradictory, and clashing strains of thought in Turkey's intellectual history, this work seeks to emphasize the elements they shared in common, as well the many thinkers who explicitly insisted on reconciling them. Even within what could be thought of as mainstream Kemalist or Islamist rhetoric, an emphasis on synthesis can be found. What is more, these labels themselves disguise the presence of intellectual currents that sought to chart out a middle ground. Thus in discussing modernity or identity, the idiosyncratic intellectual Peyami Safa sounded remarkably similar to both Bülent Ecevit, who just over a decade later became the leader of Atatürk's Republican People's Party (CHP), and İbrahim Kafesoğlu, now hailed as an influential early Islamist.

Beyond the Turban-Hat Stage

In the early 1950s, several of Istanbul's most prominent cultural and intellectual magazines devoted themselves to a heated debate about Westernization and the nature of Turkey's identity. Many of the participants specifically endorsed the Democratic Party's vision of democratic prosperity while embracing a synthetic view of Turkey's modernity and geography. Among the publications that made the case for synthesis most directly was *Türk Düşüncesi*, or *Turkish Thought*, a journal started by the publisher and intellectual Peyami Safa. Safa was unique in the way his background spanned the intellectual and political currents of mid-century Turkey, making Safa's work particularly relevant for understanding how and where those currents overlapped. Described by historian Nazım İrem as part of a small movement of "republican conservatives" or "conservative modernists" from the 1930s, Safa was at once an accepted and outspoken member of the traditional Kemalist elite.[2] In 1950 he was recruited to run as a parliamentary candidate for the CHP but following his defeat, he switched sides and became an eager supporter of the Democrats. In a sense, his views reflect both his own and the country's political trajectory.

Claiming in 1953 that current Turkish intellectual life was in a state of disorder, Safa ambitiously announced that his journal's program was to reorder it. Just as tractors did for farmers, his journal would help bring a bountiful intellectual harvest out of the ungrateful Anatolian ground. This, he thought, required rescuing the country's discourse from "every demagogue's reaction-revolution [*irtica-inkılap*] dichotomy" and creating a real discourse in the light of modern western thought.[3] Safa presented the false dichotomy he sought to escape by critiquing an outmoded vision of modernization that he claimed the West itself had abandoned:

Europe and the West, in the manner understood by some of our Westernizing [*Garpçı*] journals and thinkers who consider themselves revolutionary, can be considered long past gone. When speaking of Western Europe they cannot save themselves from the mental molds of the first three-quarters of the last century, which have been completely abandoned today .... When we say Europe, or in the broad sense the West, we reflect an understanding of yesterday's culture and civilization which is a part of history, its era having passed. We do not know that being created today is a new and vital West working to clear away this outdated past. No matter how good their intentions, those who want to force the Turkish revolution into the dead Western mold do not know how outdated the ideas they consider advanced are. The first question they must wake up from the Western dream in which they are dozing and ask themselves is, if I am not mistaken, "which west?"[4]

For Safa, then, Westernization required appreciating Europe's ongoing intellectual development. Beginning with Einstein's critique of Newtonian

---

2 Nazım İrem, "Turkish Conservative Modernism: Birth of a Nationalist Quest for Cultural Renewal," *International Journal of Middle East Studies*, Volume 34, 2002, 87–112.

3 Peyami Safa, "Program" and "Türk Düşüncesi ve Batı Medeniyeti," *Türk Düşüncesi*, Issue 1, December 1953.

4 Ibid. A contemporary author writing in the magazine *East-West* took this approach even further, suggesting that arguing about the nature of Western modernity was in fact the essence of Western modernity. "How can it be," he asked, "that the concept [modernity] which is the subject of such serious argument [in the West] doesn't produce a quarrel here?" "Gak deyince," *Doğu-Batı*, February 1955.

physics and Heisenberg's uncertainty [*kararsızlık*] principle, Safa wrote that the world had witnessed the "collapse of the dictatorship of science" and the shaking up of "not just the idea of measurement, on which the concept of positivist knowledge rested, but also the determinism on which all science and materialist philosophy rested."[5] Accompanying the rise of existentialist philosophy and the hopes destroyed by two world wars, the twentieth century had seen the end of the "dream that reason and science could not only explain everything but also give human society eternal peace and order." To succeed, then, Turkey would have to "share in the intellectual ferment [*fikir humması*] that gave the West its present dynamism" rather than "remain passive before or merely ape a frozen example."

More explicitly, Safa stated that his goal was to "surmount today's spiritual tension, its cultural and civilizational malaise [*buhran*] by articulating a synthesis, appropriate to and above Turkey's historical and geographical situation, between dichotomies like spiritual and physical, East and West, and past and future." This approach led him to criticize those who he felt were overenthusiastic or thoughtless in their embrace of the West:

Atatürk wanted to ensure that the Turkish nation entered the Western cultural family not as an imitator but in possession of its own identity and personality.... Most of our Atatürkists forget this, and what's worse, support the radical leftists who want us to forget the Turkish revolution's sincere nationalist character.[6]

What Atatürk, in Safa's telling, realized was that Turks, by looking to their own "national and religious traditions," could find "all the vital elements of the synthesis that will save the Turkish revolution from appearing to leap between aping the Arabs and aping the Franks."[7] Moreover, by presenting Turkey's intellectual and cultural challenges in the context of European trends, Safa ultimately suggested that wrestling with these problems was not part of Turkey's development but of contemporary civilization itself. That is, confronting the dilemmas of modernization made Turkey a modern country, not a modernizing one.

Safa took his argument one step further by claiming that all Westernizing countries outside of Europe had faced the same dilemma

---

[5] Ibid.   [6] Ibid.   [7] Ibid.

as Turkey and ultimately taken a similar approach to confronting it. Citing Russian and Japanese examples, he claimed that "every westernizing culture defends its own identity against excessive westernization."[8] Thus the "Asianist movement" [*Asyacılık Hareketi*] that Atatürk assumed command of had existed in Turkey since the Second Constitutional period as a national reaction to the policies of "radical Europeanism [*aşırı Avrupacılık*]." In this formulation, Turkey had always had the foresight to try to preempt the loss of identity that could befall late modernizers.

Safa's thinking, as laid out at length in *Turkish Thought*, echoes the ideas of more conventionally conservative and Islamist thinkers, save for where he positions the early Republic relative to his synthetic ideal. *İstanbul*, another prominent intellectual journal from the time whose contributors included İbrahim Kafesoğlu and the author Ahmed Hamdi Tanpınar, devoted considerable space to debates over Turkish identity, with a particular emphasis on the fact that Turkish modernization had long embraced synthesis. In one of its initial issues, literary critic Mehmet Kaplan responded directly to *Turkish Thought* by arguing that he was even more committed to synthesis than Safa. Kaplan claimed that while Safa presented synthesis as an ideal to be achieved, he saw it instead as a social necessity and already extant historical reality:

All great civilizations were a synthesis. Just like ancient Chinese, Indian, Egyptian, Greek, Roman, and medieval Western civilizations were all syntheses, Islamic civilization, and the unique Ottoman civilization within it, were syntheses. Today's Western civilization is a synthesis. And our own new civilizational movement that has been developing since the Tanzimat is nothing if not a synthesis.[9]

Kaplan then went on to explain that he was not alone in making this observation. Most of Turkey's famous intellectuals felt the same way:

Most of the Turkish intellectuals who came after [mid nineteenth-century Ottoman writer İbrahim Şinasi], that is Namık Kemal, Ziya Paşa, Ahmed

---

[8] See also Walter Schubart's "Rusya'da Avrupacılar ve Asyacılar," ibid.
[9] Mehmet Kaplan, "Edebiyatta Doğu ve Batı Sentezi," *İstanbul*, Volume 1, Issue 8, June 1954.

Midhat, Muallim Naci, Ziya Gökalp, Mehmed Akif, Yayha Kemal and others, always defended and applied the idea of synthesizing old and new, East and West ... Among these only two generations – the Servet-i Fünun generation and the Republican era's radical revolutionary generation – took a stand against national values and the past in the service of an agenda of completely imitating the West. But don't be deceived. If their works and actions are examined, [it can be seen that] they hardly went beyond the national and historical frame.[10]

A number of other pieces in *İstanbul* took the same approach, endorsing the essential elements of Safa's synthetic vision but from a more conservative position. An editorial titled "Entering the Technical Era" from one of the journal's first few issues echoed the Democratic Party's emphasis on the popular appreciation for Turkey's mechanical progress:

For many years Western civilization was widely discussed. But only a few things that changed the external face of our lives were adopted. And this newness was exclusively limited to one or two big cities. Now there is a movement that can be seen and felt across the whole country. Many more cars, trucks and buses fill our roads than before. Many more tractors work our fields .... The people, who stayed generally opposed to ideological revolutions, or even secretly resisted, are giving themselves over to technological devices. Nowhere is there the least resistance to automobiles, tractors, electricity or radios. Quite the contrary even people who still have not rescued their heads from old ideas are embracing technological civilization [*teknik medeniyeti*].[11]

Having emphasized both the technological roots and populist nature of modernity, the author went on to articulate his vision for cultural synthesis, focusing heavily on nationalist authenticity:

We do not want nationalism, religion, or tradition to be ranged against modern technology. For us, if defending the true value of our historic civilization is important, so is acquiring and mastering the tools of modern civilization .... Despite all conflict, we find it valuable to bring both together and believe that synergy [*terkib*] arises specifically from this contradiction.[12]

The similarities between *İstanbul* and *Turkish Thought*'s approach to civilizational synthesis stand out all the more for the two journals'

---

[10] Ibid.   [11] "Teknik Devre Giriş," *İstanbul*, Volume 1, Issue 5, March 1954.
[12] Ibid.

differences. Safa and *Turkish Thought* claimed to have surpassed nine-teenth-century modernity and almost arrived at a form of postmodernity, while *İstanbul* took a populist approach in claiming that the experience of modernization transcended the meaningless intellectual debates that characterized previous modernization efforts. But both journals, in their own way, positioned themselves as partisans of a more modern vision of modernity that was superior to the modernity embraced by others. They also agreed that Turkish culture was the product of synthesis, should aspire to be even more of a synthesis, and had, in fact, always been a synthesis. Moreover, for different reasons, they agreed that Turkey had now reached the stage where further debates about modernity were irrelevant: As the editors of *Istanbul* put it, some intellectuals still thought of "revolution" in terms of hats or the alphabet reform, "but these issues are already solved." The people "knew better" and recognized the real revolution was a technical one: "Today in Turkey democracy is tied to factors like land, wheat, beets, tractors and investment. It has surpassed the tur-ban-hat stage."[13]

From the other side of the ideological spectrum, Bülent Ecevit was also convinced that Turkey had proved its modernity by transcending its binaries. In his role as State Department–sponsored cultural ambas-sador to the United States, Ecevit articulated the dramatic success of Turkey's Westernization in elegantly paradoxical terms. As he explained in the draft of a speech for an audience in Washington, DC:

It would, however, be incorrect to define Turkey as mainly a European or an Asiatic country. Today, Turkey is both, she is Asia in Europe and Europe in Asia. In fact, the Turks are more conscious and prouder than ever of their Asiatic heritage, now that they find themselves regarded as a European as well as an Asiatic nation.[14]

Turkey accomplished this mission, Ecevit argued, by joining NATO while simultaneously entering into a series of alliances with Eastern

---

[13] "Yeni Meseleler," *İstanbul*, Volume 1, Issue 8, June 1954.

[14] While Ecevit himself often used the term "Orient" to refer to the East in a geographic sense, he made a point of rejecting its use as a cultural term, explaining in a note written across the back of another speech "Using 'outmoded' in place of 'Oriental' would be more appropriate" [*Oriental yerine outmoded demek yerinde olur*]. Draft speech for the Washington International Center, Personal Papers of Bülent and Rahşan Ecevit, Bülent Ecevit Bilim Kültür ve Sanat Vakfı.

neighbors such as Pakistan. Yet while there was a military and diplomatic dimension to Turkey's role that Ecevit would return to on many occasions, he insisted that there was also a uniquely cultural dimension. As he explained to Turkish readers in his weekly newspaper column:

In centuries of fighting, Turks had not been able to bring the West under the control of the East and Europeans had not been able to bring the East under the control of the West .... [But] just as Turks had begun the end of imperialism with their victory in the War of Independence, by adopting a new lifestyle they had destroyed the wall between East and West that could not be destroyed for centuries through the use of force.

Put more abstractly, he suggested that under Atatürk, Turkey had become more Western but had also, as an Eastern country, freed Westernness from the West:

As Westernness [*batılılık*] was freed from any religious, racial or geographic limitations ... it became a lifestyle that could be embraced by all nations .... As this lifestyle spread eastward, it was enriched through the addition of Eastern values. And when this development is completed, the division between East and West will be completely eliminated.[15]

Ecevit was perhaps most thorough in presenting his synthetic views on the relationship between politics, geography, and modernization when discussing art. A 1954 article on the Turks' long-standing love of poetry, for example, laid out the full contradictory scope of his narrative for an American audience. Ecevit began by explaining that this love "was natural within the framework of Ottoman culture, which was essentially Oriental, because the Oriental mind does not, in general, go in for rational thinking."[16] Despite this, though, "[m]odern Turkish poetry was born out of a rejection of the past. Like many aspects of contemporary life in Turkey, it is a product of the reforms initiated by the late Kemal Atatürk after he had founded the Republic."[17] This narrative quickly became more complicated when Ecevit suggested that one of the most harmful influences of Ottoman poetry was the overreaction it inspired in Republican poets. Against the "elaborate poetic diction of the Ottoman poets" they chose the "simplification of

---

[15] "Batı-Doğu," *Ulus*, October 30, 1956.
[16] "Poetry in Turkey, a Nation's Most Popular Art," *Sunday Journal and Sentinel*, November 21, 1954.
[17] Ibid.

diction," and "against the excessive use of metaphors and adjectives in Ottoman poetry," some sought to "avoid adjectives and metaphors altogether." Ironically, then, Ecevit concluded that it was only after these Republican era battles against tradition had been won that poets were finally free to engage in "less prejudiced experiments."[18] As evidence of this, Ecevit cited the increasingly influential poet Fazıl Hüsnü Dağlarca, whose "very complex syntax, at times recalling E. E. Cummings ... has introduced a modern brand of mysticism to Turkish poetry."

The development of Ecevit's logic over the course of a few sentences is telling. Ecevit starts out with an essentialized contrast between West and East in which Western rationality is posited as superior. He then goes on to praise Dağlarca's limited return to tradition – with which there can be "no compromise" but against which there should be no "prejudice" – and claims this actually makes his writing similar to that of the Western arch-modernist E. E. Cummings. Here, as in many other cases, drawing a dichotomy only served a prelude for deconstructing it in the service of a synthetic vision.

The same narrative appears when Ecevit tackled the subject of Turkish visual art.[19] "The ending of the Ottoman Empire," he claimed, "brought emancipation for the Turkish artist, awakening him to the beauties of nature and the joy of living." In the Ottoman era, Turks had listened to "monophonic and melancholy music" and a looked at "decorations composed of lifeless objects, abstract forms and colors that did not reflect the sun even when they were bright." With the advent of the Republic, by contrast, "[i]t was as if all the plastic elements which had been imprisoned for centuries on the lifeless miniatures and stylized tiles, away from nature and sun and human feeling, were now rushing forth into real life to associate themselves with real nature." Yet despite the liberating impact of this post-Ottoman turn toward realism, Ecevit felt that "[u]p until 1946 Turkish painters made no contributions of their own to modern art." "[W]hen the one-party regime ended and a multi-party system began," however, "a new reform took place in Turkish art," as the painter "gained his artistic freedom" and could rediscover the positive elements of Ottoman art:

[18] Ibid.
[19] Marjorie Hunter, "Ottoman Empire's End Freed Turkish Artists," *Winston-Salem Journal*, November 1, 1954.

The painters, free to experiment, could look back to old Turkish art with an open mind and it was by looking back that they became inspired by the works of the old calligraphists as a means for reviving the human element in non-figurative art. The calligraphic art of Islam, not like anything in Western art, has provided a great source of inspiration for the younger Turkish painters.[20]

Here again, revolutionary Republican reforms appear as necessary but not sufficient for Turkey's true modernization. This, Ecevit believed, could only occur once the reforms themselves had been transcended and the resonance between Ottoman and modern art could emerge.

A strikingly similar view of artistic synthesis also appeared in the nationalist magazine *Türk Yurdu*. A 1954 article on "Turkish Painting," for example, argued that Turkish art in the 1950s had so far failed to establish the ideal synthesis it was capable of:

Turks, who throughout history have exemplified art's multiple manifestations, who have proved their maturity in art . . . should be ashamed of the sad fate of their obsession with and imitation of the West.[21]

Saying that Turks were once at the artistic forefront of the Eastern and Islamic nations [*Şark ve İslam Milletleri*] and that with their unique style they had "brought nature to the level of enchantment," the author went on to argue that in order to recapture this glory it was necessary to not "look at the old decorative arts as obsolete" but instead "study the old, study old Turkish painting and create a new spirit, a new technique, a new Turkish painting style that is original and substantial and accommodates tradition."[22] Another piece from the magazine suggested Turks could recapture their artistic greatness because they had "a rich cultural heritage built on a range of interactions with different civilizations from both West and East" from whom they had "taken

---

[20] Ibid.
[21] Elif Naci, "Türk Resmi," *Türk Yurdu*, April 1954, bound compilation, 478–479.
[22] *Türk Yurdu*, ibid. To the extent previous scholars have explored synthetic cultural ideas from this period, it has largely been in reference to the Mavi Anadolu [Blue Anatolia] or Mavici movement, whose liberalism is often viewed as unique. Can Bilsel, however, argues that the group's synthetic ideas were more widespread than often assumed. He writes that "despite its marked political differences with Blue Anatolia, the officially sanctioned 'Turkish-Islam' was also intended as a 'synthesis' seeking a cohesive and organic 'culture'." "'Our Anatolia': Organicism and the Making of Humanist Culture in Turkey," *Muqarnas*, Volume 24, 2007, 223–241, 236.

and given a number of things." It was in spite of these diverse contacts, the author complained, that "in our recent history we have not been able to draw appropriately on this rich civilizational treasury to bring into being a national, homogenous and country-spanning culture that is unique to us."[23] In this formulation, national greatness and cultural borrowing were fused together, just as studying old styles and creating new ones became dual components of artistic greatness.

Ironically, many Western artists and art critics were also eager to tell their Turkish counterparts that in order to become fully modern and Western they had to embrace their own authentic history. In 1954, for example, a German critic visiting Istanbul for an art critics' conference complained that Turkish artists were not making an effort to free themselves from undue European influence.[24] To do so, he argued, "[T]hey must know how to return to their own roots [*öz kaynaklar*], in other words, ancient Islamic civilization, folklore and miniatures." "First," he explained, "they must appropriate the essence of that ancient era, of that past world's thinking; then they must apply it with a modern mentality to the [plastic] arts." In this case, the response from one Turkish artist was to explain that he and his colleagues were already making ample use of their past: "[I]s the influence of folklore among today's painters not apparent? Are miniatures, carpets, tiles, all these sources, not already being sufficiently taken advantage of?" Why should Turkish artists, he went on, be denied the chance to express their individuality and embrace contemporary trends as well? Modern Western Europeans, in other words, thought that to be more modern and Western Turkish artists needed to finally embrace their ancient, non-Western traditions. Turkish artists, in turn, felt that, having already done so, they were ready to join their Western colleagues in the next stage of modernity.

Which West?

In trying to articulate a vision for their culture that was fully modern but not unduly imitative, Turkish thinkers benefitted from their ability to play European and American modernities off against each other. Many proved eager to claim the American model as a form of

---

[23] Ibid., 421.
[24] Sabahattin Kudret Aksal, "Olaylar Arasında," *Doğu-Batı*, October 1954.

alternative modernity, one that could be used to critique unwanted aspects of European culture. Indeed, some of American culture's most enthusiastic Turkish advocates seemed to take particular pleasure in the negative reaction it inspired among pretentious Europeans who viewed both Turkey and America with condescension.

Mid-century travelogues offer diverse examples of Turkish observers contrasting American and European models of modernity – either as an opportunity to praise the former or disparage the latter. This was certainly possible before World War II, but the opportunities for it expanded dramatically afterward. In 1944, an engineer named Kemal Sünnetçioğlu published his account of a government-sponsored trip to the 1939 New York World's Fair.[25] In reflecting on his experience, particularly returning via Paris on the eve of the war, Sünnetçioğlu made the case to his readers for the superiority of Anglo-Saxon modernity over the decrepit French model. Boarding a French steamship in New York, Sünnetçioğlu said he observed the "degenerate liberalism" of the authorities on the boat, which he identified as their national disease.[26] The ship itself reminded him of a "painted Parisian floosy," in its superficial luxury, a far cry from the Queen Mary he came over on.[27] On the voyage – floating between "the splendors of America and tired Europe" – Sünnetçioğlu and a companion fell into conversation with a French lawyer. When they told him about Turkey's political accomplishments, he listened with his eyes half-open, a look that embodied the tragicomic "state of condescension with which France politely peered down at the world from its rotten, decaying tower."[28] Paris, with its cosmopolitanism, political bickering and moral decay, was even worse. It reminded Sünnetçioğlu of nothing more than the late Ottoman period, when the empire's once-formidable virtues had been rendered unrecognizable by the injection of Arab, Circassian, and Persian influences.

The lesson, Sünnetçioğlu thought, was clear. Turkey should not waste its precious time trying to imitate France, which was "swimming in the pomp, ornateness and grandiosity of classicism." The country should change course and enter the Anglo-Saxon sphere, as, he noted, France itself had. For Sünnetçioğlu, the Anglo-Saxon virtues he

[25] Kemal Sünnetçioğlu, *1939 Nevyork Dünya Sergisi Seyahat Hatıraları* (Istanbul: Güven Basımevi, 1944).
[26] Ibid., 100.   [27] Ibid., 101.   [28] Ibid., 107.

admired – industriousness, simplicity, energy – often appeared second-ary to his running disdain for the French. Thankfully, he concluded, Turkey was a country "possessing the most fundamental human vir-tues." As a result, it had the "spiritual resources" necessary to follow the Anglo-Saxon path and when it did, material success would follow.[29]

In 1946, a lawyer named Fuad Gedik was sent by the Ministry of Justice on a similar mission to study the US legal system.[30] He too came away impressed by America and eager to use its example to take aim at Europe. The comparisons began while he was still in London, which he claimed already felt more American than he remembered from fourteen years earlier. When his plane made a stop at the Shannon airport, Gedik met a British lawyer who was shocked to learn he was going to America to study its legal system.[31] Would England not be better suited? Gedik reminisced that the Englishman's view reminded him of the prejudice he had experienced with the French. For them, talking about Turkish courts would be strange. Their history books did not mention the Ottoman Empire's virtues, just its mistreatment of minorities. "I was going to see that for years America too had been a victim of this mentality," Gedik observed. "This Englishman, in spite of his polite-ness and seriousness, was unable to imagine an American legal estab-lishment. But he himself was going there on legal business."

In New York, Gedik marveled at the scale of the buildings and offered some statistics on the size of the American economy before asking whether New York could truly be called a center of style and entertainment. While acknowledging some would be skeptical, he pointed out that Paris itself was coming under the influence of a new "style and taste from across the Atlantic." Just a year earlier, for example, the world had its first American beauty queen, one whose appearance and dress epitomized this American sensibility. We can find American tastes "odd," he went on the tell his readers, but in light of America being "the most advanced country in the world," we certainly cannot find them "backward or dull." Wearing white suede and "silk ties with pictures of roosters, peacocks and naked women on them will seem truly strange to us," but "now they are even buying these ties in

---

[29] Ibid., 98 (printed as page 89, and appearing after the page 73–74).
[30] Fuad Gedik, *Amerika* (Istanbul: Cumhuriyet Matbaası, 1946).
[31] Ibid., 24–25.

Paris."[32] Ultimately Gedik concluded that Europeans were incapable of appreciating American nightlife because its will and dynamism did not feed their narcissism.[33] Early in his trip, Gedik met a Belgian named Pierrot whose hatred of New York, he felt, resembled a man "wanting to smash a mirror because he cannot see his reflection in it." Pierrot was especially critical of American women, who he found cold, and sought out Belgian restaurants for comfort. The old world, Gedik announced, "is made of these Pierrots." To his delight, New York revealed the emptiness of their souls.

Throughout his account, Gedik returned to the idea that European condescension toward America was driven by an abiding feeling of inferiority. Nothing, he suggested, epitomized this better than the American woman and her seeming indifference: "Truly, this woman isn't what Europeans understand a woman to be. This is something more than a just a woman."[34] In Asia and Europe, Gedik claimed, woman were merely seen as instruments for men's pleasure. As a result, Europeans saw American women as "frigid." But what they could not accept was that American women had gained their freedom and individuality.

Like Sünnetçioğlu, Gedik seemed taken with America as a means for Europe's comeuppance. If Europeans still thought of Americans as "big children," Gedik wrote, then "compared to old and decrepit Europe," "this country of big children stands as the guardian of humanity's rights and freedoms."[35] The tables, in other words, had turned: "Now all of Europe gazes at America not merely transfixed, but awaiting new life and inspiration."[36] Turkey, this meant, was not any less modern than France or England in its postwar embrace of American modernity. Not only did Turkey's experience of European condescension actually make it more like America, but as a result Turkey could reveal its sophistication in welcoming American modernity without the bitterness of the Europeans.

Several years later, a doctor named Perihan Çambel traveled to the United States as a delegate to the fourth International Congress of the American Cancer Society in St. Louis. Throughout her account of the journey, published in the *Women's Newspaper* [*Kadın Gazetesi*], Çambel too stressed the advantages of American modernity while

---

[32] Ibid., 37.   [33] Ibid., 38–41.   [34] Ibid., 113–114.   [35] Ibid., 218–219.
[36] Ibid., 43.

also defending American culture from European charges that it was insufficiently advanced. Comparing her experience with American professors to her pre-war experiences with their German counterparts, for example, Çambel observed that Americans prioritize freedom, openness, and being helpful rather than "crushing people."[37] She hoped this American custom would spread to Europe and regretted that in this regard, Turkey had for too long remained under German influence. The opposite side of this, she reflected, was that America was a young country, and at times its lack of culture was striking, particularly to Europeans.[38] Indeed, European visitors and immigrants were constantly telling her this. But in doing so they overlooked how eagerly and systematically America was working to advance its cultural life. Particularly important, for Çambel, were American efforts to make high culture publicly available; mobile libraries, for example, were just one innovation she thought Turkey would do well to adopt.

That same year, one of Çambel's *Women's Newspaper* colleagues praised another example of America's informal approach to modernity while going through customs at La Guardia airport.[39] In her account, after she offered the customs official a piece of Turkish delight, he winked at her and said, "I liked Turkish delight." Explaining the double entendre to her readers, she wrote, "[I]nstead of being angry, I laughed. Apparently, I was getting used to the American character." She went on to contrast the importance American officials placed on maintaining a "cheerful spirit" while working with the "seriousness" and "hung faces" of Turkish officials who would consider such a remark "impertinent." In place of an overly hierarchal academic elite or an overly stern bureaucracy, which both writers saw as European-inspired aspects of contemporary Turkish culture, America appeared to offer a more open and casual version of the West to emulate.

Of course, in learning from America rather than Europe it was still important to avoid the mistakes Turkey had made in learning from Europe. In a 1952 dispatch from New York, Oğuz Türkkan explained that things like "gum, coca-cola, the bob, jazz and English words"

---

[37] Perihan Çambel, "Haftam," *Kadın Gazetesi*, September 5, 1949.
[38] Perihan Çambel, "Birleşik Amerikadan Kültürel Haberler," *Kadın Gazetesi*, January 31, 1949.
[39] Naşide Gündeydi, "Amerikada Gezerken," *Kadın Gazetesi*, December 13, 1948.

would be easy to copy, but "we as a nation tried this kind of imitation before."[40] In Central Asia the Turks copied from China, then from the Arabs and Persians, and finally, since the Tanzimat, from Europe. "We have much to learn from America," he explained, "on the condition we adopt it for our character [*hususiyet*]." Refusing to copy, in fact, turned out to be one of the secrets of America's success. This was demonstrated by Henry Ford, who created something new, unlike Bohemians imitating the cultural habits of their French peers in Montmartre. Türkkan went on to suggest that in learning from America, Turkey could learn from Japan, which adapted American methods and techniques while preserving its culture and tradition.

At the same time that Turkish travelers heading West found opportunities to articulate a more complex model of Western modernity, travelers going (South) East on the Hajj found opportunities to celebrate Turkey's successful Westernization in a religious context. In 1947, Turkish citizens were given official permission to go on the Hajj after a two-decade hiatus. The excitement of many who had long been pushing for this change was reflected in travel accounts that appeared in religious magazines such as *True Path* and *The Light of Islam* over the next several years (see Figure 3.1). In focusing on the mechanics of modern travel and emphasizing the sophistication of the author as a modern traveler, these Hajj accounts were strikingly similar to the narratives of other mid-century writers, including those going to New York for the World's Fair or legal training. By incorporating a religious pilgrimage into their celebration of Turkish modernity, these accounts implicitly asserted a synthesis of their own.

There is a long history of Hajj narratives blending travel writing and religious experience. But some mid-century accounts made a more

Figure 3.1 "Hajj Memories," a serialized feature in *True Path* magazine, 1948.

---

[40] Oğuz Türkkan, "Amerika Mektupları: Amerika Örnek Almak ve Amerikan Taklidciliği," *Cumhuriyet*, May 18, 1950.

deliberate effort to frame the traveler and his travels in explicitly modern terms. Parliamentarian and bacteriologist Talat Vasfi Öz, for example, began his column titled "My Hajj Memories" on a reflective note, comparing the sadness he felt saying farewell to his family at the Erzurum airport with the joy he felt meeting them there several months earlier after a trip to Sweden and Denmark.[41] As soon as he was in the air, Öz took only a minute to glance out the window before he began comparing the experience of flying on a Lebanese airline to his previous experiences on Scandinavian planes. "I was immediately struck by the great difference … The ventilation was not good at all. There was no in-flight service and the plane reeked of fuel. The leather seats didn't even have seat covers." Then, seeing the tattered and varied garments worn by his fellow travelers, he lamented that "within the borders of our grand and sacred homeland we had not yet established a uniformity of dress." The low quality of their baggage and belongings also "gnawed at his insides like a worm." If nothing else, he was "confident they all could at least have obtained a proper suitcase." Then, looking out the window again, he began discussing the mineral wealth of the country spread out below. In addition to the potash and sodium hydroxide factories already in existence, there was the possibility of finding oil beneath Anatolia's salt flats. His friend Dr. Aschner, at least, had argued as much.

Later, Öz marveled at the scenery of the Taurus mountains: "the many colors seeming to compete with each other … the peaks adorned with deep green forests that kissed the clouds."[42] The view was a welcome respite from the passenger in front of him "who was wiping his nose with his hand, then wiping his hand on his pants." Unfortunately, reaching the Mediterranean they were "caught up in sea of clouds." Öz went on:

---

[41] *İslam'in Nuru*, Issue 3, July 1, 1951. 22–23. An Internet search reveals no record of Öz's devotional or travel writing but provides several links to his work on the endotoxin Tularemia. The pilgrim whose "Hajj Memories" ran in *Doğru Yol* traveled by ferry via Athens. He described bidding farewell to Istanbul's white minarets from the sparkling waters of the Bosporus, being mistaken for a Frenchman on account of his beret in Athens and then praying in the shade of one of the Parthenon's columns before returning to his boat. *Doğru Yol*, Year 1, Issue 22, December 1947.

[42] Ibid.

As always happens in these situations, the airplane began to shake like a malarial patient. But neither the steward nor the pilot gave us any warning. I wonder if my poor fellow passengers were even aware of the inconsiderate treatment they had received. In every previous airplane journey I've made, passengers are given regular updates about the conditions inside and outside the plane ... Was this, I wonder, a sign of our traveling East?[43]

Just as travelers could use a trip to New York to critique European modernity, for Öz, visiting the Arab world for religious purposes was an opportunity to indulge in anti-Arab prejudice.[44] After checking into his hotel in Beirut, Öz commented on his "childlike" desire to see the city before rushing out to explore.

In Beirut, a city where people of all religions and nations are assembled, it is impossible to be bored. There are many vehicles. Cars line up behind one another. And then the tramways and buses enter the scene, truly congesting the city. Among the aspects of the impatient [*tez canlı*] and hard-working [*çalışkan*] Arabs that most struck me was their irritable [*hırçın*] and talkative [*geveze*] nature. I guess in Egypt this temperament is even more developed. I remember the people there bickering at every step.[45]

Trying to change money led Öz to comment further on the nature of Arab businessmen, but also on the Turkish government's faulty economic decisions, which he blamed for reducing the strength of the Turkish lira. Nonetheless, Beirut's modernity impressed him, and he commented on the broad avenues and new villas along the water. Lebanon's shoreline also compared favorably to Scandinavia and the Baltic countries, which led him into a lengthy digression on the wonder and majesty of God, who created such beauty in the world.[46]

Like his counterparts, Öz also saw travel as an opportunity to reflect on the drawbacks and trade-offs inherent in modernity. Calling from Beirut, Öz discovered his family had just arrived home from seeing him off at the airport and remarked, "How civilized [*medeni*] transportation has shortened travel."[47] It was a sentiment that would be repeated, with changing emotions, throughout the trip. When they were told their departure from Beirut would be delayed till the following

---

[43] Ibid.

[44] As will be seen, this language was reminiscent of Bekir Tünay, a Turkish diplomat who, when traveling to his post in Baghdad could not help but remark on the squalor he saw around him.

[45] Ibid.   [46] Ibid.   [47] *İslam'in Nuru*, Issue 4, August 1, 1951. 27–29.

morning, Öz took it as an unexpected opportunity to spend more time in the city:

Shouldn't mature individuals ... accept unexpected events? Our forefathers gave this such a good name: *kısmet*. People are so impatient. We just left Ankara yesterday. Tomorrow by noon we'll be in Jeddah. Could there be a faster Hajj than this? This claim could be justly criticized. It is possible to leave Ankara and after a brief stop in Beirut be in Jeddah the same day. Yes, but should we not remember those who endured all the travails of this simple journey over the course of months? We had such a good time that day ... We wandered around. We saw old friends, visited mosques, and sampled Lebanon's many foods.[48]

At a time when US observers were discussing the Turkish peasant's enduring belief in *kısmet* as a sign of their traditional and premodern fatalism, Öz was already romanticizing it as the legacy of a bygone era before Turks had been swept up by the pace of modern life. By lamenting the fact that impatience prevented the modern traveler from appreciating the pleasures of traveling, Öz was giving voice to the most "modern" elements of contemporary European and American travel writing.

Hajj narratives like Öz's offered readers an image of Turkish pilgrims as sophisticated and indefatigable travelers, off to Sweden one year and Mecca the next. These were men who could be brought to tears by their love of God but also critique the poor service of Lebanese airlines while waxing eloquent about the charms of their splendid homeland. In recounting their experiences, they offered a mobile embodiment of the synthesis between religion and modernity that mid-century thinkers sought in so many realms.

I'm Ashamed of Both of You

Mid-century debates over identity were by no means limited to high-brow discussions of art, literature, and culture. As these travel accounts suggest, male writers debating modernity quickly turned the conversation to women – their character, their role in society, and their appearance. Media discussions of women, particularly Turkish women, during this period provided an arena in which writers frequently expressed their views on modernity, national identity, and Turkey's

---

[48] Ibid., Issue 4. 28.

place between East and West – reaching many of the same conclusions as colleagues debating other topics. Scholars have long recognized that modernity was regularly defined, discussed, and imposed in reference to women's status and appearance.[49] Indeed, the Kemalist project to make "modern" women through means ranging from unveiling to state-sponsored beauty pageants is well documented.[50] Just as the Republic used women as a revolutionary symbol of reform and transformation, the 1950s press saw in the ideal Turkish woman a symbol of the country's commitment to reject both religious reaction and excessive Westernization. In this context, media depictions of women provide further evidence of Turkey's mid-century synthetic discourse. At the same time, debates over decency in the media pitted a variety of conflicting visions of modernity against each other. In defending their commitment to indecency, publishers could present men's enjoyment of nudity in print as a feature of Turkey's modernization. Islamist and feminist critics, meanwhile, argued that this represented a quintessential example of misunderstanding what Western modernity really meant.

The 1950s saw writers celebrate the qualities of the "Turkish woman" that set her apart from Western counterparts, who were alternatively criticized for either their excessive sexuality or, alternatively, their coarse modern masculinity. In 1951, for example, *Zafer*'s front page featured a picture of a recently crowned US beauty queen alongside the winner of the previous year's competition.[51] An accompanying article expressed delight at the fact that recent winner, in contrast to her predecessor, appeared plumper. The author concluded that this development showed that American tastes had begun to reflect a greater appreciation for the natural and maternal qualities that defined Turkish women. A cartoon (see Figure 3.2) from the satirical weekly *Akbaba* made the point even more directly: "the Turkish woman," looking modern but modest in a polka-dotted dress, says of a woman in a bikini and another in a full chador: "I'm ashamed of both of you!" In this representation, the Turkish woman appears as simultaneously modern in relation to oriental or Islamic

---

[49] "A country's progress is measured by its women's progress" from "Pakistan Kadınları," *Kadın Gazetesi*, February 20, 1954.

[50] See, for example, Zehra Arat, ed., *Deconstructing Images of The Turkish Woman* (New York: St. Martin's Press, 1998).

[51] *Zafer*, February 3, 1951.

Türk kadını — İkinizden de utanıyorum!..

Figure 3.2 "Turkish woman: 'I'm ashamed of both of you.'" *Akbaba*, 1952.

backwardness, but also as chaste and modest in relation to the excesses of European or American sexuality.

As with other aspects of Turkey's synthetic modernity, this approach had its roots in the Kemalist era. For example, a 1936 society and lifestyle magazine asked:

What eyes could prefer a Bavarian German woman, plodding along like a camel, to the handsome Istanbul woman? Can the Viennese beauty who pronounces even her finest sounds gutturally speak as kindly as this Turkish maiden? Look at our beaches and look at the world's beaches. Where in the world would the beautiful bodies sunning themselves on the Florya sands face any competition? And even if any of theirs were taller or more beautiful than any of ours, could they be better people than ours? More close to the soul [*ruha yakın*] than ours? More ours than ours? [*bizimkiler kadar bizim olabilir mi?*][52]

The Turkish woman, in other words, was as objectively superior to Europeans in her appearance, as well as her moral and spiritual

[52] Nizameddin Nazır, "İstanbul'un Bugünkü Kadını ve Avrupadaki," *İstanbul Magazin*, Issue 3, March 15, 1936.

qualities, but would also, the author goes on to say, be superior simply by virtue of being Turkish. The author then associates the negative qualities of European women with their experience of excessive modernization: These women entered into a modern lifestyle with "natural grace, elusive beauty and good-natured, sincere bearing" but the conditions of their new lives created "a completely new type of European woman." The Turkish woman, by contrast, was able to maintain her positive qualities, not because Turkey lacked modernity but because she protected her national character in the face of the changes brought on by modernization. Here, as in other discourses, Kemalist proponents of modernization and Westernization insisted on staying true to a Turkish "national and historical frame" rather than heedlessly abandoning it in pursuit of excessive Westernization.

With the expansion of the press and press freedom in the early Cold War period, female writers engaged even more directly in debates over contemporary gender roles. Tellingly, they often came to strikingly different conclusions from their male counterparts while still insisting on the importance of Turkey's synthetic identity in similar terms. Describing a 1948 visit to Stockholm hosted by the International Alliance of Women, for example, Turkish lawyer and academic Nermin Abadan found much to praise about the country's commitment to female equality and emancipation.[53] But she also reflected at length about the dangers posed by an excessively modern or Western lifestyle. Abadan began her reflections by noting how easy it was to have simplistic notions about women based on their nationality: "[W]e are accustomed to picturing the French woman as indecent in her luxury and splendor, the Spanish woman as gripped with lust in her fiery dance and the German woman as buried in her work at the hearth surrounded by a brood of children."[54] Despite this, Abadan felt that certain generalizations could be made. She concluded, based in part on her conversations with Swedish women, that they, like Americans, did indeed suffer from an "excessively liberal mentality." She quoted one woman as saying that she regretted having ignored her parents in pursuit of freedom and behaved "so madly and thoughtlessly" by having a child at a young age. Abadan reflected that these women preferred acting "under the influence of certain literary works" to "protecting their purity."

---

[53] Nermin Abadan, *Yeşil Göller Diyarı* (Istanbul: Hilmi Kitabevi, 1950), 74.
[54] Ibid., 83–86. The image of an American woman, she believed, was of someone "matching men in every aspect of work life on one hand while ruling over their husband like a goddess on the other."

Like American women "they want to be completely free and strive in pursuit of an unrealizable happiness." As a result, "[t]he Swedish woman is truly rich from the perspective of material means, she has a clean, sparkling kitchen complete with the latest innovations of the machine age ... she possesses more freedom of action than the woman of other nations. But rather than bring her happiness and security, perhaps this distances her from them."

Abadan was not unique in her concerns. In one of the first issues of the *Women's Newspaper*, published in 1947, the editor İffet Oruz announced that among the social issues the paper sought to address was the question of whether the Western model of womanhood was really for the best.[55] Turkish women, she explained, have "departed from the model of the family woman and, especially in the cities, wrapped themselves in the mantle and customs of what we call the model of the western woman." But in doing so, she asked, "[H]ave they achieved their highest and most exalted station?" Or "by abandoning tradition have they lost their way?" As an example of what she meant, Oruz explained, "[W]e put on hats, we wore the mantle of modernity, from the perspective of social rights we were no different from men. But does this equality mean we must see dancing, playing cards and drinking, actions which civilized people use as entertainment and relaxation, as our highest calling?"

One of the most definitive answers to appear in the paper's pages came several years later, in a 1951 series called "What Should the Ideal Woman Be Like."[56] After offering a range of perspectives and suggesting that the answer had been different during earlier historical eras, the author defined the ideal women "for all ages" as one who rejected *züppelik* or Western-inspired dandyism. More specifically, this ideal woman "doesn't think being Western is just about fashion trends and promenades" but recognizes that it is actually about "shedding Eastern duplicity and backwardness."

Indeed, for feminist writers, a pointed critique of hyper-Westernized Turkish women often went hand in hand with demands for Turkish women to enjoy the same rights and respect they did in the West. In

---

[55] İffet Halim Oruz, "Davalarımız," *Kadın Gazetesi*, March 22, 1947. For a discussion of the *Women's Newspaper* and its place in the history of Turkish feminism, see Stefan Hock, "This Subject Concerns the Mass Rather Than a Group: Debating Kemalism, Labor, and State Feminism during the Transition to a Multi-Party Republic in Turkey," *Journal of the Ottoman and Turkish Studies Association*, Volume 1, Issue 1–2, 2014, 187–206.

[56] Melahat Gökmen, "İdeal Kadın Nasıl Olmalı," *Kadın Gazetesi*, October 1, 1951.

the second issue of the *Women's Newspaper*, one of the paper's columnists described meeting a friend she had not seen for a few years.[57] The friend, who she remembered as being a salt of the earth patriot, greeted her with a feathered hat, stylish fur, and the phrase "Bonjour, dear." Then, switching to English, the friend went on:

- My heart, my heart [*may hart, may hart*]
- And what's that?
- You're so backward dear, it means 'heart' in English.
- So you've started learning English
- The needs of the day. You must get a teacher as well
- I know enough already thanks.
- This is all from being close-minded.

The friend then explained that she liked to compare her manner of speaking to a stew: the new terms are the pumpkin, Arabic is the eggplant, French is the okra, and English the string beans, all coming together for a fine flavor. When the columnist expressed her disapproval, the friend responded:

- There's no need to say so, it's clear from your face. Of course, because I was born in Europe I think differently.
- You've been my friend for years, this is the first I've heard of you being born in Europe.

The friend has just enough time to explain that she was born in Fatih, on Istanbul's European side, before rushing off to a cocktail party with an "au revoir, darling." Even if she is joking, the columnist thinks, it is still disturbing that anyone would act this way.

In the following years, *Women's Newspaper* writers would return to the theme of Turkish women who were excessively fond of European languages and European luxury repeatedly (at times targeting this criticism specifically against Istanbul's non-Muslim minorities).[58] Like many male authors from the period, they believed that hyper-Westernization and improper modernization undermined the ideal model of Turkish

---

[57] Füruzan Eksat, "Türlüden Kokteyle," *Kadın Gazetesi*, March 8, 1947.
[58] See Nihal, "Medeni Değer Ölçüsü," *Kadın Gazetesi*, May 24, 1947; İffet Halim Oruz, "Moda ve Lüks," July 28, 1947; Füruzan Eksat, "Neredeyiz," August 25, 1947; Nihal, "Nasıl Derler Türkçede," March 8, 1948; Nihal, "Taklitçilik," January 31, 1949; Nihal, "Milli Kültür Meselesi," August 22, 1949.

womanhood. Yet they also believed that modernization imposed equally strict demands on the behavior of Turkish men.

While a wide range of publications articulated a synthetic vision of modernity through the attributes of the nation's women, some Turkish magazines from the period also did so more explicitly in discussing male attitudes toward women. Perhaps the most striking encapsulation of this approach came from the 1947 magazine *Çapkın*, meaning literally rake or womanizer. In an early editorial, entitled "From the Rake's Binoculars" and signed Papa Rake [*Baba Çapkın*] the editor offered his take on what made Turkish men's taste in women so modern.[59] He explained that "in the old days, women's skinniness or fatness so dominated male taste that it was rare to find anyone who deviated from conventional standards." For example, Sultan İbrahim's preference for heavy women created such a fad among high-ranking members of the court that "even in our fathers' time they loved large lively women who they called 'Ottomans.'" "Conversely," he went on, "King James I was so adamant in his preference for skinny women that his courtiers were forbidden from appearing in the company of women who were too large." As similar evidence of varied national taste, *Çapkın*'s editor noted that the Chinese were rumored to be disgusted by blond women but the Laps loved them. He then added, "What is to be understood from this is that we are the most broad-minded nation. We are infatuated with beautiful women of all colors, sizes and features." Only half in jest, he concluded the Turks had indeed turned rakishness into an art form.

While other accounts used women's physical features to define Turkish identity, *Çapkın*, however seriously, shifted toward suggesting that it was the Turkish man's attitude toward these features that served as a marker of national identity and modernity. The implication was that unlike the Ottomans, the seventeenth-century British, ancient Chinese or primitive Laps, modern Turkish men were sophisticated and cosmopolitan enough to appreciate all forms of female beauty. At a moment in time when modernity in Europe, America, and the third world was increasingly described in terms of mobility, travel, and internationalism, the Turkish womanizer proved his modernity by being familiar with and able to appreciate all the world's women.[60]

---

[59] "'Güzel Kadın' Meselesi!" *Çapkın*, February 28, 1947.
[60] See Andrew Rubin, *Archives of Authority: Empire, Culture and the Cold War* (Princeton: Princeton University Press, 2012) among others.

Çapkın ultimately found a number of ways to link nudity to modernity. A subsequent editorial on the subject of shame [*utanma*] argued that in an earlier era, all of society's sins were simply hidden behind "high walls" and "lattice-works." Entertainment and pleasure were restricted and secret, and even the "pleasures of the eye" were "a kind of privilege." As a result, people who could not access these pleasures turned to degenerate and debased ones instead. In place of shame, *Çapkın* argued that the new approach of celebrating beauty in word and drawing would not offend man's modest sensibilities but instead would encourage love and respect for beauty. Decades earlier, Kemalist reformers had argued that Ottoman-era practices such as veiling and the harem were linked to sexual perversion, and that eliminating them would in fact protect women's virtue. *Çapkın*, in essence, reprised the same argument, but as an excuse for printing semi-pornographic pictures rather than giving women a greater role in public life.[61]

Unsurprisingly, *Çapkın*'s interpretation of modernity was explicitly challenged by female authors from the period, who saw the essence of modernization as lying in a very different set of male attitudes toward women. An article in the first issue of the *Women's Newspaper* observed that "men assume they have found an opportunity to have a new plaything in this creature they now see alongside them in their work and social life."[62] But being modern, subsequent editorials explained, actually lay in developing a more sophisticated and civilized attitude toward women.[63] "For civilized people, even the term *çapkın*, which means casually expressing all one's sexual wants and desires, is an ugly, demeaning adjective."[64] As a result, it was incumbent on Turkey's leaders to give all the nation's children the culture and artistic appreciation necessary to restrain their base desires.

"What of the men who claim to criticize the Americanization of Turkish women while constantly praising American women

---

[61] "Utanmak Meselesi!," *Çapkın*, March 7, 1947.
[62] Şükufe Nihal, "Cezamızı çekiyoruz," *Kadın Gazetesi*, March 1, 1947.
[63] Another piece from this period argued that Turkish men on Cyprus showed their nationalism through their commitment to Atatürk's gender egalitarianism. Even though the British allowed them to live according to Ottoman law, they voluntarily limited themselves to one wife. Hasene Ilgaz, "Kıbrıs'ta Türk Kadınları ve Türk Erkekleri," *Kadın Gazetesi*, October 11, 1948.
[64] Şükufe Nihal, "Vahşete doğru," *Kadın Gazetesi*, May 24, 1947

themselves?" asked a subsequent opinion piece.[65] Quoting a female American teacher as an expert on the subject, the author declared that "Turkish men should know that the American woman they like so much doesn't like them at all." According to this anonymous teacher:

Allegedly men and women are equal. [But] for men, flirting is a right. For women it's immoral. For men, immorality is simply a demerit. For women, the slightest independent action is a matter of honor. Turkey's struggle over the past century has been for the togetherness of men and women. The Turkish woman, with a great effort, has achieved this, but the Turkish man is still in his old beliefs and unfortunately in Turkey the sultanate of men continues.

In short, while many men saw rakishness as the essence of modernity, women insisted it was a reactionary holdover from an earlier era.

In this regard, the mid-century press was both a medium for Turkish debates about modernity but also a subject of them. Many of Turkey's female journalists critiqued the relentless obscenity of the popular press with reference to the correct understanding of Westernization. One *Women's Newspaper* piece from 1949 spoke of the challenges facing a conscientious citizen trying to steer a path between reactionary opposition and "the morality of the press which exhibits women to the public buck naked for the sake of sales."[66] Another offered a eulogy for the cartoonist Cemal Nadir, thanking him for always taking women's spirits as his subject, never their naked flesh.[67] A piece from 1952 on beauty pageants urged newspapers to avoid objectifying photographs of contestants in their bathing suits.[68] Instead, the editorial suggested, it would be better from an aesthetic and artistic perspective to focus on their elegant dresses. Having a European mentality, the author noted, meant "addressing the most appropriate examples of civilization." "In our opinion," she concluded, "this is what the responsibility of the press demands."

Despite the objections of *Women's Newspaper* writers, *Çapkın*'s crass interpretation of modernity proved a popular one in Turkey's postwar press. Yet it has largely disappeared from mainstream debates

[65] Melahat Gökmen, "Medeniyetin, İnkılapların Dev Adımlarla İlerlemesi," *Kadın Gazetesi*, October 23, 1952.
[66] İffet Halim Oruz, "1949 Yılına ait Düşünceler," *Kadın Gazetesi*, January 3, 1949.
[67] İffet Halim Oruz, "Cemal Nadir," *Kadın Gazetesi*, March 8, 1947.
[68] İffet Halim Oruz, "İki Kıraliçe," *Kadın Gazetesi*, July 16, 1952.

over Turkish modernization. The gender politics of the 1950s have proved too retrograde to merit attention from contemporary liberals and too indecent for contemporary Islamists. As a result, contemporary scholarship on mid-century Turkish media has sometimes discussed the "popular press" largely with reference to religious publications.[69] Circulation figures from the era are hard to come by, leaving scholars free to make their own assumptions about what ordinary citizens were actually reading. But it would be a mistake to assume that, absent government censorship, Islamist papers like *The Great East [Büyük Doğu]* would have been best sellers. Indeed, many of the era's Islamists felt they were fighting a losing battle against indecency and railed against the popularity of the prurient press. One cartoon from *Akbaba* highlighted the contrast nicely: showing devotional papers like *The World of Islam* and *True Path* on one side and *Çapkın* and its ilk on the other, the caption suggested the former were the diet readers claimed to be keeping, the latter what they were actually eating [*bu ne perhiz, bu ne lahana turşusu*].

The irony, as this chapter argues, is that *Çapkın*, *True Path*, *Akbaba*, and the *Women's Newspaper* were all equally committed to presenting their rival visions of Turkish modernity as uniquely synthetic. During the 1940s and 1950s, Turkey's artistic genius, and technological advancement, not to mention the beauty of its women and the way its men stared at them, could all serve to give the country an identity that transcended the division between East and West. According to intellectuals from diverse ideological backgrounds, this unique status offered Turkey the promise of cultural superiority and political power so long as the country embraced the possibilities provided by its rich heritage instead of rejecting them, as others had done, for an outdated or misunderstood form of Western modernity. That is, by consistently distinguishing themselves from those who would blindly imitate the West, many members of an earlier generation of Westernizers embraced a rhetorical approach that their critics continue to use against them to this day.

---

[69] See, for example, Gavin Brockett, *How Happy to Call Oneself a Turk: Provincial Newspapers and the Negotiation of a Muslim National Identity* (Austin, TX: University of Texas Press, 2011).

4 | Multipurpose Empire
Ottoman History in Republican Turkey

Great Fatih ... May your spirit rest in peace. Your noble ideals will live forever with the Turkish nation and the Turkish Republic upon the sound foundation laid by Atatürk. Is it even necessary to elaborate? Look at Korea. Look at the Atlantic Pact.[1]

– Professor Şinasi Altundağ, May 29, 1953

According to many scholarly and popular accounts, the legacy of the Ottoman Empire has always been a battleground between anti-Ottoman Kemalists and pro-Ottoman Islamists.[2] Atatürk, the story goes, built his new national republic on a vigorous rejection of the Ottoman past. While condemning the Ottomans as backward and oriental, Atatürk gave his people a glorious and invented history of the Central Asian Turks to serve as a basis for their national pride. The Democratic Party (DP) supposedly began to push back for the first time in the 1950s. Then, under Erdoğan, Turkey either "reconnected" with its Ottoman "roots," or, in less sympathetic accounts, rejected the Republic in order to embrace a new ideology of neo-Ottomanism.

But as a handful of historians including Büşra Ersanlı and Doğan Gürpınar have begun to suggest, this misleading narrative fails to account for the much more sophisticated use Republican thinkers made of the Ottoman past.[3] All historical symbols, particularly those

---

[1] "Şehrimizdeki Tören," *Zafer*, May 30, 1953.

[2] See Alev Çınar, Modernity, Islam and Secularism in Turkey: Bodies, Places and Time (Minneapolis: University of Minnesota Press, 2005); Etienne Copeaux, *Espaces et temps de la nation turque: analyse d'une historiographie nationaliste, 1931–1993* (Paris: CNRS éditions, c1997); Sam Kaplan, *The Pedagogical State: Education and the Politics of National Culture in Post-1980 Turkey* (Stanford, CA: Stanford University Press, 2006); Gavin Brockett, *How Happy to Call Oneself a Turk: Provincial Newspapers and the Negotiation of a Muslim National Identity* (Austin, TX: University of Texas Press, 2011).

[3] Gürpınar, for example, argues that by the 1940s the Turkish Republic "had partially reconciled itself with the Ottoman past" leading to the creation of a "popular Ottomanism" that did not "contradict uncompromising

like the Ottoman Empire that spanned three continents and six centuries, are amenable to multiple, conflicting interpretations. As a result,
the "Ottoman legacy" was not some fixed thing to be accepted or
rejected. Rather, it was repeatedly reinvented by different political
actors, starting in the early Republic and continuing up until today.

Atatürk condemned the corrupt rulers of the late Ottoman period
while acknowledging the achievements of the Ottoman golden age and
claiming the empire's best features as "Turkish." Beginning in the
1940s and culminating with the 500th anniversary of Istanbul's conquest in 1953, Turkish politicians, academics, artists, novelists, and
journalists engaged in a thorough Kemalist reappropriation of
Ottoman history. Powerful Sultans like Fatih Mehmet II became secular, pro-Western revolutionaries while Turks of all political persuasions celebrated the Ottomans for their military might and supposedly
self-evident Turkishness. Under the influence of a new postwar rhetoric
emerging from the United States and the UN, Turkey also embraced the
rhetorical possibilities of the Ottomans' now famous "tolerance,"
especially when seeking allies in the Balkans and Middle East.
Treating the Ottoman legacy as an invented tradition on these terms
can help us better appreciate the distinctly populist nature of early
Republican nationalism as well as the distinctly political nature of
transnational history today.

Reversing the Fatal Decline

The quotes that appear most frequently as evidence for Atatürk's
uncompromisingly hostile view of the Ottoman Empire – his description of the Sultans as "madmen and spendthrifts" for example – come

republicanism and the republican contempt toward the Ottomans." Rather "A
domesticated, sterilized, and polished imagery of the Ottoman Empire,
sanctioned by the republic and compatible with republican and national mores,
does not pose a challenge to the historical legitimacy of the republic." Similarly,
Edhem Eldhem frames the late twentieth-century Islamist rehabilitation of
Abdülhamid II by noting that "Kemalist discourse . . . already agreed on the glory
of the early Ottomans" and had incorporated sultans like Fatih and Süleyman
into "the Turkish and Kemalist pantheon of great men." He cites Necip Fazıl
Kısakürek as arguing for the superiority of Abdülhamid by saying Sultans like
Mehmet "had it easy" – "they were leading an already strong and powerful
empire; Abdülhamid, on the contrary, faced the Herculean task of saving . . .
a moribund state." Ersanlı's work will be discussed in more detail later.

from a time when there was still an Ottoman Sultan enthroned in Istanbul who represented a clear political threat to his power.[4] By 1927, the most intensely anti-Ottoman claims in Atatürk's famous speech Nutuk occur when he is quoting his own statements from the debate over abolishing the Sultanate in 1922.[5] Elsewhere in the speech, he proudly declared that both under the Ottomans and before, Turks were "the strongest of Eastern peoples [*Akvam-ı şarkiye*]" at the "forefront" of their "attacks into the heart of Europe."[6] Once it was no longer necessary to condemn the Ottoman dynasty for immediate political reasons, Atatürk and his successors could rework their relationship with the Ottoman past in order to paint a more glorious history for their nation.

The rehabilitation of the Ottoman Empire began almost as soon as it was out of the way and continued apace in the following decades. By the early 1940s, there were scores of publications about Ottoman history. Yet many them have escaped notice, in part because the meaning of the word "Ottoman" itself has changed over time. As used in the Republican era, it referred much more exclusively to the royal family itself, as well as the people, policies, and practices most closely associated with the court. In time, as the term began to have more positive connotations, its meaning expanded accordingly, eventually coming to refer more generally to all of the institutions and social practices that existed during the Ottoman period.

To ask today how the Republican government could have renounced so much of the "Ottoman" past is to ignore how little of it they actually saw as Ottoman. In perhaps the most striking example, what today might be called the "Ottoman Army" was, in Republican parlance, almost always the "Turkish Army."[7] Nationalist rhetoric lauded soldiers and often commanders from Osman's time through World War I as "our heroes" who had courageously fought for "our fatherland" whether they won or

---

[4] Mustafa Kemal Atatürk, Atatürk'ün Söylev ve Demeçleri: Volume 2 (Istanbul: Maarif Matbaası, 1945), 154.

[5] Mustafa Kemal Atatürk, *A Speech by Gazi Mustafa Kemal*, 1929 Leipzig translation, 586.

[6] Ibid., 426.

[7] Typical was a work from the Military Press in 1933 saying the "Crete Campaign" was one of the most difficult in Turkish military history, but the Turks succeeded through "their strength of will." E. Yüzbaşı Ziya and Rahmi, *Girit Seferi* (Istanbul: Askeri Matbaa, 1933).

lost.[8] Typically, such rhetoric blamed the Sultans' incompetent leadership for betraying the valor of the Turkish troops: "While Turkish heroes sacrificed their lives to take Crete, Mad İbrahim took amber as an aphrodisiac so he could better busy himself with the women."[9] Cultural elements show a similar change. The shadow puppet Karagöz, for example, is now one of the three subheadings appearing in the Turkish Wikipedia entry for "Ottoman Culture."[10] In the 1930s, by contrast, Karagöz was a Turkish folk tradition whose populist spirit defined it as everything the Ottomans were not.[11] Similarly, the familiar wooden "Safronbolu" houses with protruding balconies now often referred to as "Ottoman houses" were, as seen in Cengiz Bektaş's *The Turkish House [Türk Evi]*, once thought of differently.[12] Even the bridges, fountains, and medreses that now epitomize "Ottoman architecture" were in the 1930s considered "Turkish."[13] By the time all these became "Ottoman,"

---

[8] Almost a third of the entries in the 1945 encyclopedia *Famous Turks [Türk Meşhurları]*, for example, were Ottoman, as were a substantial number of the entries in the more expansive *Famous Men* from 1935. İbrahim Alaettin Gövsa, *Türk Meşhurları Ansiklopedisi* (Istanbul: Yedigün, 1945); İbrahim Alaettin Gövsa, *Meşhur Adamlar* (Istanbul: Yedigün, 1935).

[9] Feridun Fazıl Tülbentçi, *Geçmişte Bugün* (Ankara: Akbaba, 1943). Building on Zeki Taştan's summaries of popular history books from the period, Murat Kacıroğlu concludes that while works by authors such as Turan Tan and Nizamettin Nazif were often quite critical of even famous sultans such as Fatih or Suleiman, their heroes were men such as Heyreddin Barbarossa or fictitious soldiers whose bravery secured victory for the Ottoman army and state. Zeki Taştan, "Türk Edebiyatında Tarihî Romanlar İstanbul Üniversitesi, Unpublished PhD thesis, İstanbul, 2000, as cited in Murat Kacıroğlu, "'Cehennemden Selam' Romanı Örneğinde İlk Dönem (1927–1940) Tarihi Macera Romanlarda Kanonik Söylem Yahut Angaje Eğilim," *Turkish Studies*, Volume 5/2, Spring 2010, 449–481.

[10] Wikipedia, "Ottoman Culture," http://tr.wikipedia.org/wiki/Osmanl%C4%B 1_k%C3%BClt%C3%BCr%C3%BC, accessed March 14, 2013.

[11] For example, Selim Nüzhet, *Türk Temaşası: Meddah – Karagöz Ortaoyunu*, (Istanbul: Matbaa-i Ebüzziya, 1930).

[12] Cengiz Bektaş, *Türk Evi* (Istanbul: Yapı Endüstri Merkezi Yayınları, 2013).

[13] Istanbul's fountains were a product of "Turks' benevolent spirit" (İbrahim Hilmi Tanışık, İstanbul Çeşmeleri I, Istanbul: Maarif Maatbası, 1943). Fatih Camii was a "beautiful and powerful example of Turkish artisans' aesthetic" that also showed "the development of national genius." H. Baki Kunter and A. Saim Ülgen, *Fatih Camii ve Bizans Sarnıcı* (Istanbul: Cumhuriyet Maatbası, 1939), 5. In the Bursa Halkevi Journal, Sedat Çetintaş wrote that the Ottomans had "developed a modern and advanced architecture … without falling under the influence of any foreign civilization." "Türk Mimari Tarihimizde Bursa Eserleri," *Uludağ*, Issue 32, 1935. Taking things one step further, historian İsmail Hakkı Uzunçarşılı even stressed that the empire's many mosques were

decades of nationalist rhetoric had already thoroughly convinced people of the fact that everything Ottoman was fundamentally Turkish anyways.

Recognizing that Atatürk's anti-Ottomanism was directed at a narrow political elite rather than an entire society or era helps highlight the populist nature of Republican rhetoric. By denying the "Ottoman" label, Kemalist historians were, like other nationalist movements, rejecting the *ancien régime* to better celebrate the achievements of the people who, they insisted, had suffered under it. Today, when Turkish politicians celebrate the Ottomans on populist terms, this too is a political project, not the natural reemergence of some long-dormant popular affinity.

Almost all of the varied works on Ottoman history published during the one-party era can be read as efforts to prove that Turks deserved credit for the glorious parts of the Ottoman past. Aziz Şevket Kansu, for example, is perhaps most famous for the effort to unearth Mimar Sinan's skull in order to anthropometrically prove the architect's Turkishness. In 1940, however, he published the results of an equally bizarre project, in which he used 1927 Republican census data and Bursalı Mehmet Tahir's "Ottoman Authors," to calculate the number of per capita Ottoman intellectuals that came from each Anatolian region.[14] He then compared these results to average skull measurements from each region in order to demonstrate that the regions first settled by members of the Turkish race were the ones with the highest percentage of Ottoman geniuses.

Other authors worked to prove diverse but similar claims about the role of "Turkishness" in Ottoman achievements: Turkish military genius deserved credit for defeating Napoleon in Egypt,[15] Ali Pasha, the Lion of Yanina, was not only a Turk but a Turkish patriot,[16] Piri Reis, a Turkish cartographer, discovered America,[17] and the exploits of

"social foundations" where, in addition to worshipping, citizens could hold meetings, reach collective decisions, and find out community news. İsmail Hakkı Uzunçarşılı, *Osmanlı Tarihi*, Volume 2, 284.

[14] Şevket Aziz Kansu, "Anadolu'da Türk Mutefekkirlerinin Coğrafi Yayılışı Üzerine Bir Araştırma," *Ankara Üniversitesi Dil ve Tarih-Coğrafya Fakültesi Dergisi*, Volume 1, Issue 1, September 1942, 21–30.

[15] Ziya Şakir, *Türkler Karşısında Napolyon* (Istanbul: Anadolu Türk Kitap Deposu, 1943).

[16] Gabriel Romeran, *Tepedenli Ali Paşa*, Ali Kemali Aksüt, translator (Istanbul: İkbal Kitabevi, 1939).

[17] Afet İnan, "Bir Türk Amirali," *Belleten*, Volume 1, 1937, 317.

Ottoman mariners forced "historians of every nation to confess that the Turkish race was the world's most militant race."[18] The Turkish Military Press, meanwhile, republished books like Celaloğlu Mustafa's *Tabakatü'l Memalik ve Derecatü'l Mesalik* as *The Turkish Army's Wars in the Time of Ottoman Expansion*.[19] When foreigners threatened Turkish territory, they were reminded of this legacy as well. In 1939, the poet M. Faruk Gürtunca told Italians considering an attack on Anatolia that in addition to riding on Rome with Atilla, the Turks had sunk Andrea Dorea's fleet under Barbarossa and were ready to do so again. "Ask," he suggested with reference to Ottoman incursions in southern Italy, "which lion Janissary rests in your great-grandmother's heart?"[20]

During this period the Turkish Foreign Ministry also monitored how Turkey's neighbors engaged with the Ottoman past on thoroughly nationalized terms. In 1933, for example, the Turkish Embassy in Sophia reported with alarm the production of an "anti-Turkish" film showing the "unlimited oppression" Bulgarians suffered during the "era of Turkish administration."[21] In 1942, a Turkish diplomat in Albania reported on the dilapidated state of Sultan Murat's tomb, while an Italian official sought to curry favor with the Turkish embassy by informing them that when the region had been under his control he had seen to the tomb's upkeep.[22]

Republican historians also incorporated the Ottoman Empire into their nationalist narrative. Using what Büşra Ersanlı has called the "theory of fatal decline," they identified a Golden Age lasting until the time of Süleyman followed by a period of stagnation and decline from the eighteenth century on.[23] They then argued that through the

---

[18] Ali Rıza Seyfi, Akdenizin Kurtları, Resimli Şark, No. 8, August 1931.

[19] Mustafa Celaloğlu (Sadettin Tokdemir, trans.), *Osmanlı İmparatorluğunun Yükselme Devrinde Türk Ordusunun Savaşları ve Devletin Kurumu, İç ve Dış Siyasası* (Istanbul: Askeri Maatbası, 1937).

[20] M. Faruk Gürtunca, *Bu Arslan Dokunmayın* (Istanbul: Ülkü Kitap Yurdu, 1939).

[21] Cumhuriyet Arşivi, 030–0-010–000-000–2410631-37. Hariciye Vekaleti to Yüksek Başvekalet, December 20, 1933.

[22] Cumhuriyet Arşivi, 030–0-010–000-000–233-573–22. Hariciye Vekaleti to Yüksek Başvekalet, July 9, 1942.

[23] Büşra Ersanlı, "The Ottoman Empire in the Historiography of the Kemalist Era: A Theory of Fatal Decline," in Fikret Adanır and Suraiya Faroqhi (eds.), *The Ottomans and the Balkans: A Discussion of Historiography* (Boston: Brill, 2002) 115–154.

Golden Age the empire had maintained its fundamentally Turkish character as well as the more enlightened approach to religion that the Turks had brought with them from Central Asia. Decline, when it came, resulted from the influx of "foreign elements" and the increasing power of the reactionary *ulema*. This strategy allowed the Turkish nation to take credit for the early Ottoman Empire's cultural achievements and battlefield victories while escaping blame for its later failures. As importantly, it positioned Kemalist reforms as curing the diseases that had crippled the Ottomans.

Perhaps this theory's most concise and official articulation appeared in Afet İnan's *A Study of Turkish-Ottoman History's Characteristic Features*, written for one of the earliest issues of the Turkish Historical Society's journal in 1938.[24] İnan began by emphasizing that there was a Turkish "ethnic foundation" [*etnik zemin*] for Ottoman expansion in Anatolia, and that "empires' lives are linked to the strength of their foundations." Then, in explaining the empire's phases, she highlighted the fact that Selim "added the title of Caliph to his ancestors' imperial legacy." This "made the Ottoman Empire a theocratic state and bound its political statesmen by doctrine to the unchanging rules of a religious book." With this periodization in place, İnan went on to praise the positive characteristics of the early empire. The Ottomans provided the still feudal Europeans with their first example of a centralized monarchy: "[T]he central administration [*merkezdeki idare*] knew the income potential of every small town in the entire empire and determined how it would be spent in an orderly manner."[25] Ottoman "military power and technical superiority" was also based on the empire's intellectual life: "A school was found in each village" until a "retrogression [*gerileme hareketi*]" in the entire Islamic society during the sixteenth century prevented the further development of Turkish medreses.[26] İnan also praised the Ottoman's etatist policies, pointing out that until the sixteenth century, all financial activity was "under the state's organization and control." Then, in the late sixteenth century, "the microbes of decline [*inkıraz mikropları*] began to appear in the state's healthy

---

[24] Afet İnan, "Türk-Osmanlı Tarihinin Karakteristik Noktalarına bir Bakış," *Belleten*, Volume 2, Issue 5–6, 1938, 123–132. As one of the founders of the Turkish Historical Society, İnan played a major role in articulating official Kemalist history, including preparing the "Fundamental Outline of Turkish History [*Türk Tarihinin Ana Hatları*]," which would serve as the foundation for Turkish history textbooks.

[25] Ibid., 125.   [26] Ibid., 126.

structure." Centuries later, the empire's first reform efforts failed because "Tanzimat men remained too bound to religion and opposed to free-thought," while the Young Ottomans too were crippled by their commitment to sharia.[27] İnan thus concluded that it fell upon "the greatest of all Turks to teach us through his actions that harmful practices could only be fixed with revolution, not reform."[28]

State history textbooks reflected İnan's interpretation of the Ottoman period. The 1931 edition of *Tarih*, a high school textbook often cited as the defining expression of Kemalist historiography, began by explaining that Osman's rise was a result of his being able to bring good government to the people where Byzantine princes had failed, "in addition to the unique heroism and militarism of the Turks."[29] The book pointed out that one of Osman's first acts was to cancel capitulations given to foreign merchants and stressed the Ottoman government's capacity for state-building and administration.[30] It even cited two separate instances when Germans expressed a desire to receive the blessings of Ottoman rule.[31] Şefika Akile Zorlu-Durukan's study of *Tarih* bolsters this interpretation, claiming that while Atatürk's state-building project "required the construction of the *immediate* past as worthless, corrupt, and unredeemable," this did not apply to the early Ottoman period.[32] "Criticism of the Ottoman Empire in general starts" in the late sixteenth century, she concludes, before which early textbooks suggested that "Eastern civilization maintained its superiority."[33]

This same narrative was prevalent outside of textbooks as well. In the poetic realm, Hüseyin Hüsnü prepared an eccentric Sultan-by-Sultan history of the Ottoman Empire in verse, "written from feelings of Turkishness, in plain Turkish," dedicated to the Turkish nation's "exalted savior," and published on the tenth anniversary of the Republic.[34] Hüsnü wrote that the Ottoman Empire began when "Osman unfurled the banner of Turan and caused Turkishness to come alive once more."[35] He then

---

[27] Ibid., 130.   [28] Ibid., 132.

[29] *Tarih: Yeni ve Yakın Zamanlarda Osmanlı – Türk Tarihi, Volume III* (Istanbul: Devlet Matbaası, 1931), 3.

[30] Ibid., 3, 5, 28.   [31] Ibid., 32, 52.

[32] Şefika Akile Zorlu-Durukan, "The Ideological Pillars of Turkish Education: Emergent Kemalism and the Zenith of Single-Party Rule" (Unpublished dissertation. University of Wisconsin, Madison, 2006), 158.

[33] Ibid.

[34] Kılkışlı Hüseyin Hüsnü, *Manzum Türk Tarihi* (Izmir: Yeni Matbaa, 1933), 3–4.

[35] Ibid., 95.

contrasted the empire's early days, when "[t]he Turkishness-rejecting men of God / Got a heavy dose of Osman's rod" with a later era when its rulers forgot the basic truth that "[r]eligion should not a nation steer, nor should a ship with prayer recklessly veer."[36] Alongside poets, diplomats also used this narrative when stressing the importance of Republican reforms to a foreign audience. In 1929, for example, Abdullah Zeki Polar's "Reasons for the Decline of the Ottoman Empire" began by stating that before the seventeenth century the empire's wealth and power were legendary, but decline set in because "RELIGION DOMINATED THE STATE."[37]

At the same time, prominent historians focused on the Ottomans' early success as a source of justification and inspiration for their own state-building project. Fuat Köprülü's *Origins of the Ottoman Empire*, for example, can be read as an extended effort to define the success of the Ottoman state as both secular and Turkish.[38] Rejecting the European argument that religious zeal had motivated Ottoman expansion, Köprülü wrote that though the "purest and most vigorous elements" of Turkish Anatolia who formed the Ottoman state "were generally Muslim, they were free from all fanaticism and adhered more to a simple form of their old native traditions."[39]

Not surprisingly, early Republican leaders saw national unity and centralized authority as crucial to the Ottoman Empire's rise. They condemned some Sultans for sullying Turkish with Arabic words and praised others for maintaining the vitality of the language.[40] Their interest in the Ottoman Empire's "Turkification" policies also hints at how they saw their own efforts to assimilate minorities. Republican statesmen could not openly discuss their efforts to "Turkify" any of the countries non-Turkish peoples, because this would involve admitting there were non-Turkish people to begin with. But they could readily praise the early Ottomans for their efforts to Turkify Anatolia's population or criticized the late Ottomans for not pursuing a more assimilationist national policy. Köprülü, for example, attributes Ottoman

---

[36] "Türkü bozan dervişlerle hocalar / bu hakandan yedi hayli sopalar," "Hocalarla devlet işi yürümez / Dua ile hiç bir gemi yürümez."
[37] A. Zeki Polar, *Osmanlı İmparatorluğunun Çöküş Sebepleri* (Istanbul: Ak Kitabevi, 1962), 10.
[38] Quotes from Gary Leiser's translation, *The Origins of the Ottoman Empire* (Albany, NY: State University of New York Press, 1992).
[39] Ibid., 51.
[40] See for example, Samih Nafiz Tansu, *Osmanlı Tarihi Özü* (Istanbul: Numune Matbaası, 1944).

success to the fact that "Christian immigrants" and "the Muslims of Semitic or Iranian origin who found themselves among a Turkish majority" were quickly Turkicized.[41]

The narrative of fatal decline remained central to all popular, official, and academic history from the beginning of the Republican period through the DP era. Beginning in the late 1930s, though, the number of books published on Ottoman history by official and private presses rose noticeably and there was a newfound enthusiasm for celebrating the Ottoman Empire's Golden-Age achievements rather than condemning its later failures. At least one author has speculated that Atatürk's personal hostility toward all things Ottoman facilitated a historiographical shift immediately following his death.[42] Yet it also seems possible that with the passage of time Republican leaders became increasingly confident in the permanence of their revolution and the transformation they had achieved. By the late 1930s, there was no longer any reason to fear the reestablishment of the old empire. Nor was there any reason to suspect that Europeans, whatever prejudices they still might harbor about the Turks, had failed to notice that Turkey had changed dramatically since the empire's collapse.

These trends culminated in the Turkish parliament's 1952 decision to allow female members of the Ottoman royal family back into Turkey. Making an impassioned case for their return on the floor of the Turkish parliament, Hamdullah Suphi Tanrıöver began by imagining Fatih returning on the 500th anniversary of the conquest and asking "where is my family?"[43] In allowing Fatih's descendants back into the country, Tanrıöver argued that "there was no longer any risk" because the country's "regime was strong and its survival guaranteed by an alert nation." Even if the Ottoman dynasty had produced "a traitor, a madman and three-to-five weaklings," he claimed, they had also built a new homeland for the Turks and won them fame throughout the world. Moreover, he put particular emphasis on extolling the nationalist credentials of the surviving royals themselves. Tanrıöver reminded his listeners that when asked if she spoke Turkish with her

---

[41] Köprülü, *Origins*, 54–55.
[42] Orhan Koçak, "Westernization Against the West: Cultural Politics in the Early Turkish Republic," in Celia Kerslake, Kerem Öktem, and Philip Robins (eds.), *Turkey's Engagement with Modernity: Conflict and Change in the Twentieth Century* (London: Palgrave Macmillan, 2010), 305–322.
[43] T. B. M. M. Tutanak Dergisi, 85 Birleşim, 16 VI. 1952.

children, Princess Dürrüşehvar told reporters, "[H]ow can you forget that I am a Turkish woman?" When asked about Atatürk, Princess Niloufer acknowledged that he had sent them into exile but explained, "[Y]ou must not forget that I am a Turkish woman. Until my dying day, I can only feel gratitude for the man who saved my country." Another princess, Tanrıöver continued, had moved to America. When her children were invited to join the US army, they responded, "[W]e are Turkish youth. One day our country will accept us and we will serve there. We will not become Americans." The parliament cheered and ultimately voted to take the Ottomans back.

Fetih 1953

In 1943, İsmet İnönü began preparations for the 500th anniversary of one of the Ottoman Turk's most glorious achievements: the 1453 conquest of Constantinople.[44] The celebrations that took place a decade later defined Fatih's triumph as a victory for secularism, a victory for Western enlightenment values and, most of all, a victory for the Turkish nation. Turkey's 1953 Conquest Day celebrations followed the self-consciously modern Kemalist repertoire for important national anniversaries, with commentators even looking at the contemporaneous coronation of Queen Elizabeth for additional ideas.[45] Over the course of ten days, students and faculty of Istanbul University held lectures, conferences, and seminars where countless historians discussed the importance of Fatih's achievement.[46] The students also hosted a soirée [*suare*], a garden party [*gartenparti*] and a ball [*balo*], the last of which involved redecorating the Taksim Casino in the style of a fifteenth-century madrasa and hosting a fashion show with dresses inspired by Ottoman costumes.[47] The Turkish Theatre Company performed "Tosca" in Fatih's honor, as well as a special play written about the Sultan himself.[48] The government opened new schools and libraries on the outskirts of Istanbul. With fighter planes soaring overhead, the military paraded to Fatih's tomb in the center of Istanbul's

---

[44] Hasan Ali Yücel, "Fethe Girerken," *Cumhuriyet*, May 27, 1953.
[45] Sadun Savcı, "Dolmuşta." *Vatan*, June 3, 1953.
[46] "Fetih yılı program," *Milliyet*, May 21, 1953.
[47] "500üncü Fetih Yılı Balosu," *Vatan*, May 28, 1953.
[48] "Yarın İstanbul'un 500üncü Fetih Yıldönümü kutlayacağız," *Vatan*, May 28, 1953.

old city.[49] There, a mufti said prayers for Fatih's soul, which were subsequently broadcast on the Turkish state radio.[50] The Beyazıt Library exhibited almost 500 children's drawings of the conquest. Other exhibits highlighted fine art from Fatih's time or displayed the Sultan's personal possessions. Schoolchildren read poems written by the conqueror himself. The word "Fatih" was on everybody's lips; Sir Edmund Hillary was hailed as the Fatih of Mount Everest while advertisers insisted their nylon dresses would conquer Istanbul.[51] In addition to state-sponsored wrestling tournaments, gymnastics competitions, and horse races, there was also a special Fetih soccer match played to mark the occasion (Beşiktaş defeated Fenerbahçe 2–1).[52] Mosques and historic buildings throughout Istanbul were illuminated at night. Fireworks were launched and cannons were fired. In New York, the city's 3,000 Turks gathered to commemorate the conquest with a cocktail party in the Empire State Building. Here, the *New York Times* said, they would celebrate by drinking rakı and "Istanbul Magic," a cocktail made by mixing this spirit with lemon juice and crème de menthe.[53]

More explicitly, the rhetoric accompanying all these events repeatedly emphasized Fatih's Turkish national identity, his revolutionary, pro-Western outlook, and his secularism. As repeated in page after page of enthusiastic newspaper coverage (see Figures 4.1 and 4.2) Fatih was not an Ottoman emperor, but the "great Turkish ruler" of a "great Turkish empire." Istanbul, in fact, was his "eternal gift" to the Turkish nation. In addition to this terminology, more concrete rhetoric bound Fatih to the modern Turkish state. Watching Turkish soldiers marching past Fatih's tomb "with bristling mustaches and a lion's gait," a writer for the newspaper *Cumhuriyet* concluded, these "heroic children of the Great Fatih" were proof that "heroism was truly this nation's ancestral inheritance and the legacy of its forefathers."[54]

More than just binding Fatih to modern Turkey, these displays wrote him into the narrative of the Turkish War of Independence and forged

[49] Ferdi Öner, "Fethin 500üncü yıldönümü Tören ve Şenlikleri Başladı," *Cumhuriyet*, May 30, 1953.
[50] Ibid.   [51] "Everest'in fethinin akisleri," *Milliyet*, June 3, 1953.
[52] "Beşiktaş Fenerbahçeyi dün 2–1 mağlup etti," *Milliyet*, June 1, 1953.
[53] Morris Kaplan, "Turks Here Will Sip 'Lion's Milk' to Mark Victory of 500 Years Ago," *New York Times*, May 29, 1953.
[54] Ferdi Öner, "Fethin 500üncü yıldönümü Tören ve Şenlikerli başladı," *Cumhuriyet*, May 30, 1953.

Figure 4.1 *Zafer*'s Conquest Day special insert, May 29, 1953.

a link between Fatih's victory and Turkey's ongoing struggle to preserve its national sovereignty in the face of Russian aggression. One of the most popular slogans to appear in newspapers and speeches proclaimed,

(a)   (b)

Figure 4.2 Front pages from *Vatan* (left) and *Cumhuriyet* (right) on May 29, 1953.

"Istanbul has been Turkish for 500 years and will remain Turkish for 500 more." More pointedly, on May 29 official delegations brought silver vases full of "border soil" from Kars and Edirne – cities on Turkey's Soviet and Bulgarian borders respectively – and deposited them on Fatih's grave.[55]

"Among the Ottoman Sultans, Fatih was undoubtedly the most secular minded [*laik kafalı*]," *Cumhuriyet* declared, while a *Vatan* columnist praised his Renaissance worldview [*rönesancı kafası*].[56] In 1953, secularism stood alongside nationalism as one of Fatih's defining virtues. The oft-repeated phrase used to articulate the historical importance of the conquest in papers of all political persuasions was that in conquering Istanbul Fatih had "brought an end to the Middle Ages" – marked by "fundamentalism" and "sectarian conflict" – and "opened a new era" in human history. A particularly

<hr>

[55] "İstanbul bugün Fetih yılını kutluyor," *Cumhuriyet*, May 29, 1953. See Esra Özyürek's analysis of a similar ritual during celebrations of the Republic's tenth anniversary in *Nostalgia for the Modern: State Secularism and Everyday Politics in Turkey* (Durham, NC: Duke University Press, 2006), 131.

[56] İhsan Ada, "İstanbul," *Vatan*, May 30, 1953.

ambitious, but by no means uncommon, formulation of this achievement credited Fatih with kicking off the Renaissance: "The West was shocked by Istanbul's fall, but it was also awakened. Shaking off the yoke of religious bigotry, it turned again to the life-giving source of Ancient Greek free thought."[57]

There was an explicitly pro-Western dimension to Fatih's enlightenment as well. In capturing Istanbul, the former Cumhuriyet Halk Partisi (CHP) education minister declared, Fatih definitively "turned his face toward the West," both culturally and geographically.[58] Fatih showed this Western orientation through patronage of humanistic arts and sciences.[59] Fatih made Istanbul a center of scientific research by establishing its first university and brought about a "renewal" in Turkish art and culture by, among other things, ignoring the religious prohibition on representing human figures. Fatih revealed himself to be Western and cultured through the respect he showed his teachers, through his employment of Renaissance artists like Giovani Bellini; through his knowledge of Italian, Latin, and Greek;[60] and, finally, through the rationality of his ideas.[61] A subsequent article during Celal Bayar's 1954 visit to the United States took this further, drawing out the similarities between twentieth-century America and the Ottoman Empire in its golden age: both prioritized freedom and progress, not to mention science and the arts, while rejecting religious and racial discrimination in order to evaluate individuals based on their merit alone.[62]

Learning from the West had also supposedly been crucial to Fatih's military success:

Belief and personally righteous forces were not enough for the victory . . . . The Ottomans learned [the Byzantine's] lifestyle and military techniques well. We knew well that victory cannot be achieved in a war between two nations without using the same techniques.[63]

Indeed, the innovative military tactics that Fatih used to conquer Istanbul were one of the many things that earned him the title of "revolutionary [*inkilapçı*]." The adjective appears regularly, if not frequently, in

---

[57] "İstanbul Fatih'i kucaklıyordu," *İstanbul Ekspres*, May 29, 1953.
[58] Hasan Ali Yücel, "Fethin Önemi," *Cumhuriyet*, May 29, 1953.
[59] Sami Nafiz Tansu, "Sanatkar Fatih," *Cumhuriyet*, May 31, 1953.   [60] Ibid.
[61] "Fatih'e ait seminerler devam ediyor," *Vatan*, June 6, 1953.
[62] M. Enver Beşe, "Bayarların Ziyareti," *Kadın Gazetesi*, February 20, 1954.
[63] Hasan Ali Yücel, "Fethin Önemi," *Cumhuriyet*, May 29, 1953.

descriptions of Fatih, who revealed his innovative spirit by dragging his fleet overland in order to circumvent Byzantine defenses on the Golden Horne. This rhetoric was particularly pronounced in *Ulus*, the semiofficial paper of the CHP. According to one writer, Fatih's approach showed "he was a totally new kind of person, one who believed in newness and in the innovators [*türetler*] of the age. He was not satisfied with the methods of his ancestors. He was not tied to old ideas."[64]

In this context, it is no surprise that many writers made the comparison between Fatih and another enlightened, secular, revolutionary, and pro-Western Turkish leader even more explicit. "Fatih's portrait, like Atatürk's, should be hung in our houses and offices with respect," claimed one *Cumhuriyet* columnist, adding that if the government subsidized the distribution of these portraits, it would gladden the spirits of both men.[65] Many other authors drew a parallel between the service both had provided to the Turkish nation: "It was the Istanbul Fatih took that Atatürk saved twice, once by stopping the enemy at Çanakkale, once by driving him back after Dumlupınar. At each end of Istanbul's five-century existence as a Turkish city is a great Turk."[66] In making these comparisons, authors specified that they were praising Fatih for all the ways he was like Atatürk, not trying to supplant one with the other. Indeed, to show there was no contradiction, several quoted Atatürk's supposed response to a colleague who had belittled Fatih: "Quiet. Who is Fatih? And who are you? Take that great man's name to your lips with reverence [*aptest alıp da ağzına öyle al*]."[67]

Much like Atatürk's, Fatih's legacy came complete with an array of anecdotes and legends that could be used, at times straightforwardly, at times with some contortion, to prove or refute any interpretation of his character. The range of these stories allowed authors to pick and choose, including whichever ones gave Fatih the worldview they found appropriate.[68] Testifying to Fatih's secularism was a story about his

---

64 Ataç, "Yeni," *Ulus*, May 31, 1953.
65 İsmail Habib Sevuk, "Fatih ve Dar-üs-şefeka," *Cumhuriyet*, May 27, 1953.
66 "Times'in Fatih ve Atatürk yazısı vesilesile," *Cumhuriyet*, June 10, 1953.
67 İsmail Habib Sevük, "Fatih ve Dar-üs-şefeka," *Cumhuriyet*, May 27, 1953.
68 Promoting a secular reading of Fatih's accomplishment required not just telling the right anecdotes but policing those who told the wrong ones. On May 29, 1957, for example, the Istanbul police detained a "youth by the name of Mesud Yavuz Bilgin" for reading a poem at an unofficial ceremony in Eminönü, which used "emotional language" to criticize Ayasofya's transformation into a museum. "Fethinin 504. yıldönümü dün törenle kutlandı," *Cumhuriyet*, May 30, 1957.

confrontation with several holy men who claimed that God answered their prayers by giving Istanbul to the Turks. "This," Fatih responded gesturing to his sword, "is sharper than your prayers." Other stories testified to Fatih's respect for education and his elders: When Fatih entered the city, Byzantine women and children began offering flowers to his advisor Akşemsettin, believing the older, bearded man to be their new conqueror. Akşemsettin directed their praise and gifts to Fatih, who directed them back to Akşemsettin: "I am your conqueror," he explained, "but that man is more important. He is the conqueror's teacher."[69] Another legend, explicitly told to demonstrate Fatih's commitment to the positivist ideal of artistic verisimilitude, began with Gentile Bellini presenting Fatih a canvas showing a dead man's face. Fatih told him the face was not waxen or droopy enough to be a dead man's. Then, to prove his point, Fatih took the artist to see the head of a recently executed criminal. Bellini was shaken but enlightened.[70]

Beheading and artistic advancement also came together in a unique traveling exhibition put together by the Museum of Modern Art (MoMA).[71] In 1954, MoMA prepared a selection of Turkish school-children's paintings of the conquest received from the Beyazıt Library, which were then sent to colleges and museums across America. Turkish painter Bedri Rahmi Eyüboğlu praised the students' "brave" use of color while other artists hailed Turkey's newfound commitment to teaching art and creativity in the schools. Among the many pictures, one student had painted a scene of a soldier bringing the Byzantine emperor's head to Fatih. After reviewing the proposed caption, Turkish officials asked the museum to specify this had been an "unauthorized decapitation."

Alongside discussions of Fatih's pro-Western worldview, the conquest also provided an opportunity to reconsider the role of women in Turkish history. Authors at the *Women's Newspaper* lamented both the neglected state of Fatih's mother's tomb and how little scholars knew about Fatih's views on women.[72] At a Dolmabahçe garden party,

---

[69] "Fatih ve Topkapı'daki törende yüzbinlerce İstanbullu bulundu," *Vatan*, May 30, 1953.

[70] Sami Nafiz Tansu, "Sanatkar Fatih," *Cumhuriyet*, May 31, 1953.

[71] ICE-D-4–54. International Council and International Program Records Subseries I.B: International Program SP-ICE Exhibition Files, through Series VI: International Council Administrative Records. The Museum of Modern Art Archives, New York.

[72] Leman Arslan, "Hüma Hatun Fatih Sultan Mehmedin Annesi Midir?," *Kadın Gazetesi*, May 28, 1953; İffet Oruz, "Fatih ve Kadın," ibid.

a reporter from the paper found herself watching a performance of Ottoman military music alongside Turkey's 1952 Miss Europe. "In the hall that night," she reflected "were such beautiful women as to entrance Europe and the world. Their faces radiated the honor of a womanhood which had mothered both Fatih and Mustafa Kemal."[73]

Finally, Conquest Day offered Istanbul residents the chance to express previously stifled feelings of nostalgia in an appropriately modern way.[74] As present-day writers like Cengiz Çandar and Orhan Pamuk vividly remember, the unrivaled purveyors of old Istanbul's charms were historian Reşat Ekrem Koçu and the illustrator Münif Fehim Özarman.[75] During the ten days leading up to May 29, for example, the newspaper *Cumhuriyet* ran a series by Koçu filled with legends and anecdotes romanticizing Istanbul life in the previous centuries, while *Hafta* magazine published nostalgic pieces such as "Entertainments of Old Istanbul."[76] The success these features enjoyed helped inspire Haluk Y. Şehsuvaroğlu's *Istanbul through the Centuries*, another old-Istanbul compilation celebrating the beauty of "our houses, our possessions, our costumes and our means of transportation" as well as "the elegance and dress of our women."[77] In a similar feature, author Ahmet Hamdi Tanpınar described how Istanbulites had discovered pleasures of the Bosporus a century ago, while waxing eloquent about the Princess Islands and the beach at Şile.[78]

This nostalgia went hand in hand with using the conquest celebrations to show off the Republic's ongoing infrastructure development. A map from the Highways Directorate, for example, depicting all of the country's newly paved roads, included a laurel-framed seal of Fatih directing his navy's overland transportation.[79] Even more explicit were

---

[73] Cahide Divitçi, "Dolmabahçe sarayında garden-parti," *Kadın Gazetesi*, June 11, 1953.

[74] See Orhan Koçak on the emergence of such nostalgia in the 1940s in "Westernization against the West."

[75] Cengiz Çandar, "Muhteşem Tehlike," *Radikal*, November 28, 2012; Orhan Pamuk, *İstanbul: Hatıralar ve Şehir* (Istanbul: İletişim, 2003), 157–158.

[76] Mustafa Rona, "Eski İstanbul Nasıl Eğlenirdi?," *Hafta*, Issue 92, May 29, 1953.

[77] Haluk Şehsuvaroğlu, *Asırlar Boyunca* (Istanbul: Cumhuriyet Gazetesi Yayınevi, 1953), 173.

[78] Yahya Kemal, Abdülhak Şinasi, and Ahmet Hamdi, *İstanbul* (Istanbul: Doğan Kardeş Yayınları, 1953), 59–79.

[79] Karayolları Haritası, 1953; Atatürk Kitaplığı Map Collection, Hrt_003544.

government publications like *A General Look at Public Works on the 500th Anniversary of the Conquest*, which insisted that the DP government was doing just as much to serve the Turkish nation as Fatih had.[80] In fact, years later, Şevket Sürreyya Aydemir would recount being "forever moved" by hearing Adnan Menderes's views on this subject: "We're becoming one homeland, one nation again. Just like in Fatih's time. Fatih united Anatolia's diverse Oğuz tribes. We also have to unite this country, rebuild it. Cities are out of touch with each other. There are no roads, no paths."[81]

Many authors have suggested that whatever new enthusiasm the Ottoman past enjoyed in the 1950s was a product of the DP's more tolerant approach to public religiosity.[82] In reality, the CHP proved as eager to exploit the political potential of Conquest Day as its opponents. In fact, CHP members repeatedly complained that the DP's "dull" and "wretched" ceremonies were an insult to Fatih's memory on this "sacred" and "lofty" occasion.[83] The CHP specifically criticized the DP for failing to follow through on İnönü's elaborate anniversary preparations. In a June 7 speech, CHP district president İlhami Sancar described the "great sadness" Turkish citizens felt over the government's trivialization of May 29. He promised that, if brought back to power in 1954, the CHP would put on a ceremony worthy of Fatih himself.[84] Newspapers criticized the government over its handling of the celebrations as well. Cartoonists showed Istanbul's mayor instructing his doorman, "If Fatih calls, tell him I'm out," or contrasted the prime minister's presence at Queen Elizabeth's coronation in London with his empty chair in Istanbul.[85] *Cumhuriyet* argued the government's embarrassing performance was a missed opportunity to

---

[80] *Beş Yüzüncü Fetih Yılında Devlet Çalışmalarına Umumi bir Bakış* (Istanbul: Parsadan Basın, 1953).

[81] Şevket Süreyya Aydemir, *Menderes'in Dramı* (Istanbul: Remzi Kitabevi, 1969), 214.

[82] For example Feroz Ahmad, *Turkey: The Quest for Identity* (Oxford: Oneworld Publications, 2003) or most explicitly Yılmaz Çolak, "Ottomanism vs. Kemalism: Collective Memory and Cultural Pluralism in 1990s Turkey," *Middle Eastern Studies*, Volume 42, Issue 4, July 2006, 587–602.

[83] "Fetih yıldönümü için Meclise bir soru önergesi verildi," *Cumhuriyet*, June 2, 1953.

[84] "Fetih Şenlikleri dün sona erdi," *Cumhuriyet*, June 8, 1953.

[85] *Cumhuriyet*, May 28, 1953; *Cumhuriyet*, June 3, 1953.

show the world how civilized and advanced Turkey was. It could have
been "like Cannes," one author mused, "the Venice Biennale or
a French Colonial exposition."[86]

CHP supporters even went as far as to suggest that the DP had
deliberately downplayed the 500th anniversary in order to placate
Greece and America, asking:[87] "Why was Ayasofya not lit up like
every other mosque or museum in the city?"[88] and "Do we get indig-
nant when the Greeks celebrate the independence they won from
us?"[89] The Istanbul University Student's Union published an official
complaint in *Vatan* warning that those who downplayed the celebration of Fatih's victory in order to "win or placate friends" committed
a mistake that might "endanger the future" by calling Istanbul's
Turkishness into question.[90]

In fact, there may have been some truth to these seemingly conspir-
atorial accusations. Reporting on a meeting with President Celal Bayar
in January 1953, Patriarch Athenagoras told the US consul:

[T]he Turks were a "kind people" and were certainly intelligent enough to
realize that now was not the time to offend Christian nations. Consequently,
the present government would play down the celebration this spring and
handle it in a tactful manner.[91]

When the Patriarch added that he himself would be willing to
participate in the ceremonies, Bayar "was most gratified" and told
him that "it would, of course, be necessary to hold the anniversary celebration, but it would not be on a large scale and the
Greeks should not feel sensitive about a matter of such ancient
history."[92] In fact, government rhetoric went out of its way to
minimize any element of Turkish-Greek rivalry. The Ottomans'
defeated foe was always referred to as the Byzantines, never the
Greeks. Newspapers were quick to remind "our Greek friends"

---

[86] Samih Nafiz Tansu, "500üncü Fetih yılında neler olmazdı," *Cumhuriyet*,
    May 23, 1949.
[87] "Fetih yılına dair Meclis'e iki takrir verildi," *Vatan*, June 2, 1953.
[88] "Terbiyemiz bakımından Fetih," *Cumhuriyet*, June 8,1953.
[89] Sadun Savcı, "Dolmuşta," *Vatan*, June 3, 1953.
[90] "Fetih yıldönümü törenleri bitiyor," *Vatan*, June 7, 1953.
[91] Frederick Merril, "Phanar and Five Hundredth Anniversary of Conquest of
    Constantinople," Despatch No. 445, January 15, 1953, Turkey, Istanbul
    Consulate General, Records Re The Patriarchate, Box 1, G 84, NARA.
[92] Ibid.

that the alternative to the Turkish conquest of Istanbul was never continued Byzantine rule but rather Slavic domination and Byzantine incorporation into the "State of Moscow."[93]

In this Cold War context, politicians and journalists were eager to wrap Fatih's mantle around Turkey's participation in the Korean War as part of the United Nations' forces. Saying Fatih's achievement was much more than just a military victory, Istanbul Mayor Fahrettin Gökay told a crowd assembled on May 29 that Fatih had in fact given the world an example of the United Nations 500 years before its time.[94] In a subsequent speech, professor Şinasi Altundağ declared:

Great Fatih ... May your spirit rest in peace. Your noble ideals will live forever with the Turkish nation and the Turkish Republic upon the sound foundation laid by Atatürk. Is it even necessary to elaborate? Look at Korea. Look at the Atlantic Pact ... We, Fatih's children, show our greatest display of being worthy of him through serving the cause of world peace with our soldiers' blood in Korea today. Now we bow with honor before all of our holy martyrs who, beginning with Fatih, have died for their country and who now give their lives for world peace under the United Nations in Korea today.[95]

Columnists, too, made similar comparisons, with one asking, "[W]hat difference is there between Ulubatlı Hasan, who first raised our flag over the walls of Istanbul, and the commander who went into battle in Korea wrapped in the Turkish flag?"[96] Some US accounts echoed this rhetoric as well. Visitors to the MoMA Fetih exhibit, for example, learned that Fatih's empire was "a veritable 'united nations' of people." As a result "[t]he great heroism of the Turkish troops in Korea expresses not only the enduring fighting qualities of the Turks but the success of this 500-year-old experiment in international living."[97]

More dramatically, legend had it that Turkish troops serving in Korea were actually aided by the spirit of the "happy soldiers" who died in Fatih's conquest. In 1952, a young soldier returning from Korea to Diyarbakır reportedly stopped into a coffee shop in the Fındıklı

[93] "Türk İstanbul," *Cumhuriyet*, May 31, 1953.
[94] "Fatih ve Topkapı'daki törende yüzbinlerce İstanbullu bulundu," *Vatan*, May 30, 1953.
[95] "Şehrimizdeki Tören," *Zafer*, May 30, 1953.
[96] Mümtaz Faik Fenik, "Seferihisar'da Genç Ulubatlı Hasanlar," *Zafer*, May 30, 1953.
[97] ICE-D-4–54. MoMA, ibid.

neighborhood of Istanbul. Looking around, he announced that he had come to see the Sofu Baba and asked if anyone could show him the man's home. The customers were shocked. "Son," one of them said, "there's no one alive here by that name. He's one of our saints. You can find his tomb." Even more shocked, the soldier explained that he had met the Sofu Baba in the heat of battle. Surrounded by Communist troops and facing death, he and his comrades had begun to lose hope. Suddenly, a radiant, bearded old man appeared. The man stroked his back, imparting a feeling of indescribable warmth, and asked why he was afraid. "It doesn't suit you," he said, "now fight." When the soldier asked the old man who he was, the man said, "I'm the Sofu Baba. From Istanbul. I live in Fındıklı. Come find me after the war." He then disappeared into the smoke as the men launched their assault.[98]

The Origins of Ottoman Tolerance

Turkey's Cold War geopolitical needs also help explain one of the most distinct and enduring developments in Ottoman historical rhetoric that occurred in this period: the emergence of "tolerance" as a featured aspect of Ottoman rule. A number of factors came together to fuel the popularity of "Ottoman tolerance." Turkish statesmen were well aware of the criticism their country faced, both in America and the Soviet Union, for its historic treatment of Christian minorities. Turkey also faced accusations from its new Western allies that its neutrality in World War II been motivated by ideological sympathy toward fascism. The rhetoric of tolerance sought to respond to these criticisms and justify Turkey's place in a new Western world order defined by international cooperation and freedom.

Returning from a 1950 UNESCO conference consisting of "professors from all the world's democratic countries," a representative of the Ministry of Education wrote that Turkey would need to "facilitate the teaching of a broader historical viewpoint in keeping with UN ideals." This viewpoint should be based on "the reality of nations ever-growing economic, political and civilizational ties and their dependence on one another," in place of "our previous flat,

---

[98] One version of this legend is related by the Turkish Ministry of Religion outside the tomb of the Sofu Baba, located on the Fındıklı Yokuşu in Istanbul's Cihangir neighborhood. It can also be found at: www.smartbeyoğlu.com/firma/23015/ sofu-baba-turbesi.html.

narrow [*dar*] and extremist [*müfrit*] national views and teachings."[99] Among other things, this effort (which, he noted, also required other countries to purge their schoolbooks of anti-Turkish prejudice) would promote world peace, end national rivalries, and, most importantly, help defeat the spread of Communism. The author cited American history textbooks written "without religious prejudice" as examples that could serve as a "guide" in the creation of a "united world."[100] He then lamented that "if we had had the power in the Seljuk and Ottoman eras, we ourselves could have served as exemplars of the humanitarian ideal."[101] In this context, the discourse of Ottoman tolerance offered a way to nationalize the era's internationalism and give a patriotic gloss to the spirit of global peace.

The discourse of Ottoman tolerance also echoed US attacks against Soviet "religious persecution," suggesting that Turkey's historic embrace of religious freedom marked it as a part of the free world. In 1948, an article in Ankara University's *Faculty of Language, History and Geography Journal* argued that Ottoman Christians had always been happy compared to Russia's Muslims[102] and explicitly contrasted the lack of religious compulsion in Islam with the mandatory atheism prescribed by Communism.[103] The author also concluded that the Ottoman Empire had never been at war with Christianity, only the Slavs. In the sphere of public rhetoric, Celal Bayar gave voice to these sentiments when he declared, "Fatih began the practical application of the ideas of religious freedom and freedom of conscience for which people still struggle today."[104] One of the few officials conquest publications translated into English in 1953 was a pamphlet called "The Importance of the Conquest of Istanbul for Mankind and Civilization," which explained that "[t]he respect of the Turks for

---

[99] Osman Turan, "Milliyet ve İnsanlık Mefkurelerinin Tarih Tedrisatında Ahenkleştirilmesi," *Ankara Üniversitesi Dil ve Tarih-Coğrafya Dergisi*, Volume 10, Issue 1–2, March–June 1952, 209–239, 210.

[100] Ibid., 212.   [101] Ibid., 225.

[102] Bekir Sıtkı Baykal, "Şark Buhranı ve Sabah Gazetesi," *Ankara Üniversitesi Dil ve Tarih-Coğrafya Dergisi*, Volume 6, Issue 4, September–October 1948, 219–258, 252.

[103] Ibid., 233.

[104] *Beş Yüzüncü Fetih Yılında Devlet Çalışmalarına Umumi bir Bakış* (Istanbul: Parsadan Basın, 1953), 67.

all religions, even in the days before Mohammedanism, is no[w] proved by recent research."[105]

The regional politics of the early Cold War also played a role. Among other justifications used to bolster Soviet claims to northeastern Anatolia was the argument, advanced by two Georgian scholars in 1945, that Ottoman Turks had "spread violence and death" across Georgia, "imposing their religion and language by sword."[106] Şinasi Altundağ set out to rebut these claims at the Fourth Turkish Historical Society Congress with a vigorous defense of the Ottoman Empire's tolerance.[107] Citing the "emotion and loyalty [*his ve bağlılık*]" the Georgians felt toward the Ottomans, Altundağ went to explain that the Ottomans' cultural policies were clear: "Today, are languages like Greek, Bulgarian, Serbian, and Albanian not still around? Did the Greeks, Bulgarians, Serbs, and Georgians re-learn their languages and Christianity after leaving the Ottoman Empire?"[108] "A tolerance reigned in the Ottoman Empire that was the envy of other nations . . . . To steal a Christian's chicken or pasture a horse on a Christian's field was equivalent to a murder and punishable by death . . . . Once ten Janissaries were executed for the unjust killing of a Christian."[109]

Celebrating Fatih's religious tolerance went hand in hand with celebrating his supposed secularism. Several authors went as far as to suggest that in making Ayasofya into a mosque, instead, presumably, of destroying it, Fatih was not only showing his secular ideals but his respect for Christians culture as well. Despite the ruined state in which the Byzantines left Ayasofya, Fatih admired its mosaics of the Virgin Mary and violently intervened to stop a Janissary from damaging the marblework. Some authors went as far as to claim that

---

[105] İsmail Hami Danişmend, "The Importance of the Conquest of Istanbul for Mankind and Civilization," translated by E. A. and B. M. (Publications of the Istanbul Society for Celebration of the Conquest No. 15). This rhetorical outreach was sufficiently effective that the *New York Times* noted, "The modern Turk believes his was the first country to establish a legal basis for the co-existence of all religious and racial groups." Morris Kaplan, "Turks Here Will Sip 'Lion's Milk' to Mark Victory of 500 Years Ago," *New York Times*, May 29, 1953.

[106] S. Djanasia and N. Berzenisvili as quoted in Şinasi Altundağ, "Osmanlı İdaresi ve Gürcüler," *Ankara Üniversitesi Dil ve Tarih-Coğrafya Dergisi*, Volume 10, Issue 1–2, March–June 1952, 79–90.

[107] Ibid.   [108] Ibid., 79.   [109] Ibid., 81.

in turning the building into a museum, Atatürk was acting on the same impulse that had inspired Fatih.[110] In a particularly striking effort to recast Fatih as an exemplar of religious tolerance, Ecevit offered American readers the following anecdote in January 1955:

> In [Ayasofya] were some of the finest mosaics that Byzantine artists had executed ... Yet representation of the human form was forbidden by the Mohammadan religion. So the new rulers of the city, who were of the Mohammadan faith, had no choice but to destroy them. Could Mehmet the Conquereor, the liberal Sultan who was later to bring over the famous Italian artist Bellini to his court to do his portrait allow such an act? For nearly five centuries the whole world believed that he did! But a few years after Turkey became a secular republic ... it was discovered that Mehmet the Conqueror had only had those mosaics covered with sheets of durable cloth ... So when the plaster and the sheets of cloth were removed, the mosaics were there – as fresh as they were in 1453.[111]

Later that same year, in the fall of 1955, a pogrom targeted Istanbul's Christian population, destroying stores and churches and leaving at least a dozen people dead. Ecevit was one of the few authors to see a contradiction with the lofty rhetoric of the 1953 celebrations. In a column titled "Fatih, Forgive Us," he lamented that the destruction visited on Istanbul's minorities was a painful rejection of the principles Fatih had demonstrated entering the city 502 years earlier.[112]

Ottoman Nostalgia Today

Speaking at Dolmabahçe palace on his first trip to Istanbul after the War of Independence, Atatürk declared that the royal residence no longer belonged to the Ottoman dynasty, those "specters" or "shadows of God." Now, with the founding of the Republic, it was "truly

---

[110] Damat Mehmet Şerif Paşa, Ciğercan Tarih Kitapları Serisi No. 5, *Fatih Sultan Mehmed Han-ı Sani ve İstanbul'un Fethi* (Istanbul: Hilmi Kitabevi, 1953).

[111] "Istanbul a Beautiful City of Many Names Haunted by Its Long Hectic Past," *Sunday Journal and Sentinel*, January 2, 1955.

[112] Bülent Ecevit, "Fatih, Bizi Affet," *Ulus*, September 9, 1955. In the course of the column he also argued that this was true even if Turkey's cause was justified and the Ottoman Empire's minorities had in fact betrayed it.

the palace of the people [*millet*]."[113] As a result, he declared, "I am elated to be here as one of the people, a guest of the people." Almost a century later, similar sentiments would be echoed by President Erdoğan when he inaugurated a massive new presidential palace in Ankara intended to replace the earlier one built by Ataturk. After welcoming his guests "to the people's house, to your house [*milletin evine, sizin evinize*]," Erdoğan declared that "the Presidential complex within which we find ourselves is a symbol of the fact that the Republic now belongs to the public not any institution or social class."[114]

Where Atatürk once championed the Turkish nation against a decadent, out-of-touch and fundamentally foreign Ottoman elite, Erdoğan now draws on a romanticized version of the Ottoman past to condemn Atatürk's Republican elite on the same terms. Appreciating this, and the many ways Ottoman history has been reinterpreted over the past century, makes it easier to understand how the empire's memory is used today. After 1953, the more concrete Ottoman legacy, existing in economic, institutional, and personal relationships from the time of the empire itself, gave way to a legacy that is better understood in terms of invented tradition. The popular image of the Ottoman Empire that was consolidated in the 1950s – mighty but just, tolerant but undeniably Turkish – has proved remarkably enduring in films, museums, and popular culture; even as a range of different political movements have refined their own versions of the Ottoman past. Current Islamist invocations of Ottoman piety, just like liberal invocations of Ottoman multiculturalism, both count on the same fundamental continuity between the Ottoman and Turkish states articulated by early nationalists. At the same time, the malleability of the Ottoman legacy can help explain its contestation in popular culture today.

On May 29, 2010, for example, Istanbul celebrated Conquest Day with speeches, reenactments, and multimedia pageantry. Along the city walls, men dressed in Janissary costumes and fake mustaches marched

---

[113] "Büyük Gazimiz İstanbul Halkın Mümessillerine Hitaben bir Nutuk," *Hakimiyet-i Milliye*, July 2, 1927. Quoted in Ryan Gingeras, *Eternal Dawn: Turkey in the Age of Atatürk* (Oxford: Oxford University Press, 2020).

[114] Speech by President Recep Tayyip Erdoğan on October 28, 2015 as published on the official presidential website. www.tccb.gov.tr/haberler/410/35788/cum huriyetin-sahibi-milletimizin-kendisidir-sembolu-de-cumhurbaskanligi-kulliyesidir.html.

alongside uniformed military academy students and drum majorettes. The Justice and Development Party (AKP) mayor of Istanbul stressed the fact that within three days of taking the city, Fatih ordered the Janissaries back to their barracks to restore order. Fatih, it seemed, supported the AKP in its struggle to establish civilian control of the military. A Turkish military officer, by contrast, spoke about the many characteristics Fatih and Atatürk shared. Later, everyone headed to the Golden Horn for a laser light show with rainbow colors to symbolize Fatih's tolerance.

After it debuted in 2011, commentators regularly cited Mutehşem Yüzyıl, a popular soap opera about the life of Suleiman the Magnificent, as a prime example of Turkey's AKP-inspired Ottomania.[115] In 2014, however, the show suddenly found itself accused of romanticizing the past the wrong way. Months after the actor who played Süleyman appeared at the Gezi Park protests, Erdoğan lashed out at his character, questioning whether a man portrayed as spending more time in the bedroom than on horseback could be a suitable role model for a new generation of Turkish children. Suddenly, academic historians who had long worked to desexualize popular accounts of the harem were forced to publicly point out that the Ottoman sultans had, in fact, slept with their many concubines. In the aftermath of this controversy, a new set of Ottoman-themed TV series appeared, offering viewers a more martial version of the past to match the country's darker political mood. For nationalistic viewers, there was Diriliş Ertuğrul, a gritty take on the empire's founding. For those who wanted something with Islamist sensibilities, there was Payitaht, the story of Abdülhamid defending his realm against scheming Europeans and Jews.[116]

On May 29, 2019, Istanbul's CHP mayoral candidate Ekrem Imamoğlu shared a video on Twitter in which he quoted Fatih as saying that he "came to conquer hearts, not land."[117] Imamoğlu then promised that, like Fatih, he would again make Istanbul a city where residents of all faiths and languages lived together in peace and justice. Meanwhile, AKP supporters spread accusations that Imamoğlu was

---

[115] Elif Batuman, "Ottomania: A Hit TV Show Reimagines Turkey's Imperial Past," *New Yorker*, February 17 and 24, 2014.

[116] See William Armstrong, "What a TV Series Tells Us about Erdogan's Turkey," *New York Times*, May 17, 2017.

[117] Ekrem İmamoğlu, May 29, 2019. https://twitter.com/ekrem_imamoglu/status/1133603511013392389?s=20.

secretly Greek and warned that his victory would be a triumph for Turkey's "internal Byzantines." One paper called on him to deny that he spoke Greek in order to lead "the city conquered by Fatih."[118] A year later, Imamoğlu won widespread praise from his secular constituency for purchasing a Gentile Bellini painting of Fatih that went on sale in London. The pro-AKP press, in turn, condemned him for wasting money on a drawing done by an infidel.

In the realm of foreign policy, the Ottoman legacy has proved equally malleable. Observers argued for almost a decade over whether the AKP was rejecting Atatürk's legacy by turning its back on the West in favor of the Muslim East or whether the party had instead finally realized Turkey's historic role as a bridge between the two. For advocates, the AKP's "neo-Ottomanism" represented a long-belated recognition of the "strategic depth" that Turkey possessed on account of its unique geography and history. Yet others, including Greeks, Armenian-Americans, and Washington conservatives, used "neo-Ottoman" instead as an epithet almost akin to neo-Nazi, shorthand for some form of Islamic irredentism. Yet even for critics, the term proved ambiguous. Erdoğan's efforts to cozy up to Syrian leader Bashar al-Assad before the Arab spring were initially cited as proof of his neo-Ottoman ambitions. Then, after 2010, Erdoğan's support for anti-Assad rebels was instead. Subsequently, critics have attached the neo-Ottoman label to Turkey's cooperation with Russia and Iran, countries that are not famous for having gotten along well with the Ottoman Empire.

The discourse of Ottoman tolerance, in Turkey and abroad, also offers a fascinating study in the politicization of history. While historians have been quick to identify the relationship between knowledge and power among nineteenth- and twentieth-century nationalist historians, they have seldom explored how a similar relationship contributes to contemporary critiques of nationalist historiography. Beginning in the 1990s, for example, transnational institutions such as the European Union used their resources to help transform the Ottoman Empire into a symbol of religious and cultural tolerance. At the risk of oversimplifying, where nineteenth-century nation-states promoted the work of nationalist historians who provided embellished accounts of their nations' historic origins, transnational institutions

---

[118] "Ekrem İmamoğlu'nun 'YOKMUŞ' gibi davrandığı cevapsız sorular," *Sabah*, May 29, 2019.

promoted the work of historians whose accounts of a pre-national, multicultural past seemed to offer a model for overcoming current conflicts. The EU, which has an obvious interest in promoting stability and international cooperation along its borders, has funded museums, conferences, books, and universities that promoted a version of Ottoman history conducive to this goal. In these accounts a romanticized version of Christian-Islamic syncretism replaces the old myth of five centuries of Turkish-Greek hatred. Karagöz has become "Ottoman" in the sense of being part of a shared regional culture, while Mimar Sinan's Armenian ancestry can now serve as evidence of Ottoman pluralism.

In the face of the ugly, xenophobic, and militarized version of Ottoman nostalgia all too widespread in Turkey today, the multicultural alternative will likely remain appealing to those in search of a liberal antidote. But we should be aware that this too is a political project and one subject to distortions of its own.

5 | Making the Past Modern
Popular History in Print

[T]he old European section of Istanbul glittered at the end of the broad half-mile of bridge with the slim minarets lancing up into the sky and the domes of the mosques, crouching at their feet, looking like big firm breasts. It should have been the Arabian Nights, but to Bond, seeing it first above the tops of trams and above the great scars of modern advertising along the river frontage, it seemed a once beautiful theatre-set that modern Turkey had thrown aside in favour of the steel and concrete flat-iron of the Istanbul Hilton Hotel, blankly glittering behind him on the heights of Pera.

– Ian Fleming, *From Russia with Love*, 1957[1]

Completed in 1955, the Istanbul Hilton was intended to serve as a preeminent symbol of Turkey's modernization.[2] The very contrast that caused Bond such disappointment was, for many Istanbul residents, exactly the point. Trams too served as markers of the city's progress. They were prominently featured in many mid-century drawings of Istanbul's famous monuments, passing alongside a historic mosque or fountain, as if to remind viewers that these buildings were located in a modern metropolis, not in some timeless oriental fantasyscape.

This chapter examines the unique challenge faced by non-Western nationalists who sought to celebrate their country's history and rural geography in a way that would not call their modernity into question. In the face of orientalist depictions of Turkey as irrevocably traditional or mired in its past, mid-century Turkish writers, artists, and architects perfected a range of techniques for celebrating their history without being seen as a part of it. The British never had to worry that tourists

---

[1] Ian Fleming, *From Russia with Love* (London: Signet, 1957), 81.
[2] For more on the Hilton as a symbol of modernity, see Sibel Bozdoğan, *Modernism and Nation Building: Turkish Architectural Culture in the Early Republic* (Seattle: University of Washington Press, 2001) as well as Begüm Adalet, *Hotels and Highways: The Construction of Modernization Theory in Cold War Turkey* (Stanford University Press: Stanford, 2018).

would think the Beefeaters represented the pride and strength of their country's army. When Turks sought to revive their Ottoman-era marching band, however, they were just the slightest bit concerned. The wholesale reappropriation of the Ottoman past discussed in the previous chapter represented the most comprehensive ideological approach to this challenge, but there were a number of other cultural, intellectual, and artistic responses as well, all intended to establish a modern relationship between Turkey and its history.

This chapter begins by looking at the use of modern features like trams in visual representation of Ottoman-era monuments to set them in a modern context. Civic efforts to surround these same monuments with parks, gardens, and fences were, I argue, part of a parallel architectural approach to setting them apart from the modern city. In magazines, authors writing about history also used literary and visual techniques to position readers as modern individuals investigating their past from a self-confidently modern perspective. The frequent use of nineteenth-century European Orientalist motifs was itself one of these techniques. In the realm of geography, this chapter also examines similar approaches to depicting Eastern Anatolia and proclaiming its Turkishness in mainstream, almost exclusively urban, publications. One long-standing approach presented Eastern Anatolia through the lens of scholarly investigation, using academic inquiry as a pretext for visiting the region and using the results to assert its Turkishness. The second approach presented the region through the lens of tourism. During the 1950s, many publications implied that by seeking out less-developed parts of the country, city dwellers were actually demonstrating their modernity.

We Must Know How Foreigners Have Seen Us

Before examining how Turkey's mid-century writers, artists, and urban planners worked to present their country's history from a modern perspective, it is worth briefly outlining what they were up against. As many Turks, particularly those elites who most regularly interacted with foreigners, were acutely aware, the perception of Turkey as an "oriental" country was still widespread in the 1940s and 1950s. Whether articulated by Ian Fleming or the anonymous creator of the drawing below (see Figure 5.1), Turkey's "oriental" essence was still regularly described with explicit reference to the Arabian Nights well into the opening decade of

Figure 5.1 "Istanbul 10 Miles." Mid-century folk art from the US Navy.

the Cold War. While initial contacts with American soldiers and diplomats might have gradually changed American perceptions about Turkey, they quite often provided Turks with further evidence, whether it was needed or not, of how their country was viewed.

This image was sold as a piece of early Cold War "folk-art" by a collector at the U.S. Naval War College. The slightly washed-out caption reads, "Pardon effendi Charles, but all my goods are black ... please ... the only blonde is coffee-hanume!!! But if effendi wishes so, she will also be available." The sign in the lower right reads, "Istanbul, 10 miles."

In 1947, the battleship *Missouri* returned the body of Ambassador Münir Ertegün to Turkey for his funeral (or, in the words of one diplomat "whatever the Turks do upon such an occasion").[3] At the level of geopolitics, the *Missouri*'s visit marked an important show of American support for Turkey in the opening stages of the Cold War. But at a social level it also provided an opportunity for an unprecedented degree of personal interaction between ordinary Americans and residents of Istanbul. Reflecting positively on the occasion in an article titled "While Bidding Farewell to Our Esteemed Guests, the American Naval Units" a *Vakit* journalist nonetheless observed:

---

[3] February 8, 1947. Stanley Woodward to Edwin Wilson. Unclassified General Records, U.S. Embassy, Ankara. Box 100, RG 84, NARA.

It cannot be claimed that there no longer exist today Americans who think that the Turks still wear the shalvar and the fez. As a matter of fact, a picture in one of the sailors' cabins of the Missouri shows a sketch of Istanbul with baggy trousered and fezzed people on it."[4]

Indeed, an article from the same day quoted a sailor from Chicago saying:

We have been living in fairy tales for the past three days. When I was a small boy, my mother used to tell me stories and one of them was about a country where one had only to whistle to make all his wishes come true. Here, your wishes seem to come true the moment you start thinking about them. It really is a dreamland.

With such reactions in mind, the US government began an instructional manual given to incoming staff – "Guide to Turkey: A Land for Pioneers" – by saying: "Turkey may make you think of sultans and veiled women, of men in baggy trousers and red fezzes, of Turkish delight, Turkish coffee and Turkish baths."[5] Bülent Ecevit, for his part, offered a lighthearted take on the way American soldiers and diplomats responded when these expectations were dashed:

To many of them the name Turkey implied an exotic oriental country, with low divans covered with oriental rugs, hookahs, large braziers with burning charcoal in the middle of rooms, round brass trays on low stands with shining brass pitchers on them containing the attar of roses, walls decorated with tiles and miniatures, women wearing long pants in the harem style, and so forth .... Well, we did not have any of these any more .... Our friends from the New World would not stand so much disappointment. Something should be done about it. With no help coming from the Turks, they took the initiative in the true pioneer spirit. They cleared the old bazaars of all the articles left on the shelves from the old days. They bought old rugs, hookahs, brass pitchers, braziers and trays .... Now when a Turk wants to show his son the way his forefathers furnished and decorated their homes, he takes them to some of his American friends in Ankara.[6]

---

[4] H. Sağnak, *Vakit*, April 9, 1947. Article and translation from the U.S. Istanbul Consulate's press reports. Unclassified General Records, U.S. Embassy, Ankara. Box 100, RG 84, NARA.

[5] "Turkey: A Land for Pioneers," Unclassified General Records, U.S. Embassy, Ankara. Box 88, RG 84, NARA.

[6] Americans in Turkey Really Go Turkish. *Winston-Salem Journal*, October 17, 1954.

It was against the prevalence of these associations that many Turkish authors exercised particular care in presenting their past. As publisher Ahmet Banoğlu explained in his preface to the first issue of his reissued *History World* [*Tarih Dünyası*]:

In foreign countries there are hundreds and hundreds of works published about Turkey, thousands upon thousands of articles, and we still haven't been able to collect all of them. We must know how foreigners have seen us throughout all of history so that we may direct our response to them. [*Yabancıların bizi, bütün tarih boyunca nasıl gördüklerini bilmeliyiz ki, biz onlara karşı hareket tarzımızı idare edelim.*][7]

In some sense, Banoğlu anticipates Said, but as a nationalist call to arms. He also offers a reprise of Atatürk's famous conversation with Afet İnan, in which Atatürk's daughter discovers a French textbook describing Turks as members of the yellow race and he responds that in that case they must write a new history themselves.[8] Yet Banoğlu, rather than see the mission as a matter of correcting false scholarship with more accurate research, instead presents a more explicitly politicized mission couched in the language of public relations or image-management. And indeed, these were the terms in which many Turkish writers, politicians, and artists took it up. In planning, recording, and transforming Turkey's urban fabric, in photographing historic reenactments, designing museums, and promoting tourism, participants in creating Turkey's mid-century visual culture relied on an overlapping, mutually reinforcing set of artistic and rhetorical techniques in order to proclaim their own modernity and that of their country's past.

In the 1940s and 1950s, much like today, newspapers and magazines published in Istanbul were always eager to write about Istanbul. In doing so, they consistently sought to present the city in ways that simultaneously emphasized its modernity and its history. In a 1951 feature called "Istanbul Yesterday and Today," *History World* sought to highlight Istanbul's transformation over the previous half century with a celebration of all the things that ruined its "Arabian nights" magic for James Bond. Pairs of photographs showed identical buildings and locations fifty years apart with captions explicitly mentioning the presence of cars, electric trams, and buses as well as the "civilized"

---

[7] *Yeni Tarih Dünyası*, Volume 1, Issue 1. 1953.
[8] Ayşe Gül Altınay, *The Myth of the Military-Nation: Militarism, Gender, and Education in Turkey* (New York: Palgrave MacMillan, 2004).

[*medeni*] outfits on the pedestrians. One caption, for example, states: "In front of Sirkeci station 50 years ago was a space where drifters and stray dogs wandered." On the right, it reads, "The same space today has become a car park, and nothing resembling its state 50 years ago remains." In these photographs the historic buildings – Yeni Cami, Sirkeci, and the British Consulate – serve to mark the city's identity. They are the essence of Istanbul against which the city's modernization, as defined by the appearance of cars, trams, and even parking lots, can be measured.

Of the many efforts to frame Istanbul's history by presenting it alongside visual markers of modernity, one of the most striking comes from a collection of press and publicity photos taken to document an early performance of Turkey's Mehter band during the 1953 Conquest celebrations. As an employee of the Turkish Military Museum, İbrahim Hakkı Konyalı was instrumental in reinventing the Mehter tradition as a celebration of the nation's martial history.[9] His pictures of the Mehter performance consistently highlight, rather than conceal, the modern context in which these historical reenactors moved. A number of them show uniformed members of the modern Turkish military inspecting or reviewing the Mehter troop (see Figure 5.2) In several others, the band is posed against an urban backdrop, standing in front of a block of apartment buildings or walking along the road to the site of one of their performances. Finally, several photographs show other photographers standing prominently in the shots with their cameras. In one of these images, the journalists are joined by two contemporary workers who have stopped to watch the spectacle with shovels on their shoulders; another shows a line of janissaries parading underneath a large sign for Beykoz brand shoes on a wall above them. All of these elements, in short, served to highlight that this was a performance of Turkish military history, set off from the present by the actions of the observing soldiers, journalists, and workers.[10]

As shown most colorfully by the image on the cover of this book, midcentury magazine illustrations frequently hint at a similar framing, where

---

[9] Mehter bands were a part of the Janissary corps during the Ottoman golden age whose kettle-drum heavy music accompanied troops into battle. They reappeared in symbolic form first briefly in the Turkish war of independence and then again for the 500th anniversary conquest celebrations. Photos: Konyalı Archive, Document Nos. 280–281.

[10] The photographs of the event that appeared in newspapers at the time also featured similar juxtapositions. An image in *Cumhuriyet*, for example, showed the Mehter troop face to face with a number of well-dressed attendees at a Dolmabahçe Garden Party.

Figure 5.2 Turkish officer inspects a member of the Mehter band in İbrahim Hakkı Konyalı's photograph, 1953.

the artist seems to be providing visual cues for how readers should position themselves vis-à-vis the history under discussion. An even more explicit example is the drawing (see Figure 5.3) with which illustrator Münif Fehim introduced the 1935 serial *Famous Men*. Here, a young man sits at his desk holding the work itself and day-dreaming about the historic characters contained within. The man is wearing a dinner jacket. On the desk are a telephone and a bust of Atatürk, while another picture of Atatürk hangs on the wall. The images in the man's mind are Cleopatra, perhaps Antony or Caesar, and finally Barbarossa, an Ottoman figure set in a pantheon of established historical greats. The image seems intended to identify the reader of the book as a thoroughly modern Republican youth whose enjoyment of history from a twentieth-century vantage point is a perfectly healthy pastime.

Figure 5.3 Münif Fehim's illustration for the introduction to *Famous Men*, 1935.

A similar framing appears throughout the 1950s in images of men standing beside Istanbul's historic columns. Much as such figures served to show visual perspective, they also, with their suits and bowler hats, offer a parallel form of chronological perspective as well. A man shown looking up at the Kız Taşı in an illustration for *Istanbul through the Centuries*, for example, can again stand in for the viewer, a modern Istanbul resident with a natural curiosity about his city's history.[11] The image also features a row of modern apartment buildings visible behind the column, while another, from *History World*, shows a gentleman in a suit, bowtie, and umbrella in front of a different ancient column.[12]

More strikingly, urban redesign in 1950s Istanbul served to physically impose a similar frame on the city's historic buildings. Between 1956 and 1957, Menderes and the Democratic Party (DP) undertook an urban redevelopment program that dramatically transformed Istanbul's old city. Widely criticized today for the damage it did to the city's history, the project led the government to bulldoze large swaths of historic neighborhoods to open new, straight avenues through the city's historic peninsula. Several dozen Ottoman-era buildings, including some by Mimar Sinan, were destroyed. The gate through which Fatih supposedly entered the city was torn down to

11　Şehsuvaroğlu, *Asırlar Boyunca İstanbul*, 11.
12　İbrahim Hakkı Konyalı, *Tarih Hazinesi* [bound volume] (Istanbul: Ülkü Kitap Yurdu, 1951). 171.

make way for the Avenue of the Nation, while a new avenue rising from Beşiktaş was named after Hayrettin Barbarosa. At the same time, the government sought to restore the city's most prominent Ottoman monuments. This involved both renovating them and drawing greater attention to them by clearing away nearby structures. Thus monuments from the Ottoman golden age – Mimar Sinan mosques or Rumeli Hisarı – were restored and rebuilt while the nineteenth-century wooden buildings near or even in them were demolished as part of the same process. When this was done, the historic buildings were usually surrounded by fenced-in parks, setting them off from the rest of the city's urban fabric and marking them as distinct historic sites. As Nur Altınyıldız argues, in restoring Ottoman monuments, the government sought to "return them to their past majesty and display them in their new contexts ... Each would be viewed like a carefully framed easel painting, from vistas created along the roads and between the newly constructed buildings bordering them."[13] The frame, in a sense, was modernity.

After first tearing down wooden houses, often still inhabited and built literally up against the walls of historic structures, then replacing them with parks, the government highlighted its efforts in tourist brochures and election propaganda, thereby enhancing the symbolic importance of these changes. Removing nineteenth-century buildings made the link between Istanbul as a modern city and its idealized, ideologically sanitized Golden Age all the more direct by cutting out the physically and chronologically intervening evidence of oriental decay and backwardness. In short, the DP government decided to destroy the city's crumbling wooden structures for the same reason these structures supposedly appealed to nineteenth-century orientalist painters – because they symbolized the decline of a once-great civilization and the dilapidated modern state into which the East had sunk.

Though it is impossible to martial more specific evidence for this reading, both the language through which these urban redesign projects were promoted and the reactions they inspired among foreign observers bolster its plausibility. In discussing what should be done with such little historical architecture as the city of Ankara possessed, Bülent Ecevit argued it was necessary to renovate Ankara Castle while destroying the decrepit neighborhoods around it:

---

[13] Nur Altınyıldız, "The Architectural Heritage of Istanbul and the Ideology of Preservation," *Muqarnas*, Vol. 24 (2007). 281–305.

In Ankara's old neighborhoods it is impossible to live in a healthy, civilized manner compatible with Turkey's Westernization [*sıhhi, medeni, ve Türkiye'deki batılılaşma hareketine uygun bir hayat sürülemez*]. Preserving some neighborhoods or buildings because they are important from an architectural, historic or archeological perspective is one thing. Trying to preserve their livelihood as an anachronism is something else. However admirable the first is, the second is as useless an effort.[14]

Ecevit insisted that before these neighborhoods were emptied, ample provisions must be made for their "low income" residents to achieve the conditions of modern life elsewhere. Then, the castle, which "might be the site of Ankara's best views," could have its slopes planted with trees and, following "some work and expenditure," would beautify Ankara to no end:

In its current state, Ankara Castle is a poor, unhealthy marginal neighborhood trying to continue its existence despite having outlived its allotted time. But by clearing it out and making it an open-air museum, this place could become Ankara's most beautiful and interesting spot, and the Republic's capital would gain in touristic value.[15]

Ecevit's effort to enhance Ankara echoed the response of the US Consul in Istanbul when Menderes took a similar approach to the old city.[16] Commenting on the "raising and removal of hundreds of old, wooden houses that line Atatürk boulevard," Robert Miner declared, "They were, in the opinion of such old-fashioned people as myself, picturesque, but I suppose they were also unsightly, and they certainly were, or would shortly become, unsafe."[17] In acknowledging the illegitimacy of his own orientalist appreciation for the "picturesque," Miner both tacitly accepted the government's practical interest in "modernizing" this aspect of the city's architecture and also implicitly justified their cultural or symbolic motives.

A cartoon from the period appearing in *Cumhuriyet* reinforces the idea that the valuable, "historic" aspects of Istanbul were distinct from those that made the city appear unmodern. Flying over the city, one

---

[14] Bülent Ecevit, "Ankara Kalesi," *Ulus*, June 23, 1955.   [15] Ibid.

[16] Ecevit also shared the consul's concern that in its haste to demolish old buildings, the government failed to find alternative housing for the displaced.

[17] Letter from Robert Miner to Counselor of Embassy John Goodyear, September 12, 1956. General Records of the Department of State. Misc Lot Files, Lot File no. 58 D 61, Subject Files relating to Turkey. Box 2, RG 59, NARA.

aviator says to his copilot, "[T]he Beyoğlu side is being improved, why is the Istanbul side [Fatih] being ignored?" The copilot responds, "If it isn't ignored and left in this shabby, ruined state how will it be obvious that it's the historic district." The joke lies in the absurdity of thinking things had to be run down to be historic or, in other words, the idea that one might confuse the two by mistaking the "shabby" architectural legacy of late-nineteenth-century Istanbul with the truly important parts of its history. As both Ecevit and the cartoon's author implicitly understood, taking a modern approach to one's history required having the ability to distinguish between the ruined and the historic.

More broadly, tourist literature from this period consistently reinforced the idea that careful a policy of renovation could demonstrate a country's modernity by transforming the old into the historic. As early as 1952, for example, the Ministry of Education published a book showing all that the DP government had done since coming to power to modernize Istanbul and develop the "touristic importance of its historic richness." Among other things the work mentioned was that now in the Spice Market "a variety of things" could be purchased "within a modern market setting" [*modern çarsı dekoru içinde*]. Publicized side by side were the government's efforts to restore Istanbul's old water fountains and develop a new infrastructure to deliver water with modern pipes and a modern dam.[18]

This approach also found favor in the magazine *Tourism World* [*Turizm Alemi*], Turkey's first publication devoted to promoting domestic and foreign tourism. As *Tourism World* declared in its first issue, "Tourism is an important endeavor taking its place among our many development questions."[19] In this context, restoring old buildings was seen as an extension of building a modern city around them. In Konya, for example, "[a]longside modern buildings, old monuments are being restored. Behind them, factories, economic, agricultural and business enterprises, art schools, sports clubs, a stadium, a velodrome, parks and gardens give the city a modern, civilized countenance."[20] As a result, the editors stated that

[i]ncluded in our proposed program is taking necessary precautions to preserve our historic monuments from ruin ... In connection with this it is also necessary to bring into existence attractive and original entertainment

---

[18] Rakım Ziyaoğlu, *İstanbul Albümü* (Istanbul: Milli Eğitim Basımevi, 1952).
[19] *Turizm Alemi*, Issue 1, Editor's preface.   [20] *Turizm Alemi*, Issue 1, page 6.

districts [*gayet cazip ve orijinal eğlence mahalleri*] where tourists will spend money freely.

Moreover, the magazine implied that Europeans had long understood the link between being modern and preserving one's history:

[The French] look after the most minor structures from the Gothic period like a delicate bride .... This means that to protect, beautify and restore monuments is not only a condition for being a nation but at the same time one of the highest honors bestowed by membership in the civilization.

Tourism World also promoted the idea that bridges, roads, and other staples of modernization were crucial for making Turkey's historic and natural beauty accessible to tourists. Even Lake Van, to take the most remote example, could become a "tourist center" with the addition of a "wide, up-to-date asphalt road" ringing its shore. Likewise, visitors to Akşehir could not only enjoy the tile work on the Eşref Oğulları Mosque but also "one of central Anatolia's most modern beaches" built on the lake's shore.[21] Tourism was, after all, a "matter of organization."

Finally, documenting the country's historic monuments for tourists offered yet another opportunity to embed them in a modern context. The French, for example, not only preserved their history, "but have written volumes of articles about the cathedrals in every corner of the country, and published grand, grand catalogues of them." Thus renovation and documentation were seen as interrelated aspects of modernizing history. After restoring historic buildings "useful things like photograph or model exhibits, brochures, paintings, and post cards should be prepared" in order to help "every city's youth to recognize their own monuments."

Once again, with reference to Europe, writers insisted that taking advantage of these modern techniques for documenting and publicizing historic cities and monuments provided a means to elevate Turkey's history and culture to the level of their Western counterparts. The author lamented that "[a]nyone with any knowledge of the world" would instantly recognize pictures of European cities, "but in our own country, even the most educated among us still don't know our cities well enough to tell Erzurum from Sivas, Diyarbakır from Mardin, Kayseri from Konya or even Bursa from Edirne." To remedy this, the

[21]   Ibid.

government should "publicize their profiles with photographs, pictures, designs or any of the many other means available." "What a pity," he concluded, "it is not even possible to find clear and well-taken postcards of all of Anatolia's monuments, or even those in Istanbul."[22]

In order to demonstrate the stakes involved in modernizing Istanbul's tourist infrastructure, *Tourism World* included an interview with one of the directors of France's tourism bureau. In the piece, Mr. Miraud explained:

Today for Turkey to become a tourist country is a dream. Two years earlier I went to Istanbul. It had historic and natural beauty, but I only stayed two days. And I have no intention of going back. Because you can't even find a restaurant with good vegetables or a hotel with a good view .... Istanbul just has nature and history. Besides that, you can't find anything.[23]

To make Istanbul a tourist city, he explained, a few key changes were needed. Specifically, in the neighborhoods of Beyoğlu, Harbiye, and Karaköy, he recommended: "a) legal gambling b) establishments open till dawn c) permission for naked 'variety' shows d) all kinds of liquor freely sold e) all hotels open to men and women f) free exchange of all money." He also recommended that Turkey become more oriental. "In Istanbul nothing remains of the legendary East," Miraud complained: "Think about it. In Paris there are plenty of places showing Eastern dances that are open every night. People who go to Istanbul expecting to see better ones will be shocked."

If nothing else, Mr. Miraud's comments offer another reminder that, even in the 1950s, the obsession with appearing modern was hardly the product of some internal Turkish complex operating in the absence of any external provocation. More importantly, they reinforced both the limitations and the possibilities of embracing a modern, touristic vision of history. Yes, this approach required well-cooked vegetables, nudity, and freely flowing liquor. But for people with no objection to any of these things, it also meant that as soon as a country opened a few of the right sort of bars, restaurants, and clubs, its old monuments, be they palaces or even mosques, would be transformed from relics of a retrograde Oriental civilization into legitimate sources of national pride.

[22] Ibid.
[23] "Türkiye'nin Turistik Durumu Nedir?" *Turizm Alemi*, March 1954, page 7.

History World

In reminiscing about reading the popular history of Reşat Ekrem Koçu as a child, Orhan Pamuk writes that while he found this work delightful, even arousing, at the time, he subsequently realized that it represented Koçu's failed imitation of Western modernity.[24] Koçu, the author of such compendiums as *Turkish Istanbul, From Osman Gazi to Atatürk*, and the never-completed *Istanbul Encyclopedia*, offered readers a broad range of historical fact and anecdote, discussions of daily life and popular dress interspersed with tales of the macabre and bizarre, all illustrated with a consistent style of pen and ink drawings. Koçu, Pamuk claimed, aspired to write in the Western encyclopedic style but never realized the importance of prioritizing fact over anecdote.[25] Yet an alternate reading of Koçu is possible, one in which he improved on the modern genre of popular history while also incorporating serious research. In Turkey, popular history came into its own as the generation that had been the focus of early Kemalist literacy campaigns reached maturity. Moreover, with the improvement in Turkey's economic circumstances after World War II and a newfound emphasis on free enterprise, publishers could not only obtain basic staples like paper and ink but also make a profit from selling newspapers and magazines to a reading, paying, advertisement-consuming public. The rise of Turkish popular history in the 1950s also built on and responded to Western models. Koçu's "Strange and Curious Things from History" appeared at roughly the same time that *Ripley's Believe It Not* was translated and syndicated in the newspaper *Cumhuriyet*.

Yet Koçu also sought to demonstrate that instead of simply importing sensational material from the West, Turkish scholars could find even more wondrous tales in their own Ottoman archives. At a time when many American intellectuals were horrified that the aspect of their culture that seemed most appealing to foreign audiences was lowbrow pulp fiction, it is striking to see Turkish authors offering a more scholarly approach to sensationalist history.[26] Illustrations of Kara Mehmet Pasha, "the vezir whose head was used as a football," and the cross, "a terrifying method of execution," were squarely in line with the Ripley's tradition. Yet in Koçu's work such features appeared

---

[24] Orhan Pamuk, *İstanbul: Hatıralar ve Şehir* (İstanbul: İletişim. 2002), 157–158.
[25] Ibid. [26] See Rubin, *Archives of Authority*.

alongside his own extensive research into more serious topics such as Istanbul's architectural history or detailed accounts of court life. They also appeared alongside patriotic glorifications of Ottoman-Turkish heroes, especially in connection with Istanbul's 500th anniversary celebrations. As discussed in the previous chapter, Fatih, Ulubatlı Hasan, and Barbarossa turned up regularly in Koçu's work. Ideologically, Koçu's approach also fit well with the theory of fatal decline. He used the Ottoman golden age as a source of national pride while mining its later centuries for titillating tales of moral decay.

Alongside Koçu, one of the most famous popular history writers of the time was Feridun Fazıl Tülbentçi. In addition to his historical radio show, Tülbentçi wrote a number of novels. In 1948 the newspaper *Ulus* serialized *Barbarossa Is Coming [Barbaros Hayrettin Geliyor]*. For the equivalent of 450-odd pages, Tülbentçi's "ruddy Turkish mariners" fight to defend the Muslims of North Africa, many of whom are refugees from Spanish cruelty in Andalusia, against the machinations of Christian rulers.[27] The Barbarossa brothers enjoy drinking wine – in moderation – and carousing – chastely – with slave girls, even while fighting a "jihad" on behalf of their "religious brothers."[28] Effortlessly seducing foreign women while saving his country from nefarious plots, Tülbentçi's Barbarossa resembles no one so much as a sixteenth-century Ottoman James Bond, fighting not against Communist Russia but the Pope (see Figure 5.4).

Like Koçu, Tülbentçi offered readers a mix of Turkish nationalism, ideologically appropriate religious themes, and scantily clad women that fit well with a new genre of popular history magazine which flourished in the 1950s. Diverse titles such as *Turkish History [Türk Tarihi]*, *Voices from History [Tarihten Sesler]*, and the *Illustrated History Journal [Resimli Tarih Mecmuası]* wove together Ottoman nostalgia, tributes to Ottoman modernity, glorification of Ottoman military might, and investigations of Ottoman faith, all the while trying to appeal to buyers with bizarre tales and muted eroticism.

---

[27] Tülbentçi, *Barbaros Hayrettin Geliyor* (Istanbul: İnkılap Kitabevi, 2008).

[28] The Barbarossa brothers had a loyal Christian ally as well, a former priest named Danilo. Danilo provided comic relief as something of a coward and a boor but also used his quick thinking and foreign language skills to save the Turkish heroes. He eventually undergoes a half-hearted conversion to Islam, after which his companions acknowledge he is "not a full Muslim ... but a good man." Ibid., 366.

Figure 5.4 "Is there no good Muslim left to save me from the hands of these infidels?" from Tülbentçi's serialized Hayrettin Barbarossa novel in *Ulus*, 1948.

Among these magazines, *History World [Tarih Dünyası]* and *History Treasury [Tarih Hazinesi]* stand out as the two most revealing, both for their popularity, enduring commercial success and the running rivalry between their publishers (see Figure 5.5).

History World was the creation of publisher Niyazi Ahmet Banoğlu. Banoğlu began his career writing short pieces of Ottoman-themed historical fiction such as "The Slave-Girl Galleon" for *Istanbul Magazine* in the 1930s. He then collaborated with Münif Fehim to tell the stories of prominent Ottoman and Republican figures in the *Turkish Heroes [Türk Kahramanlar]* series during the 1940s.[29] In the 1950s, *History World* gave him the opportunity to work with historians like İsmail Hakkı Uzunçarşılı and Ahmet Refik to cover such topics such as "Sultan Abdülmecit and the Intrigues of the Palace Women," "The Anniversary of Coffee in Turkey," "The Sultan's Hammam in the Harem," "Poison and Poisoning in History," and "Marie Antoinette's Secret Love." In keeping with the magazine's contents, Banoğlu's covers generally featured either heroic portraits of Sultans, battle scenes with valorous Turkish soldiers, or European depictions of dancing girls.

In one of his first pieces for the new magazine, Banoğlu retold the story of an adulteress's stoning from Ahmet Refik's *Women's Sultanate*

---

29 "Esir Kızlar Kalyonu," 12 Teşri Nisan, Issue 23. This was followed by "Gökten Düşen Kız" on 19 Teşri Nisan (Issue 24), and on 25 Sonteşrin (Issue 36) a story about a heart-broken Circassian dying for his beloved.

Figure 5.5 President Celal Bayar reading *History World*, undated.

[Kadınlar Saltanatı] in colorful fashion, complete with a "young and beautiful wife," her "shrill and soul-piercing cries," and a bloodthirsty crowd intent on killing the "dirty, treacherous ... harlot."[30] The exploits of Ottoman Kadıs gave *History World* another opportunity to combine serious historical research, Kemalist ideological critique, and prurient detail: "After the end of the Ottoman Empire's Golden Age the Kadıs ... [did] whatever it took to weaken and destroy this multi-continent empire."[31] An account of all the Kadıs' "hair-raising" verdicts would "surpass even a 20th-century murder novel in bloodiness." In fact, the magazine planned to offer readers just this, with stories of Kadıs "feeding human flesh to dogs, hanging women from their breasts and men from other parts, and chaining men by the nose as if they were bears."

---

[30] *Tarih Dünyası* [bound volume] (Istanbul: Şaka Matbaası 1950) 404, 400, 443, 448, 453, 550, 37.
[31] Derviş Karamanoğlu, "Osmanlı Tarihinde Kadı Şekavetleri," ibid., 40.

But while he entertained readers with these accounts, Banoğlu also acted as the voice of national virtue. In addition to challenging European depictions of harem life, he took issue with the content of mainstream historical films. Under the headline "They Are Killing History,"[32] he condemned the Turkish film industry's enthusiasm for romantic dramas featuring Ottoman sultans: "If these people had a love of history, if they had a pride in their Turkishness inspired by the past, they wouldn't grasp at these themes ... To reduce men who made history like Yıldırım Beyazıt, Fatih, Yavuz Selim, Barbarossa, and Kanuni Süleyman to indecisive characters on the silver screen is an unforgivable sin." Worse yet were the costumes. Of one film he declared: "Hürrem Sultan's headgear makes her look like a gypsy dancing girl."

But Banoğlu's moments of moralism were not enough for İbrahim Hakkı Konyalı. After collaborating with Banoğlu for six issues and authoring such articles as *"Cariyeler* and the Slave Bazaar," Konyalı left to start his own magazine, *History Treasury [Tarih Hazinesi]*, citing ideological differences.[33] From the outset, Konyalı, who worked for the Turkish Military Museum while also contributing to the controversial Islamist paper *Büyük Doğu*, took a more religiously nationalist tone. "Every Turkish state or political organization was a link in the timeless chain of Turkish history," he declared in the magazine's first issue, but the Ottoman State was the "most civilized," a "sparkling jewel set in this chain."[34] The "necessary anger" that must be felt against the last few "degenerate [*dejenere*] Sultans," he insisted, should not sully six and a half centuries of "glowing" history.

Alongside pieces about Istanbul's prostitutes and "The Drunkard's Holiday," Konyalı published a number of articles that others at the time would have characterized as reactionary.[35] He wrote that Turkey's ability to stand on its feet after World War I was a tribute to its faith in Islam and that the Turkish nation had finally "found itself" with the 1950 "Democratic revolution."[36] Konyalı praised Abdülhamid for chastising the CUP leaders who suggested he flee Istanbul during World War I and suggested in a later article that had Abdülhamid stayed in power he would have been too wise to enter the

---

[32] *Tarih Hazinesi* November 26, 1952.   [33] Ibid., Issue 1, November 15, 1950.
[34] Ibid.   [35] *Tarih Hazinesi* [Bound Volume], 281 and 254.
[36] *Tarih Hazinesi*, Issue 2, December 1, 1950.

war in the first place.[37] In subsequent issues he blamed the Republican regime and its reforms for the dilapidated state of Istanbul's mosques and tombs, writing, "[I]f Turks are not afraid before God they should at least be embarrassed in front of tourists."[38] More pointedly, he told readers that Fatih had wanted Ayasofya to remain a mosque for all eternity "and asked God to curse those who didn't fulfill this order."[39]

In writing mid-century popular history, Turkish authors struggled with the tension between sexualizing the past in pursuit of better sales and defending the nation's honor by countering European tropes of Oriental depravity. Ahmet Banoğlu's discussions of harem life, however, provided a clever resolution to this tension by inverting the logic of European orientalism. For European orientalist artists, harem scenes offered an opportunity to show naked women while distancing themselves from the responsibility for doing so by presenting their work as the reflection of a sensuous, exotic, Eastern reality. Banoğlu, by contrast, regularly republished orientalist images of naked women while distancing himself, and his magazine, from them by explaining that he was simply reprinting inaccurate, even offensive, European fantasies. Banoğlu, in other words, could offer readers with all the exoticism of European accounts of Ottoman history while presenting himself as a responsible, objective, and nationalistic critic of this very approach.

Much as the story about a woman stoned for adultery, with which Banoğlu opened his magazine, featured a caveat stating that this practice was un-Islamic and exceptional, Banoğlu's stories about harem life always included a passage criticizing European views of the institution. One of *History World's* first issues featured an article entitled "Inside the Harem," which began, "The most mysterious part of the palace, and because of its mystery the most intriguing, was certainly the harem."[40] The author then went on to explain that most stories about the Harem were lies and that readers should just think of it as a place where women were "imprisoned for their whole lives." With this disclaimer out of the way, he then launched into a story about a eunuch who was caught having sex with one of the women he was supposed to be guarding. A later article about odalisques[41] pointed out that these harem women were "no different from mistresses in western palaces" and in fact, "if there were differences, they

---

[37] "Abdülhamid'in İttihatçılara ve Sultan Reşad'a Verdiği Ders," *Tarih Hazinesi* [Bound Volume], 8.
[38] Ibid., 512.   [39] Ibid., 828.   [40] *Tarih Dünyası*, Volume 1, page 67.
[41] Ibid., 1512.

were in odalisques' favor." Odalisques, for example, unlike mistresses, were not married to anyone else. As Kemal Baykal explained in another article,[42] "every great ruler from Solomon to Napoleon has had a mistress" but because the word "odalisque" was of Turkish origin "famous paintings called odalisques done by great artists like Ingres, Delacroix and Boulanger also featured Turkish décor." The article, accompanied by several examples of these paintings, went on to note that the word "odalisque" "awoke mysterious things in the minds of earlier Europeans" and still "has the same effect today." If it had the same effect on the magazine's readers, editors seemed to believe, so much the better.

When *History World* reopened after a brief hiatus in 1953 as *New History World* [*Yeni Tarih Dunaysı*], its editors doubled down on this approach to covering the Ottoman harem. The first issue of the new magazine featured a reprint of a European odalisque painting titled simply, "Here is the harem as it appeared in the imagination of Western artists." Then, following shortly on the heels of "Letters from the Harem," another article titled "Secrets of the Harem"[43] showed that even the act of debunking harem myths could serve to reaffirm them. The author began by asking, "[H]ow true were the stories about harems and women being naked in them?" He then went into great detail about the lack of reliable historical sources, saying it was hard for scholars to figure out exactly what was going on. In the absence of reliable sources, he argued, one still could not trust European accounts because they lacked access to the harem and therefore lacked accurate information about it. Among the few concrete details he included was the fact that men "couldn't look at faces of harem women when talking to them" and had to place their own face to the ground if they accidentally did so. Somehow, in the course of a few paragraphs, the article deftly transformed an explanation of why European accounts of harem life could not be trusted into an opportunity to reaffirm its essential exoticism. By playing up the paucity of sources about harem life and the inability of foreigners to observe it, the author succeeded in once again emphasizing its mystery.

Looking East, Being Western

Much as historians sought to counter Western orientalism when discussing Turkey's national history, Turkish writers exploring the rural

[42] Ibid., 1545.   [43] Ibid., 74.

parts of their country's geography felt a parallel need. In celebrating the history of Istanbul, Turkish writers and politicians highlighted, as well as physically enhanced, the city's modern elements. In celebrating Anatolia, however, they were acutely aware that many of the physical markers of Istanbul's modernity – the tramways, the apartment blocks, even the men in suits – were absent. If Istanbul's history carried the threat of Arabian Nights exoticism, rural Anatolia threatened the image of Turkish modernity through its lack of development. Here it was the Anatolian villager, his traditional lifestyle and farm animals, that risked confirming another Orientalist image whose popularity in the West Turks were all too aware of: the unchanging Middle-Eastern peasant still carrying on his millennia-old agricultural existence.

The response of Turkey's educated elite to this challenge was not to insist on the modernity of the Anatolian peasant – something they were seldom themselves convinced of – but rather to take additional measures to position themselves as modern in their relations with their country's "un-modern" geography. This section considers two principal ways through which they sought to do so, academic and touristic. The first, found in journals well predating the 1950s, used a scholarly approach to sustain the discourse of Turkish modernity by viewing Anatolia through the lens of academic study. The second, popularized in 1950s magazines, engaged with the region through the language of domestic tourism. Crucially, both approaches enabled writers to interact extensively with the region and also praise it effusively, while positioning themselves at a distance from it. In the first instance, they could approach it as scholars, analogous to the Western researchers who came to study their country. In the second instance, they approached it as modern tourists, analogous to the Western visitors who expressed endless fascination with their country while traveling through it.

In 1947, the *Ankara University Faculty of Language, History and Geography Journal* published an "expedition report" by Afet İnan detailing a "historic trip" between Ankara and Samsun that took place over the course of two weeks.[44] The report and the scholarly journey it described were in many ways typical of those that had been

---

[44] Volume 11, Issue 41, 1947, *Ankara University Faculty of Language, History and Geography Journal*, 120.

regularly conducted by the members of the country's intellectual establishment over the previous decades. İnan led a group of twelve students
and professors to visit historic monuments in the central and northern
Anatolian regions. They toured castles, tombs, caravansaries, archeological digs, and prehistoric sites with the assistance of local mayors
and governors. Rather than being arranged by the chronology of their
trip, the itinerary was written up according to the historical age of the
sites visited. İnan explained that, having prepared before the trip, at
each stop "one among us lectured on the history of the place, while
those who could attend had a chance to listen." She also added that the
results of their previous study were included in her article so that
readers could "make a historic journey along with us." Readers were
then directed to further sources on the sites. As the article concluded:
"by seeing the works of our own and earlier ages firsthand in this way
useful information was obtained."

In İnan's narrative, appreciation for Anatolia's history, landscape,
and geography, as well as its specifically Turkish character were filtered
through the lens of academic study and intellectual understanding.
Even the group's emotional reactions were set in terms of intellectual
appreciation:

This caravansaray, in both its comfort and monumental grandeur, was
certainly a principal example of the works of Selçuk civilization ... As we
departed from [it], we could not restrain ourselves from looking back
repeatedly.[45]

But being a tourist, or even reading tourist literature, could play the
same role as scientific inspection in letting modern citizens appreciate their country's less modern regions. Crucially, in this context the
act of participating in tourism – whether as a traveler or a reader –
became itself a marker of modernity. *History and Geography World*,
another offering from Ahmet Banoğlu, gave readers in Turkey's
major cities a chance to do just this. In the first issue, the caption
below a picture of a pine nut garden near Bergama read, "[E]scaping
from the chaos of the city and its nerve-wracking lifestyle to relax in
the embrace of nature is one of the uniquely sought-after and most
intensely felt needs of modern individuals."[46] These words deftly
transformed the "undeveloped" character of rural Turkey from

[45] Ibid.   [46] *History and Geography World*, Volume 1, Issue 1, April 15, 1959.

a source of potential shame into something that readers could enjoy precisely because they were so modern. This was reinforced by the explicit comparison of Turkey's undeveloped natural areas with recognized areas of natural beauty in Western countries. The Seydişehir mountains, for example, were just one of the many areas to be declared a "Turkish Switzerland." In discussing the natural beauty that could be found on the outskirts of Istanbul itself, another magazine declared, "Canada, that land whose lakes and forests we've fainted at in films, with all its wild beauty, its greens and its sparkling blues waters ... was here."

Scholarship on politics and history of tourism has identified the practice as a product of the modern nation-state. In the United States, for example, one author argues tourism was a response to the anxieties of industrialization and urbanization.[47] Other works advance the idea that "oriental" travel in particular enabled Western Europeans and later Americans to escape the noisy intrusion of the modern by visiting countries perceived as being in the past.[48] That is, it fulfilled the stated desire of people from the developed world for "less-developed locales" or the desire of city dwellers to find a rural "escape" from the "density, poverty and corruption of the cities."[49] The Turkish case offers an intriguing appropriation of this approach, in which a country aspiring to be urban, industrialized, and developed embraced tourism – as an idea if not actually as a practice – precisely because it was associated with the escapist desires found in more modern countries.

Alongside Turkey's mid-century ideological reinvention of the Ottoman Empire, the visual and rhetorical strategies employed during the 1940s and 1950s helped nationalize the Ottoman past and Anatolian countryside. During the 1920s and 1930s, many aspects of the Kemalist reform program reflected a commitment

---

[47] Marguerite Shaffer, *See America First: Tourism and National Identity 1880–1940* (Washington: Smithsonian Books, 2001), page 37. Eugenia Afinoguénova's *Spain Is (Still) Different* (Lexington Books, 2008) suggests that in an inversion of this process, the Franco regime actually advertised Spain's appeal as a tourist destination based on a celebration of its lack of modernity, using the phrase "Spain is different."

[48] Derek Gregory, "Colonial Nostalgia and Cultures of Travel" in Nezar Al Sayyad (ed.) *Consuming Tradition, Manufacturing Heritage* (Psychology Press, 2001), 125 and 153.

[49] Ibid., 157.

to changing fundamental aspects of the nations' appearance and behavior to thwart Western perceptions of Turkey as an Oriental country.[50] Yet the magnitude, and success, of these more dramatic projects should not overshadow subsequent efforts to change the way the nation was viewed.

[50] Hale Yılmaz, *Becoming Turkish: Nationalist Reforms and Cultural Negotiations in Early Republican Turkey* (Syracuse, New York: Syracuse University Press, 2013.)

6 | Ottomans, Arabs, and Americans
Geography and Identity in Turkish Diplomacy

Bekir Tünay served as the Democratic Party (DP) government's military attaché to Baghdad between 1953 and 1955. In his memoires, he recounts his personal relationship with Iraqi regent Abdul Ilah and its role in building Turkish-Iraqi ties. Amid descriptions of Iraq's material backwardness, the Iraqi people's lingering respect for the Turks, and the admiration even Kurdish nationalists held for Atatürk, Tünay describes how his friendship with Abdul Ilah blossomed.[1] They first met at a banquet following a military exercise Tünay had attended:

The banquet was inside a large tent. There was every kind of liquor. I was by the buffet. Suddenly at my side I saw Emir Abdul Ilah with two glasses in his hand. He offered one to me. "We don't drink at the King's banquets. But I heard how much you liked Iraqi raki and so I am breaking with tradition for the first time for you. I very much like Turkish rakı, especially Club Rakı.

"Shocked, touched, excited and overwhelmed" by the king's behavior, Tünay offered him a cigarette: "At that time, on account of Fatih's 500th year, or rather the 500th anniversary of Istanbul's conquest, a FATİH cigarette had been put out. I praised them." The king responded, "I like these cigarettes. They were well made." Tünay then wrote home to urgently request a kilo of Fatih cigarettes along with two kilos of Hacı Bekir lokum for Abdul Ilah's Turkish mother. In Tünay's telling, it was the start of a beautiful relationship.

Because of this bond, Menderes subsequently requested that Tünay accompany Abdul Ilah on his 1954 visit to Turkey.[2] Following a string of events and receptions, Tünay recalled a particularly late dinner at an Izmir nightclub, after which Abdul Ilah remarked:

---

[1] Bekir Tünay, *Menderes Devri Anıları* (Nilüfer Matbaası, 1968).

[2] Tünay, for his part, proudly cited his casual, personalized approach to diplomacy as a more modern, American-inspired alternative to the stiff, Oriental formality of his superiors.

- [Menderes] seems happy with his life. I looked, the singer's eyes were on him all night. There must be something between them. What do you say?
- I doubt it.
- You didn't look carefully. Menderes's eyes never left her.
- The Prime Minister appreciates Turkish music.
- My God she could sing well. She truly was a Turkish music virtuoso. I suppose we were drunk. Honestly, I was so busy looking at her I couldn't follow any of the others.[3]

Abdul Ilah then asked the singer's name and the men moved on to talking about the dancers. Later he remarked: "I like Menderes for several reasons. He really knows how to work like a Western statesmen and how to enjoy himself like one too [*Batılı devlet adamı gibi çalışmasını da, eğlenmesini de çok iyi biliyorlar*]. We Easterners don't know how. We know only excess and excessive restraint." Recording this observation, Tünay reflected that it was completely true.[4]

Another night of drinking awaited them on their return to Istanbul, which, in Tünay's telling, was the high point of the visit. Asked if there was anything else he wanted before leaving Turkey, Abdul Ilah, who often spoke of his childhood years on the Bosporus, admitted: "I want to listen to a handful of the best Turkish musicians on our terrace. We should start after midnight and continue till morning." Having been given an unlimited budget by Menderes to entertain his guest, Tünay quickly arranged it; they ate and drank to the "enchanting sounds of the instruments" until "the half-bronzed red of dawn played over the shimmering waves."[5]

The irony, which Tünay himself remarked on, was that the Iraqi with whom he felt such personal rapport was a member of the Hashemite family that had betrayed the Ottomans during the Arab revolt. But these were also the Arabs who, on account of their own elite backgrounds, shared a cultural connection with Republican diplomats like Tünay.[6] Kemalist ideology had not fully severed Turkey from its Ottoman past and its Arab neighbors, nor did Islamic piety serve as the primary force bringing them together. In this regard, Tünay and

---

[3] Ibid., 205.   [4] Ibid., 207.   [5] Ibid., 207–210.
[6] Tünay was from Adana but had enjoyed himself in Istanbul as a student at the military academy.

Abdul Ilah's shared nostalgia for Istanbul nightlife provides a telling entrée into the cultural politics of Turkey's early Cold War diplomacy.

This chapter investigates how beliefs about geography and history influenced Turkey's foreign policy in the 1940s and 1950s. The diplomatic history of Turkey's involvement in NATO and its relations with the Arab world during this period has been thoroughly written. Yet a renewed look at the rhetoric that informed these relationships can still offer several new insights about the malleability of ideas in the face of diplomatic necessity. In the debate over Turkey's entry into NATO, diplomats deployed their views about Turkey's geography and the Turkish people's character in unexpected and sometimes contradictory ways. On the question of Middle East defense, Turkish anti-imperialism, specifically as directed toward the British, also played an important and often overlooked role. Many accounts portray Turkish policy during the early Cold War, particularly under the DP, as motivated by an almost sycophantic pro-Western attitude, while other popular narratives present Turkey's eagerness to join NATO as a product of Kemalist pro-Western sentiment.

In fact, Turkish leaders under both the Republican People's Party (CHP) and DP regularly appealed to a historically rooted anti-imperialism in rejecting British defense proposals, and US policymakers regularly worried this attitude would be an impediment to US-Turkish cooperation. As a result, while both American and Turkish diplomats insisted Turkey should serve as "a bridge between East and West," they meant this in very different ways. Ankara often saw its role as warning the United States against policies that would alienate Arabs, while Washington expected Turkish diplomats to help convince Arabs to accept these same policies. During this period, Turkish statesmen routinely exploited the paradoxical possibilities of their geographic and historic links with the Middle East as well. Turkish leaders cited shared religion, culture, and history when addressing Middle Eastern leaders. At the same time, Ankara insisted that in its dealings with Arab states Turkey always appear as an equal partner of the Americans, French, and British.

Finally, looking back at Turkey's early Cold War diplomacy forces us to rethink the political importance of Turkish attitudes toward Arabs. While Turkish anti-Arab prejudice has often been cited as a motivating factor in Turkey's policy toward Arab states, a closer examination suggests that this prejudice, though very real, was largely subordinate to Turkey's geopolitical interests and anti-imperial instincts. Turkish public opinion was often quite sympathetic to Arabs when they appeared to be victims of European imperialism, but this sympathy quickly turned to hostility when Arab states began to appear complicit in Soviet imperialism instead.

Will They Weasel?

As detailed by Ekavi Athanassopoulou, when Washington extended aid to Turkey under the Truman doctrine, US leaders genuinely feared that Soviet political and military pressure would lead to Turkey's incorporation into the Soviet sphere of influence, thereby facilitating further Soviet expansion.[7] This led Washington to provide diplomatic and military support to protect Turkey and create a necessary "barrier against Soviet penetration into the Middle East."[8] Yet several years later, by the time NATO membership became the subject of trans-Atlantic discussions, these short-term fears about Russian expansion were no longer a driving force in US decision-making. At this point, Washington agreed to extend NATO membership to Turkey in order to secure its "wholehearted co-operation" in the event war occurred elsewhere in Europe.[9] Melvyn Leffler has explored the many long-term strategic benefits that US officials in the State and Defense Departments expected to obtain from Turkey's membership.[10] Yet if this account explains America's desire for Turkish membership, it is also important to understand the question from Turkey's perspective. This means considering how Turkish statesmen convinced their counterparts in Washington that Turkey would only offer America its "wholehearted co-operation" if it was made a NATO member.

Turkey's push for NATO membership is often discussed with reference to Kemalist westernization, implying that in joining the alliance Turkey sought to solidify its European status. But whatever widely divergent opinions may have existed in the 1940s on the vexed question of whether Turkey's culture or geography qualified it as "European,"

---

[7] Ekavi Athanassopoulou, *Turkey, Anglo-American Security Interests 1945–1952: The First Enlargement of NATO* (London: Frank Cass, 1999.)

[8] Ibid., 238. [9] Ibid.

[10] Leffler, Melvin. Strategy, Diplomacy, and the Cold War: The United States, Turkey, and NATO, 1945–1952. *Journal of American History*, Vol. 71, No. 4 (March 1985). 807–825.

no one up to that point had ever suggested that Turkey was a North Atlantic state. In fact, from diplomatic discussions that occurred at the time, the process through which Turkey became a part of NATO had more to do with NATO transcending its geographic identity than with Turkey adopting a European one.

Turkey's desire for a formal American defense commitment preceded, in both chronology and importance, considerations of the geographic context in which this would be offered. Indeed, the Turkish government was quick to express this desire as soon as it learned that Washington was considering a new set of European alliances. In early 1948, US diplomats repeatedly told their Turkish colleagues that the new commitments under consideration represented a radical departure from their country's long-standing desire to avoid entangling alliances and, furthermore, that their government was hesitant to weaken its position by overcommitting itself. Only later, as Western Europe and the North Atlantic became the focus of Washington's new alliance did geography become the most obvious explanation for denying Turkey membership. Responding to an enquiry from the Turkish government, Ambassador Wadsworth informed President İnönü in December 1948, "It is very doubtful ... that Turkey, which is neither in Western Europe nor on the Atlantic, could be considered to form geographically a part of this regional group."[11]

US statesmen argued that rather than representing the sum total of their defense commitments, the North Atlantic alliance could be augmented by other regional alliances centered in the Mediterranean or the Middle East. This formulation, however, quickly raised concerns in both Washington and Ankara, not to mention Athens and other capitals. Americans worried that making a formal commitment to defend Western European states from Soviet aggression without making a similar commitment to Greece and Turkey could encourage Soviet ambitions in the Eastern Mediterranean by calling American commitment to the region into question. In July 1948 Turkey's Foreign Minister Necmettin Sadak told the US ambassador that:

---

[11] Enclosure to despatch No. 483, December 23, 1948 From Embassy Ankara. Department of State. Top Secret Records. Box 1, RG 84, NARA. In keeping with instructions received from Washington on December 17, Telegram No. 588, ibid.

[h]is preoccupation remained the same, namely, if and when assurances are given by [the] U.S. of military support for [the] security [of a] Western Europe[an] group of powers and no similar assurance [is] extended [to] Turkey, this will be regarded as [an] invitation by Soviets to step up pressure on Turkey .... [I]t would be [an] indication to Soviets that [the] U.S. [was] less interested in [the] Security of Turkey and [the] Middle East than in [the] Security of West Europe and might well lead [the] Soviets to embark on rash movements or proposals re[garding]Turkey.[12]

US officials, though sharing this concern, initially remained optimistic that something less than full alliance membership could assuage it:

[The] Dep[artment] further stated its realization ... that [the] conclusion [of the] Atlantic Pact of which Greece obviously could not be [a] member because [of its] geographic location might discourage [the] Greek people and encourage [the Soviets] to undertake more aggressive action against Greece. [The] Dep[artment] [is] in [the] process [of] developing [a] formula to avoid this danger by making clear to Greece, [the] U.S.S.R and [the] world that [the] conclusion [of the] Atlantic Pact does not signify [a] lessening [of] U.S. support for Greece [or] of [the] importance [the] U.S. attaches to [the] security of Greece.[13]

Yet Turkish statesmen remained concerned that any alliance consisting of Western European states would inevitably come to be seen as America's strategic priority and thus that inclusion in other potential regional alliances would be inadequate. As Foreign Minister Sadak told the State Department, "the problem therefore can be stated in these terms: how can [the] U.S. under [the] Vandenberg resolution associate itself for security purposes with Turkey in [the] same manner as [the] U.S. evidently intends to associate itself for security purposes with the countries of Western Europe."[14]

Crucially, the decision to include Italy in the nascent alliance recast the question. Both Turkish and American policymakers realized that once the alliance was no longer limited to the North Atlantic, the question of Turkish and Greek membership became even more urgent. With Italy in, leaving Greece and Turkey out could no longer be explained by geography and thus would appear to more blatantly

---

[12] Despatch from Ankara Embassy to Secretary of State, July 6, 1948, Department of State. Ibid.

[13] Despatch from Secretary of State to Ankara Embassy, February 4, 1949, ibid.

[14] Despatch from Ankara Embassy to Secretary of State, July 6, 1948, Department of State. Ibid.

signal a lack of US interest in their security. In November 1949, five months after Italy had become a founding member of the alliance, the Turkish ambassador explained succinctly, if not entirely accurately, that "Turkey would not have come into the picture if we [the Americans] had kept the North Atlantic group confined to the North Atlantic; it was when Italy was included that Turkey felt obliged to put forward her interest."[15] Among US officials, this argument received considerable sympathy. The US ambassador in Moscow, for example, weighed in noting:

As we understand it, the admission of Turkey would be a departure from the original concept of a unified grouping of countries belonging to the North Atlantic community. On the other hand, the admission of Italy at the outset was a broadening of that concept.[16]

After Turkey had been accepted into NATO, it became a staple of US and Turkish discourse that NATO membership in some way ratified Turkey's claim to a Western or European identity. But when membership was still up for debate, there was little suggestion on either side that NATO's geography carried this sort of cultural connotation. Italian membership may have intensified the link between NATO membership and European identity. But the language used by both Turkish and American statesmen emphasized Turkey's security interests instead, arguing that the borders of NATO were coterminous with the area that Washington was most committed to defending. Indeed, the very possibility that NATO would be perceived this way led the Turkish government to redouble its campaign for membership and ultimately led Washington to grant it. In short, by admitting a country that was clearly not, geographically speaking, part of the North Atlantic region, Washington stripped the alliance of its geographic specificity. This, in turn, made Turkish membership appear all the more necessary to many in Ankara and subsequently in Washington as well.

As noted earlier, Washington ultimately accepted Turkey's request for NATO membership not because it believed doing so would forestall

---

[15] Memorandum of Conversation, "Renewed Inquiry by the Turkish Ambassador Regarding Possible Closer Treaty Relationship between Turkey and the United States," November 15, 1949. State Department. Top Secret Records, Box 1, RG 84, NARA.

[16] Despatch No. 8 from Moscow Embassy to Secretary of State, August 31, 1950. State Department. Top Secret Records, Box 4, RG 84, NARA.

a Russian take-over, but because it feared that failing to do so would risk Turkish cooperation in the broader Cold War struggle. Thus in the American debate over Turkish membership, questions of Ankara's future behavior and Turkish psychology were central. As discussed by Athanassopoulou and Leffler, American planners were eager to secure access to bases on Turkish territory and secure Turkish participation in case of a full-scale war in Western Europe. But was granting Turkey NATO membership necessary and sufficient to secure these interests? Some US policymakers argued that Turkey would cooperate even without a formal defense commitment. Others, by contrast, worried that even with such a commitment Turks might still find a way to stay neutral as they had in World War II. The debate over whether Turkish cooperation was really contingent on NATO membership then involved questions of history, democracy, and Turkish psychology. And Turkish diplomats, for their part, did their best to exploit the ambiguities inherent in all these questions in order to achieve their goals.

George Wadsworth, the US ambassador between 1948 and 1952, most clearly stated the case for Turkish membership, arguing that "unless we are really prepared to come through with a commitment of real value to the Turks they would repeat last war's 'friendly neutrality' policy, block the straights, trade with both sides and hope we would defeat the Moscovs."[17] Or as a subordinate commenting on Wadsworth's draft put it: "I also believe that, given certain conditions, the Turks might 'weasel' on us."[18] That this negative characterization of İnönü's behavior during World War II actually served as an argument in favor of accepting Turkey into NATO hints at the contradictions and ambiguity that would come into play when the question turned from Turkish history to the Turkish character.

As ensuing discussions made clear, for many US diplomats the would-they-weasel question was, at its "core," "essentially psychological."[19] Thus General Arnold, the commander of the Joint Military Mission for Aid to Turkey (JAMMAT) at the time, argued that

---

[17] Note stapled to draft material for Chiefs of Mission's Conference, February 1951, General Records of the Department of State. Misc. Lot Files, Subject Files relating to Turkey, Box 1, RG 59. NARA.

[18] Ibid, written on draft material for Chiefs of Mission's Conference, February 1951, ibid.

[19] Comments of Charles Lewis on draft of material for Chiefs of Mission's Conference, February 1951, ibid.

NATO membership was "desirable and essential if we are to have the guaranteed right to utilize Turk facilitates and bases for action against the U.S.S.R.," because "doubts of our determination to continue assistance" might "weaken Turkey's intention to resist."[20] The perceived cultural characteristics underlying Turkish thinking quickly came to the fore. Admitting Turkey into NATO, for example, "would make them feel proud and would encourage their traditional martial spirit," while refusing them would "in all probability ... have a deleterious effect on Turkish amour propre and public morale."[21] "[T]he Turks are proud and suspicious and they have already suffered one psychological blow through their exclusion," one diplomat explained in support of Turkish membership.[22] But in another case orientalist stereotypes served to explain why Turks would fight even without an American guarantee:

That a simple peasant folk like the Turks need to be fortified morally by being allied to the "giaour," I would doubt. I believe that the basic reactions of the Turkish peasants who constitute 80% of the population will be, in time of war, the "Kismet" which comes both from the historical process as well as his faith, and the satanic pleasure which comes to any Turk when he sets about killing Moscovs.[23]

In other words, the Turk's oriental character would supposedly make him less willing to fight absent a formal US defense commitment or, alternatively, as satanically willing as ever.

With Turkish psychology at the center of the debate, it is not surprising that American statesmen would also assess the impact of Turkey's emerging democracy in determining how this mass psychology would translate into policy:

There is no question but that the nation as a whole will fight if attacked but as in any other democratic country its leaders are sensitive to public opinion and public opinion is wavering because of a feeling that their contributions and sacrifices to the United Nations have reaped no tangible reward in the form of political commitment. There is a growing feeling throughout the country that

---

[20] Despatch No. 582 from Secretary of State to Ankara Embassy, October 10, 1947. State Department. Top Secret Records, Box 1, RG 84, NARA. "For your background info Army considers that planned Turk reduction in force prior to time Aid Program becomes effective would definitely weaken Turk capacity to resist attack but concurs our feeling that attack unlikely and acknowledges that advantages of reducing military burden may outweigh purely military considerations."

[21] Ibid., Charles Lewis.   [22] Ibid.   [23] Ibid.

neutrality maybe preferable to an aggressive attitude which might bring on an attack without any assurance of allied assistance in that event. The desire of all Turks to stand with the western world is as unquestionable as their courage and determination but they also have the universal desire for survival.[24]

The ambiguity inherent in such an assessment was something Turkish diplomats were quick to emphasize, as it proved incredibly useful in enabling them to play on American fears while still reiterating their commitment to Western defense. It let them threaten, in essence, that American refusal might come at the cost of Turkish cooperation while simultaneously defusing responsibility for what might otherwise appear their own government's uncooperative attitude. In May 1948, for example, the Turkish ambassador told Secretary of State George Marshall:

Any action on the part of the United States displaying greater interest in the security of Western Europe than in that of Turkey would undermine the morale of the Turkish people and strengthen the minority group which insists upon the hopelessness of Turkish resistance. ... The Turkish government would continue, of course, to resist Soviet pressure. Nevertheless, the effectiveness of this resistance would be weakened.[25]

Indeed, even before becoming fully democratic, the Turkish government was quick to pick up on the diplomatic benefits of invoking public opinion to negotiate. At least in the reports of several US officials back to Washington, this approach seems to have resonated:

While we do not believe that unfavorable decision would weaken determination of Turks to resist any Soviet encroachment on Turk sovereignty, we think there would be [an] increased tendency of Turkish public opinion to insist that [the Turkish government] follow [a] policy of less cooperation with U.S. and Western democracies, [a] policy tending toward neutralism. We think [the] present [Turkish government] is fully convinced of [the] necessity continuing its present policy of active cooperation with West but its own position would be considerably weakened by [the] apparent failure

---

[24] Despatch from CINCNELM TO CNO, State Department. Top Secret Records, Box 3, RG 84, NARA.

[25] Memorandum of Conversation, "Turkish Desire for American "Guarantee to Turkey against Aggression," May 11, 1948. State Department. Top Secret Records, Box 1, RG 84, NARA.

[of] its much publicized efforts to enter into closer security arrangements with [the] Western democracies.[26]

Another factor that came into play while discussing the trade-offs involved in Turkish membership was the role of Turkish anti-imperialism in limiting the degree of cooperation Turkey would be prepared to offer the United States. Both before and after 1952, US discussions about Turkey's role in NATO and Middle East defense inevitably made reference to the country's sensitivity to matters of national sovereignty and its deeply felt anti-imperialism. After Turkey joined NATO, US forces ultimately engaged in close cooperation with their Turkish counterparts and made considerable use of military facilitates on Turkish soil. This, of course, had been a dominant consideration in accepting Turkey in the first place. Yet in many cases US diplomats appeared surprised at the degree of cooperation they received. Immediately following Turkey's entrance into NATO, Americans were not even certain that the US military would be given rights to use Turkish airfields, even those constructed with US aid money and technical supervision, in anything less than an all-out war. A lower-level embassy employee assigned to investigate the topic concluded:

In the absence of any information to the contrary, I do not know of any reason to believe that the Turks would be prepared to turn over bases within their territory to us or any other power, short of hostilities. I've always assumed that we were proceeding on the theory that it was desirable to help the Turks build up bases for their own use, which would be available to us in an emergency. I have checked over the verbatim record of the military talks here in October (Bradley Mission), and other pertinent papers, and find no reference whatever to the establishment or utilization of bases in Turkey.[27]

Among other evidence that led US diplomats to this conclusion was a 1952 Speech in the Grand National Assembly in which Foreign Minister Köprülü declared:

---

26 From SECSTATE, June 23, 1951, No INTEL Top Secret Records, Box 4, RG 84, NARA.
27 Letter to Mr. Keith from Mr. Wendelin, "Use of Military Bases in Turkey," January 24, 1952. Top Secret Records U.S. Embassy Ankara, Box 4, RG 84, NARA.

I do not conceive it possible that any observer with good intentions could fail to admit that we do not by any means contemplate giving bases to others in our territory and that only in the event of aggression shall we use our own bases within the framework of the necessary cooperation with our allies.[28]

Assessing the speech, the embassy noted that it was met with applause and "greeted with cries of 'Bravo.'" The State Department's conclusion, based on Köprülü's comments, was again that

[i]n the light of the Turk's historical experience with foreign imperialism and the characteristic ingrained distrust of the Turkish people for anything suggesting possible foreign intervention, it seems evident that the Turkish Government would be extremely reluctant to consider outright granting of bases in its territory, unless and until it were confronted at least with the imminent threat of Soviet aggression.[29]

The correlation between Turkey's NATO membership and America's access to Turkish military facilities was always filtered through sometimes-conflicting assessments of Turkish psychology and domestic politics. If Turkish anti-imperialism raised the possibility that even in NATO Turkey would not provide US planners with the strategic assets they desired, even greater fears raised by the – carefully cultivated – prospect of Turkish neutrality still made accepting Turkey appear to be the wiser decision.[30]

The North Atlantic in the Middle East

Ultimately, the impact of Turkish anti-imperialist nationalism was most fully felt after Turkey had joined NATO, in the subsequent debates over how Turkey and its new partners should engage with the Middle East. During these debates, Turkish statesmen and the press showed how readily Turkey's geography and history could be re-

---

[28] Memorandum from Mr. Wendel[in]. Top Secret Records U.S. Embassy Ankara, Box 4, RG 84, NARA.

[29] Ibid.

[30] Moreover, by 1952, the changing nature of the Cold War and America's already-manifest commitment to Turkey's defense meant that American officials could no longer imagine a scenario where a Soviet attack on Turkey would not lead to or be part of a larger European war. This reality mitigated the additional risks that Washington would take offering Turkey a formal defense commitment, making the ability to acquire specific strategic benefits all the more enticing.

interpreted in keeping with their interests. When Turkey joined NATO, parliamentarians declared it a vindication of Turkey's Western identity and a reminder of Turkey's responsibilities to the Middle East. Ankara was eager to emphasize its shared historical ties, cultural values, and anti-imperialist legacy in approaching Middle Eastern states, while also wanting to appear as an equal partner with the other imperial powers in NATO. Turkish public opinion, in turn, was malleable enough to accommodate both these positions. While Arabs were often viewed sympathetically in the immediate aftermath of World War II – when they were still seen as victims of British imperialism – by the mid-1950s they were often seen as willing accomplices of the Soviet's imperial ambitions. Initially, Turkish diplomats sought to convince Washington to be more sympathetic to Arab anti-British sentiment. Yet Washington hoped Turkey would use its cultural and religious affinity with the Arabs to convince them of the regrettable necessity of cooperating with Britain. In time, as Arab nationalism took a more pro-Soviet direction, Turkey closed ranks behind its new American and British allies. Only at this point did Turkish diplomats, writers, and cartoonists deploy the full force of their anti-Arab prejudice in condemning Arab governments for their pro-Russian attitudes.[31]

Commenting on Turkey's geopolitical role and identity in 1951, Turkey's Washington press attaché told an audience at Princeton University that Turkey was "truly a Western power" yet "it would be ignoring history and geography to exclude Turkey altogether from the area of the Middle East." In fact, he concluded, "[T]he Turks believe that the Middle East is but a continuation of the Continent of Europe."[32] When Turkey joined NATO in February 1952, it offered Turkish politicians an opportunity to both celebrate their newly

---

[31]   The contours of this dynamic were largely anticipated in a 1946 report from the US embassy: "Generally speaking, there appears to be a strong undercurrent of sympathy for the national aspirations of the Arab states, despite the commonly felt Turkish attitude of superiority towards Arabs. Coupled with this sympathetic feeling, however, there is the realization that Arab nationalism is mainly directed against Turkey's ally, the United Kingdom, and is susceptible of exploitation by the Soviet Union." Despatch No. 639. March 1, 1946. State Department, Classified General Records 1936–1950, Box 19, RG 84, NARA.

[32]   "Turkey's Vital Role in the Global Context, an Address by Mr. Nuri Eren," General Records of the Department of State. Subject Files relating to Turkey, Box 2. RG 59, NARA.

ratified Western identity and embrace a new role in the Middle East. In negotiating Turkey's NATO accession, Turkish diplomats had insisted that the country's membership be unconditional, rather than dependent on participation in Anglo-American Middle East defense plans. This matter was sufficiently sensitive that, amidst the enthusiasm surrounding Turkey's entrance into NATO, opposition deputies repeatedly pressed an exasperated Foreign Minister Köprülü to assure them that there were no secret stipulations to this effect.[33] Then, as soon as Turkey's unqualified membership in the alliance had been secured, the question of the country's responsibilities to its eastern neighbors took on a newfound urgency.

Explaining the CHP's position in December 1951, Faik Ahmet Baratçu stressed "the great importance of the Middle East" for the Atlantic system, as well as the "first order interest" it held for Turkey "jointly with the other Atlantic states."[34] Yet he stressed that Turkey must enter NATO on "completely equal terms" with other members, as this was a "separate matter" from Middle East defense. Finally, he added that Turkey must not neglect its ability to "play the friendliest and most helpful role in calming the stormy winds blowing across the Middle East," along with "the impact of our natural understanding, in the spirit of the Lausanne agreement, for the Arab states' national struggles."

When Turkey finally joined NATO several months later, Barutçu's DP rivals were quick to stress the need for Turkey to take on a more active role in the region, appealing to both Turkey's religious and Kemalist values. Noting that Atatürk had sought to establish Turkey's security with the Balkan Pact in the West and the Saadabad Pact in the East, Zeki Erataman announced, "[W]e believe Atatürk's spirit is happy with our having joined the systematic security system he wanted to found in the West."[35] Now, he argued, "[W]e have an immediate duty to come to an understanding with the Eastern nations and take a leadership role among them." There was, he concluded, "a bloc of 150 million Muslims that must not be forgotten." In a similar vein, DP deputy Burhanettin Onat explained that the global front

---

[33] Köprülü also reassured the parliament that, despite malicious rumors to the contrary, the terms of the NATO treaty had been changed on Turkey's account so that the entire country, and not just Thrace, would be covered under Article 5. T. B. M. M. Tutanak Dergisi, 19 Birleşim 19. XII. 1951 Çarşamba.

[34] T. B. M. M. Tutanak Dergisi, 19 Birleşim 19. XII. 1951 Çarşamba.   [35] Ibid.

against communism had "an open Eastern flank" that would remain open if Turkey did not "quickly complement the Atlantic pact with a similar Eastern pact." In more grandiose fashion, Onat declared that "[j]ust as people have responsibilities, so do nations," and God had "ordained" Turkey "president" of a "spiritual world" stretching from the Atlantic to the Pacific:

At one point we resigned this, but the East didn't accept our resignation. In various places nations have been formed and won their independence, all of their eyes are on us. All of them use the Turk's name and Atatürk's picture like flags in their liberation and revolutionary movements. Unfortunately, today we are not in a position to make the most of this duty, this advantage.[36]

The rhetoric of Kemalist anti-imperialism – wherein Turkey was an inspiration to the East because it had defeated the West and become Western – captured the contradictory role Turkey now hoped to play, which required being both fully Western and fully Eastern as needed. Alongside Atatürk the Westernizer, this rhetoric invoked a different Atatürk, the one "who declared Asia's first jihad for freedom."[37] This was the Atatürk whose address, Nutuk, "was like a scared book for Asian intellectuals," whose spirit "spread over the whole East like the glow of dawn," and whose victory at Dumlupınar "showed other Muslim nations the road to salvation."[38]

Press coverage from the period featured writers from a range of political backgrounds invoking similar rhetoric in calling for a greater Turkish role in the Middle East. In 1949, for example, the journal of the Zonguldak Peoples' House offered a nationalistic celebration of Pakistan's recently won independence:

Sooner or later, the truth that Asia belongs to the Asians will be realized . . . The new Turkey, as Turkish as possible in spirit, as Western as possible in mentality, positioned between the continents so as to create an Asian renaissance, salutes every positive and forward movement in Asia with praise and affection.[39]

In doing so, the journal's writers sounded remarkably similar to Ahmet Emin Yalman praising the DP's foreign policy in 1950:

---

[36] Ibid.
[37] Behçet Kemal Çağlar, "Doğu'dan Doğu'nun Yeni Devletlerine Selam!" *Doğu*, Cild 15, Yıl 8, Sayı 82–96, September 1949–October 1950.
[38] Ibid.   [39] Ibid.

A new sun has risen for all of Asia and mankind at large ... It will be remembered that there was a time when we for a while followed the course of denying our relations with the East, with a view to assimilation with the Western world. Our natural role, however, consists in serving as a bridge in the moral and material sense between East and West.[40]

And while Yalman criticized Atatürk himself for neglecting the Middle East, Hüseyin Cahit Yalçın endorsed the same policy – while denying that Turkey had ever denied its relations with the region. Explicitly citing Atatürk's Saadabad pact, Yalçın called for a more "active" and "dynamic" policy in the region. This, he argued, would enable Turkey to "completely achieve its task as the champion of western civilization in the Near East." If successful, "Turkish diplomacy will have done a great service to the cause of civilization by establishing a stable, freedom-loving, democratic network of friendship in the Near East."[41]

Just as parliamentarians and journalists invoked Kemalist anti-imperialism in calling for greater solidarity with the Arab world, so did mid-century Turkish feminists. In 1951, *Women's Newspaper* editor İffet Halim Oruz led a committee of journalists to Aleppo, declaring that they had come as "children of Atatürk" to find not a French colony but the Syrian government and people.[42] Even stronger than the cultural and family ties between these two countries, she argued, was the understanding between a nation that had fought against imperialism and a nation that had subsequently gained its freedom. As a result, she concluded by observing that "the countries which shared an Islamic culture, as well as those that did not" should constitute a force against imperialism and exploitation. Similarly, Süreyya Ağaoğlu, Turkey's first female diplomat under the DP, was equally convinced that Turkish women had an important role to play in liberating the East.[43] Women's progress, she argued, had been opposed

---

[40] *Vatan*, August 17, Despatch 1803, ibid.
[41] *Ulus*, July 13, 1950. Among the positive steps he cited as having been taken to improve Turkey's relations with the region were "the Foreign Minister's demarches with the Arab states" and "the progress recently made in establishing closer relations with Israel."
[42] İffet Oruz, "Gazeteciler Heyeti Halep'te," *Kadın Gazetesi*, May 14, 1951.
     In 1949 *Kadın Gazetesi* ran back-to-back articles in 1949 on "The Role that Pakistani Women played in the [Pakistani] Freedom Movement" and "The Role that Indian Women Played in the Indian Freedom Movement." August 22, August 29.
[43] Sürreyya Ağaoğlu, "Şarkta Kadın" *Kadın Gazetesi*, September 6, 1948.

not just by Arab men but by colonial governments that consciously benefited from religiously justified oppression. "However cultured a country's women are," she explained, "that is how much its people are raised to love freedom and liberty." Thus, "so long as Eastern societies do not give women rights, they will never achieve independence."

For their part, US diplomats consistently commented on the prevalence of these anti-imperial sentiments during their reporting on Turkey's relations with the Middle East. "You do not find here today a marked warmth of feeling for Great Britain,"[44] Ambassador Wadsworth wrote in 1951. As Washington sought to bring Britain, Turkey and the Arab states together in a joint anti-Soviet alliance, this sentiment became a regular cause of concern for US diplomats in Turkey. Wadsworth subsequently drew up a hand-written memo titled "reasons for Turk[ish] dislike and distrust of Brit[ain]." British behavior in World War I was "not forgotten," he wrote, while Turks believed the British "still have imperialist ambitions in the Middle East" and think of Turkey and others as "colonials."[45]

As US diplomats noted at the time, the depth of anti-British sentiment helped reconcile remarkably condescending and sympathetic attitudes toward the Arab world in the minds of Turkish policymakers. "Turkey's relations with the Arab States and with Persia are on a friendly basis," but "in their hearts and minds [Turks] regard them as of inferior character," the ambassador wrote in 1951.[46] Indeed, DP Foreign Minister Fuat Köprülü, widely seen as the most outspoken

---

[44] Chiefs of Mission's Conference, February 1951, General Records of the Department of State. Misc. Lot Files, Subject Files relating to Turkey, Box 1. RG 59, NARA.

[45] And on top of this there was Britain's increasingly apparent weakness: Turkish concern, Wadsworth wrote, also stemmed from the fact that "[the British] are not able to make substantial contribution to military defense in ME." France meanwhile, suffered the indignity of being more frequently ignored than condemned in discussions of European imperialism. When it was mentioned, though, the sentiments were generally similar: "French attempt to maintain dominant position in Syria and Leb had merely succeed in making them appear ridiculous. Prestige is not something that can be developed artificially. QUOTE it is like a shadow, when you turn to it, it disappears UNQUOTE." Despatch No. 1326, May 26, 1952 State Department, Classified General Records 1936–1950, Box 5, RG 84, NARA.

[46] Chiefs of Mission's Conference, February 1951, General Records of the Department of State. Misc. Lot Files, Subject Files relating to Turkey, Box 1. RG 59, NARA.

advocate for improved Turkish-Arab relations in the early 1950s, had no end of disparaging remarks about Arabs. Meeting with Dean Acheson in 1951, for example, he "readily agreed" that Arab states were "weak and suffer from jealousy among themselves."[47] Ambassador Warren wrote up another conversation where Köprülü made an "incidental comment touching chiefly on [the] emotional susceptibilities of other Arab Govts and peoples."[48] Köprülü, who at one point described the Egyptians as "twisty and suspicious by nature,"[49] concluded in his most charitable moments that

[h]e was certain that the contempt in which the Arab States and Arabs in general are held by the present generation in Turkey would gradually disappear ... although he admitted that the time required for such a development might be long indeed.[50]

Yet alongside this prejudice, Turkish diplomats and writers showed considerable sympathy for the Arabs as well. This was particularly pronounced on the issue of Palestine: In October 1947, the US embassy reported that "it continues to be clear that Turkey is sympathetic to the Arab viewpoint," and then in December, "[o]utcry in the Turk[ish] press over Palestine partition becoming more violent and more directly critical [of the] U.S. role."[51] In 1951, Wadsworth explained for a meeting of regional US ambassadors:

On the explosive Palestine issue, Turkey expressed sympathy with its Moslem brothers of the Arab League to the extent of voting against partition in the General Assembly but has made it plain that it will not allow that issue to jeopardize its close collaboration with the U.S. ... Turkey's sympathies

---

[47] Memorandum of conversation between Fuat Köprülü and Dean Acheson, November 12, 1951, Top Secret Records, U.S. Embassy, Ankara, Box 4, NARA.

[48] Despatch No. 310 from Ankara Embassy to Secretary of State, ibid.

[49] Telegram No. 244, September 29, ibid. Interestingly, his full claim was that Egyptians were "twisty and suspicious by nature formed by historical experience." In a striking example of the contradictory deployment of prejudices, Köprülü pairs a generalized trait attributed to a group's "nature" with a reference to specific historical circumstances, in this case the experience of British colonialism, which explains that "nature."

[50] Memo – to GTI Roundtree from Mr. Moore, "Turkey and Its Near Eastern Neighbors – the Problem of Leadership." General Records of the Department of State. Misc. Lot Files, Lot File No. 58 D 61, Subject Files relating to Turkey, Box 2. RG 59, NARA.

[51] Despatch No. 1893, October 22, 1947; Despatch 932, December 5, Unclassified General Records, U.S. Embassy, Ankara, Box 100, NARA.

have been with the Arab states on the Palestine question. Turkey voted against the Partition Plan and is uneasy over the implications of a Jewish state ... Turkey, nevertheless, maintained a strictly hands-off attitude and forbade its citizens under penalty of loss of nationality to participate in the struggle on either side.[52]

Among other things, it should be noted that feeling on this subject was bipartisan in Turkey. Before the DP came to power, for example, CHP Foreign Minister Necmettin Sadak told Ambassador Wadsworth:

Israel was a fabrication of the United Nations (particularly a fabrication of the United States). The creation of this state was a mistake as he, the Foreign Minister, had informed Mr. Wadsworth's predecessor.[53]

His language was almost the same as that used by a friend of Köprülü's, speaking before an American audience several years later with the minister's endorsement:

When Palestine was occupied by the British during the First World War, the Balfour Declaration promised a home for the Jews in Palestine. In my opinion it was a mistake. It was a mistake to try to put a foreign element in the middle of [an] Arab-dominated area. The mistake continued until we had the Israel Government and the Israel State.[54]

During this period, visiting Arab statesmen regularly created enthusiasm in the Turkish press when they invoked, sincerely or not, the Ottoman past as an example of Turkish-Arab brotherhood or Turkish regional leadership.[55] Official visitors from the Arab world often

---

[52] Chiefs of Missions' Conference, February 1951, RG 59 General Records of the Department of State. Misc. Lot Files, Subject Files relating to Turkey, Box 1.

[53] Memorandum of Conversation, April 21, 1950. State Department, Classified General Records 1936–1950, Box 3, RG 84, NARA.

[54] Lecture by Hazım Atıf Kuyucak January 24, 1955 Air War College, Maxwell Alabama. General Records of the Department of State. Misc. Lot Files, Box 1, RG 59, NARA. Kuyucak had showed the text to his "good friend" Professor Köprülü who was "said to have expressed general agreement."

[55] Speech by Azzam Pasha. Classified General Records, U.S. Embassy, Ankara, Box 3, NARA. "The main object of my visit to Turkey is to consolidate an old friendship between two people who have a shared a common inheritance of more than a thousand years ... This nation, which has always been the advance post of the Moslem world, and which as always fulfilled its civilizing and organizing mission for centuries with great courage and which has attracted my admiration since my earliest youth is still occupying that admiration now forty years later."

referred to their personal experience of the Ottoman era as a source of solidarity with Turkey and were widely quoted when they did so. In 1947, for example, the Grand Mufti of Jerusalem told the newspaper *Vatan* that "when Palestine constituted a part of the Ottoman Empire, she was one of the most loyal members of that empire. It is very natural that our relations with Turkey in the future will, as previously, be established on the principals of loyalty and friendship."[56] On the same visit, Dr. Halidi, Secretary General of the Palestine Arab Committee, told *Vatan* that Atatürk "is indeed like a torch burning in the hearts of all Arabs," and "until a few years ago, Atatürk's picture was to be found in every street in Palestine"[57] Later that year, Emir Abdullah of Transjordan told the Turkish press that while he regretted being unable to read Turkish he felt an emotional bond with Turkey and listened to Turkish news on the radio.[58] Perhaps more convincingly, Sheikh Senusi of Libya told Turkish journalists about the "happy times" when Libya was part of the Ottoman Empire:

Before the Italian war we were not ruled by foreigners. The Turks ruling our country did not represent a foreign country. The Turks ruled Tripoli in keeping with the wishes of the people. In those times, it was not the Turkish government which forced its will upon the people. The government only carried out the people's will.[59]

In keeping with this rhetoric, Turkish writers were also quick to claim that Turkey had voluntarily given Arab states their independence. In 1945, for example, *Ulus* editor Hüsein Cahit Yalçın wrote of Syria and Lebanon that "Turkey gave up these parts of the motherland in order that they might live in freedom and under the regime and government of their own choice."[60] In *Yeni Sabah*, meanwhile, Ömer Rıza Doğrul explained:

[T]hese countries seceded from Turkey with our full consent. Consequently, we feel certain responsibilities with regard to these brother states. In fact, we

---

[56] Quoted from *Vatan*, May 4, 1947 in Despatch 1622, May 8, 1947. Unclassified General Records, U.S. Embassy, Ankara, Box 100, NARA.

[57] Ibid, May 3.

[58] Quoted from *Tasvir*, October 27 and 29, 1947, US press clippings, Unclassified General Records, U.S. Embassy, Ankara, Box 91, NARA.

[59] Quoted from *Cumhuriyet* April 12, in Despatch No. 1565, April 15, 1945, Unclassified General Records, U.S. Embassy, Ankara, Box 106, RG 84, NARA.

[60] Quoted from *Tan*, April 20, 1945. Unclassified General Records, U.S. Embassy, Ankara, Box 91, RG 84, NARA.

relinquished these territories in order that they should become independent and free, and not in order that they might be turned into colonies . . . . It is not the principle of Kemalist and Republican Turkey to watch with folded arms events in adjacent countries. Consequently, it is our right to demand from our Government a more active policy on this matter.[61]

Finally, in his treatment of "foreign relations in the Republican Period" professor and diplomat Nihat Erim explained that Turkey and Iraq had "no unsettled problems left between them" and "were closely attached to each other by a 400-year long life together." Similarly, he wrote, "[A]s it has with every country which detached itself from the Ottoman Empire, the Turkish government has always nourished well-purposed intentions toward Syria and has sincerely wished that she win her independence."[62]

Both Sides of the Bridge

In the early 1950s, several diplomatic crises pitted US and British Cold War interests against colonized or semi-colonized Middle Eastern states. The following section examines several of these: An initial stage, in 1952, of what would become the Suez Crisis, followed by the crisis surrounding Iranian oil nationalization and finally the tense, if not crisis level, negotiations over the fee for US basing rights in Libya. In every case, Turkish diplomats pushed the United States, and in turn Britain, to be more accommodating of regional anti-imperial concerns. Yet in every case Turkish diplomats ultimately proved willing to close ranks behind America and Britain in the face of a perceived Soviet threat.

When a standoff first developed between Britain and the new Egyptian regime of Gamal Abdel Nasser, the State Department sought a solution in having Britain and Egypt come together as partners in a joint Middle East Command. The optimistic and always pro-Turkish George McGhee promoted the idea that Turkey was uniquely positioned to overcome Egyptian skepticism and sell this idea to Nasser. "I welcome Department's recognition of Turkey as [an] important element in [a] 'new deal' approach to ME states," he wrote; "[The] association of Turkey, as a neighbor with strong ME ties and no

---

[61] Quoted from *Yeni Sabah*, June 4, ibid.
[62] Quoted from *Ülkü*, November 1, ibid.

justified suspicion of colonial intent, should greatly assist in proving bona fides of other powers in [the Middle East Command] approach."[63] As McGhee explained in another telegram, it was "the multilateral nature of the Middle East Command, and [in] particular [the] participation of Turkey as a founding member," which would have the "greatest appeal" for Egypt.[64]

Ankara, for its part, was eager to promote its unique ability to play just this role. But Turkish statesmen repeatedly made it clear that success depended on the plan really being a multilateral one with no latent colonial intent. One of the first times McGhee raised the question of participation in the command, Prime Minister Menderes emphasized that "he envisaged not simply [an] allied command to mask [the] existing situation but [a] true inter-allied organization and command."[65] Köprülü, likewise, stressed that

[i]f object is simply to strengthen Brit position in ME (e.g. to maintain Brit troops in Egypt to reestablish historic British position of "occupation"), we shall get nowhere with Egypt or other Arab States. Otherwise put, if MEC is designed to mask political objectives, we shall be wasting our time. For Arab countries, question is primarily political and psychological.[66]

Similarly, in regard to the question of whether the command would be led by a British general, President Bayar explained:

Egypt, like other newly independent countries this area, is highly sensitive to presence of foreign troops. Egypt is particularly sensitive because British troops there seem continuance of historic occupation .... Today we have only good intentions, but it is difficult make Egypt understand. Our ForMin has long sought similar formula which, while not offending national feelings, will assure strategic position.[67]

The Turkish army's chief of staff put the Turkish case even more emphatically in discussing the Middle East Command with

---

[63] Despatch No. 994, March 31, 1952, State Department, Classified General Records 1936–1950, Box 5, RG 84, NARA.

[64] Untitled Memorandum, Ankara September 27, 1951, State Department, Classified General Records 1936–1950, Box 4, RG 84, NARA.

[65] Despatch No. 289 from Ankara Embassy to Secretary of State; from Ankara September 25, 1951. Top Secret Records, U.S. Embassy, Ankara, Box 4, RG 84, NARA.

[66] Telegram No. 244, September 12, ibid.

[67] Despatch No. 283 from Ankara Embassy to Secretary of State September 24, ibid.

a counterpart from the US Navy. After saying that "[n]ot only Egypt but [the] entire [Middle East] was definitely anti-British," the Turkish general explained he and the Turkish people felt very much the same way:

At one point near end conversation he stated "Royson, I tell you frankly again, Turkey will not accept a British General as commander of the Middle East Command – an American Lieutenant yes, but British General, No! ..." I then inquired if this was his (Egeli's) own personal opinion or was it also shared by Turk Govt. His reply was: "It is the decision of the Turkish people"[68]

Americans were not unreceptive to Turkey's concerns about the British and often seemed to find them flattering. But on the specific issue of the Middle East Command's leadership, American diplomats remained willing to overlook these concerns and accommodate London's expectations. The result was a series of exchanges that elucidate the respective Turkish and American approaches to balancing British and Egyptian sensibilities. Washington continued to not only push for a British commander, but also urge Ankara to try to sell Egypt on the idea. When told, for example, by the Turkish ambassador in Washington that "a British Supreme Commander would be unacceptable to the Egyptians," McGhee responded "that he recognized the difficulties involved in obtaining Egyptian acceptance of the MEC idea and a British Supreme Commander," but Washington was nonetheless "counting on the Turks to help us to convince them of the desirability of this proposed solution."[69]

The Turkish Foreign Ministry also tried to convince Washington that accommodating British colonialism would undermine the struggle against communism. Köprülü told McGhee, for example:

---

[68] Despatch No. 299, September 27, 1951. Ibid. Commenting on this, Ambassador Wadsworth wrote: "Gen. Egeli has made similar statements upon several occasions during the last six months, but he has never been quite as emphatic. I do not give full credence to all his statements, but discounting his last evening statements 50%, there still exists evidence of very strong anti-British feeling in Turkey which cannot be brushed off lightly." Wadsworth on memo by Col Royson, chief of JAMMAT plans group. Ibid.

[69] Memorandum of Conversation, "Turkeys relationship to NATO and MEC; Feridun Erkin, Turkish Ambassador; McGhee, Robert Moore, GTI," September 28, 1951, Top Secret Records, U.S. Embassy, Ankara, RG 84, NARA.

Rising nationalism in ME exploited by Commies utilizing also reactionary and chauvinistic elements. Situation greatly worsened, however, by pursuit Western Powers their own special interests which result in lack of common policy. Western Powers must abandon "old methods" in dealing with States of area. Essential to harmonize policies on basis friendship with ME States, which offers only chance obtaining their cooperation.[70]

Ambassador McGhee, not surprisingly, tried to justify Britain's approach with reference to the same Cold War goals:

Brit treaty systems with Jordan, Iraq and Egypt considered by ME States, rightly or wrongly, as relic of colonial era. In my judgement Brit would have been prepared to abandon these treaty rights in normal times. Now, however, in midst of Cold War, to do so would invite instability in whole area and open invitation to Sov aggression or subversion.

Köprülü's response, again, captured the nature of Turkey's disagreement with the United States. He quickly agreed that it was "important that Brit prestige be built up and Suez defended," before seeking the final word: that the "Middle East command had a chance of acceptance only if it was, in fact, what it purported to be, and not subterfuge for covering up a defense of British interests."[71]

The Turkish government was less actively involved in the confrontation between Britain and prime minister Mohammed Mossadegh over Iranian oil nationalization, but the same dynamic quickly showed itself there as well. Through 1952, the Iranian cause garnered significant sympathy in the Turkish press, while Turkish diplomats consistently argued that greater Western support for Mosaddegh's position was crucial to forestalling the rise of Communist influence in Iran. Throughout the crisis, though, Turkish sympathy was quick to evaporate when Mosaddegh went too far in seeking support from communists either in Iran or Moscow. Indeed, as the situation became more polarized, and Mosaddegh appeared increasingly forced to seek such support, Ankara began to back the Anglo-American position. Nonetheless, this alignment was only reached after considerable public and private advocacy for a more accommodating course of action.

During a 1951 conversation with Dean Acheson, for example, Köprülü said that "the U.S. should do all it can to prevail on Britain

---

[70] Despatch No. 673 from Ankara Embassy Secretary of State, January 26, 1952. Top Secret Records, U.S. Embassy, Ankara, Box 3, RG 84, NARA.
[71] Ibid.

to be reasonable because Russia must be prevented from entering the area through the Tudeh party."[72] He would voice similar sentiments a year later, telling Ambassador McGhee that the Americans "must do something to help bolster Mosaddegh's position [in] Iran." When McGhee then cited the "shortcomings of Mosaddegh on [the] oil question and his leanings toward neutralism," Köprülü "agreed" but explained that he "felt Mosaddegh was now [the] only element of strength in Iran which can successfully oppose a seizure of power by communists."[73] Even in conversations with the British, Ankara urged greater accommodation with Mosaddegh, telling the British ambassador, for example to "pursue a moderate course." The British, in turn, responded by "suggesting that the Turkish Government might find it appropriate to make similar suggestion to [the] Iranians."[74]

Subsequently, the US embassy tried to put a positive spin on the Turkish position by noting:

Most of press, while sympathizing with Iran's desire to nationalize oil industry, expresses view that Iran govt has submitted too often to pressure of extremist elements and has not been willing to make reasonable compromise. Press unanimously deplores recent reported Iranian approaches to U.S.S.R.[75]

Yet the press reaction quoted in this same embassy report shows how outspoken such sympathy could be. *Zafer*, the DP paper, declared proudly, if slightly defensively, that "Turkey has shown the road of freedom to many eastern nations enslaved by foreign influences," in this case of the British economic variety.[76] More striking, though, is that while Köprülü was privately appealing to the United States and Britain to be more accommodating, the Foreign Ministry came under attack in the press for publicly standing behind its Western allies. An editorial in *Yeni Sabah*, for example, declared:

We regret to observe that in UN as elsewhere [the Turkish Foreign Ministry] continues under influence of Britain and France. We enjoy a brilliant and

---

[72] Memorandum of Conversation, Fuat Köprülü, Dean Acheson. General Records of the Department of State. Misc. Lot Files, Subject Files relating to Turkey, Box 1, RG 59, NARA.

[73] Ibid.

[74] Despatch No. 31, May 23, 1951, Classified General Records, U.S. Embassy, Ankara, Box 63, RG 84, NARA.

[75] Despatch No. 338, October 10, 1951, Classified General Records, U.S. Embassy, Ankara, Box 63, RG 84, NARA.

[76] Quoted from *Zafer*, October 5 in Despatch No. 338, ibid.

prominent position in East but when we use our influence against eastern nations we run risk of falling into position only of [guardians of] Anglo-French colonialism in this part of world.

Then, offering a more pointed critique:

What Iran is doing is just what Atatürk did 20 years ago in Turkey. By voting against Iran we are voting against Atatürk. When will our [Foreign Ministry] wake up from its lethargy and try to be worthy of leadership of the East.[77]

Ironically, the lack of access to Turkish diplomatic archives on this subject has made it easier for modern-day observers to critique the Turkish government's approach to the conflict on the same grounds as contemporary newspapers. Undeniably, the Menderes government ultimately sided with Britain. But, as State Department records make clear, for the Turkish Foreign Ministry this was very much a case of geopolitical pressures – British power and the Soviet threat – taking precedence over more deeply felt sympathies. Perhaps this dynamic was best captured by a single edit the US ambassador made to the draft text of a 1951 telegram: "If it came to losing Iranian oil to Russians" then "British intervention would be ~~accepted~~ palatable" for Turkey.[78]

A year after covert British and American intervention removed Mosaddegh from power, the United States and Libya became embroiled in a much less dramatic conflict over the appropriate rent for the Wheelus Airbase, located near Tripoli. Turkey's relationship with the regime of King Idris Senussi had been considerably better than with other Arab states. Libya was more closely aligned with the United States and did not perceive Turkey as constituting any kind of threat to its territorial integrity. Additionally, the fact that many of Turkey's founders had fought with King Senussi against the Italians in 1912 provided a more positive recent history on which to build ties than the experience of World War I in the Middle East. Indeed, Libya's first defense minister was a Turkish citizen by birth and the country's first foreign minister had lived in Turkey and worked at the Turkish Foreign Ministry.

As tension between Washington and Tripoli intensified, the relative closeness of Turkish-Libyan relations seems to have increased both

---

[77] Quoted from *Yeni Sabah*, ibid.
[78] Circular Telegram No. 178 from Ankara Embassy, August 23, 1951. State Department, Classified General Records 1936–1950, Box 5, RG 84, NARA.

Turkey's sympathy toward Libya's position and Washington's expectation that the Ankara could convince the Libyans to back down. Turkey, the Americans were happy to note, appeared eager to demonstrate its importance by helping to resolve the conflict. The Turkish Foreign Ministry, the embassy concluded, "will savor with pleasure both the feeling of paternalism for weak Libya and the choice of Turkey to reconcile American limitations of patience with the bazaar-type bargaining of the Libyans."[79]

Ankara was certainly eager to play this role, though a split quickly became apparent in what US and Turkish diplomats thought that entailed. Americans very much hoped that Turkey could reconcile King Senussi to their demands, while Ankara sought to achieve reconciliation by lobbying both the Americans and Libyans to make concessions. Shortly after tensions began, the US ambassador, acting on instructions from Secretary of State Dulles, explained to his Turkish counterpart that he would be

most grateful to the Minister of Foreign Affairs for his efforts with the Libyan delegation . . . to make clear the value of American friendship . . . [and] for the thoughtfulness which prompted the Turkish government to observe to the Libyan visitors that American Friendship in Turkey (as elsewhere) is not measured in dollars.

Dulles's original instructions, in fact, make the nature of the US request more explicit.

Would be grateful if the Turkish Government were inclined to pass to His Excellency . . . [that] it is contrary to American policy and is distasteful to the American temperament to have the American contribution to the military security of the free world hinge on the size of a financial grant.[80]

Yet the Turkish Foreign Ministry seemed inclined to accept the assessment of their ambassador in Libya, who felt that the US government might do well to be more flexible:

Turkish minister to Libya is currently in Ankara. He had passed on to the Foreign Office a request that the Turks, as good mutual friends of both the Americans and the Libyans, intervene to secure a more favorable deal for the Libyans. Mr. Birgi said obviously the Turkish Government could not

[79] Despatch No. 11, "Visit of Libyan Prime Minister to Turkey," July 8, 1954. Classified General Records, U.S. Embassy, Ankara, Box 63, RG 84, NARA.
[80] Aid memoire, Dulles, ibid.

intervene in such a matter or presume to tell us how we should spend our money. On the other hand, they were sure that we recognize as they do that Libya is one of the few Middle Eastern States which has shied away from neutralism and shown itself prepared to collaborate with the West ... [A] relatively minor increases in aid to states willing to cooperate might have very beneficial psychological effects on those tending toward neutralism.[81]

The US ambassador to Libya, for his part, worried Turkey was acting as an advocate for the wrong country. Citing a memo expressing Turkish hope that the "U.S. assume sympathetic attitude toward compensation," he wrote, "Turkish good offices ... might help forestall present trend wherein they appear to be assuming [the role of] Libya's sponsor vis-a-vis United States."[82]

Yet in response to repeated suggestions that the crisis might prove an "excellent opportunity for Turks if they are willing to act as moderating influence,"[83] Turkish diplomats continued to push the United States to change its behavior. The US embassy in Ankara reported that in discussing this suggestion:

[Turkish Ambassador to Libya] Birgi indicated understanding our exasperation [over] continued Libyan bargaining on subject. At same time, he ... indicated Turks continue believe it would have good effect on Arab neutralist tendencies if they see tangible benefits accrue to those who grant bases and otherwise cooperate with us.[84]

Or as Köprülü elegantly explained to the US embassy, "if Libyans can be prevailed upon to move away from spirit of bargaining ... a slight increase in [America's] current offer might well provide a solution."[85]

In the end, despite continuing to push both sides toward concessions, Turkish diplomacy played almost no role in the resolution of this dispute, just as it was of little consequence to the outcome of the Suez Crisis or the Anglo-Iranian oil dispute. Yet an important conclusion nonetheless emerges from the US-Turkish diplomatic exchanges they produced. In all three cases, both American and Turkish diplomats wholeheartedly embraced the idea that Turkey could serve as a bridge between East and West, but interpreted the metaphor in fundamentally different ways. Essentially, American statesmen expected Ankara to use its influence with the Arab world to sell Arab leaders on the

---

[81] Despatch No. 358, May 11, 1954; Despatch No. 520, February 1, 1954. Ibid.
[82] June 16, Tripoli No. 2, ibid.   [83] June 17, 1954, No. 1392, ibid.
[84] June 22, No. 1365, ibid.   [85] June 24, No. 1380, ibid.

desirability of American policies by overcoming Arab concerns about Western imperialism. Turkish statesmen, however, believed that their "bridging" role involved telling Washington that US polices would, if not modified, meet with Arab hostility or rejection, thereby convincing Washington to adjust these policies to win Arab support. In the end, throughout the 1950s, Turkish diplomats proved no more adept at warning Washington about policies that would provoke anti-imperialist sentiment among Arabs than they were at convincing Arabs to accept these policies.

Indeed, at times the DP government acknowledged the limits of their influence in the region just as US diplomats acknowledged the contradictions of Turkey's position there. Following a tour of the Arab world, for example, Köprülü offered an assessment of the strength and limits of Turkish-Arab cultural ties. He said that he had

found a warm and sincere response from Arab leaders. Many were old friends and pupils in his university days. He had spoken to almost all of them directly in Turkish ... He did not pretend, however, that this had any conclusive significance.[86]

American diplomats, in turn, were eager to enhance Turkey's influence in the Middle East but recognized that this might require Turkey taking a more anti-Western position. In 1951, McGhee wrote to US ambassadors in Arab capitals asking what steps Turkey might take to build Turkish prestige. In response to this query, the US ambassador to Saudi Arabia explained that the Turkish Government "should not endeavor to approach the Arabs as agents of the West, they must identify themselves with the interests of the area."[87] The ambassador from Syria, meanwhile, suggested that the United States

encourage the Turks to greater latitude than previously in [regard to issues such as] Palestine, Tunisia, Suez, etc. If occasionally they do not vote with us at UN, and vote with the Arabs, it could do much to improve their prestige and counteract the charge, not commonly believed, that they are America's "stooge." I remember the Suez issue for example, the Turks firmly believed the UN resolution was against their and our interests in the Middle East, but because their vote was needed to carry the day and because they wanted to

[86] General Records of the Department of State. Misc. Lot Files, Subject Files relating to Turkey, Box 1, RG 59, NARA.
[87] American Embassy Jidda Saudi Arabia, October 28, 1952, *George C. McGhee Papers*, Georgetown University Library Special Collections. Series XXIV, Box 1.

defer to our wishes, they voted against the Arabs. That one vote caused their prestige heavy damage in Arab circles.[88]

Paradoxically, while the Americans were at times eager to have Turkey act so as to appear in greater solidarity with their Eastern neighbors, Turkish leaders remained worried even after becoming full members of NATO, that their efforts to do so might prove too successful. At the same time Turkish diplomats stressed their cultural ties to the Middle East in conversations with Americans and Middle Easterners alike, they also worked hard to ensure that in their diplomatic relations with the countries of the region they would appear as full partners of the Western powers. Not only did they seek to ensure that their relations with Middle Eastern states would not make them appear more Middle Eastern themselves, they also saw that these dealings could represent an opportunity to present themselves as more Western.

Perhaps the most concise statement of this dynamic came in a State Department memorandum prepared before the visit of the Libyan Prime Minister in 1954:

Turkey [has] hosted leaders of a number of European countries .... This aspect of Turkey's aggressive and alert foreign policy has enabled her to make progress toward goal of identifying herself as the ally, and not subordinate, of the leading powers. Recently then, Turkey has felt herself to be in a position of demonstrating readiness to lend a hand to the smaller and less powerful countries. [The PM's visit] is an example of the latter attitude.[89]

In discussing the Middle East Command, US officials took it as given from the very outset that this attitude would govern Turkey's approach. An early memo on the subject, for example, stated: "Turk Govt will be prepared to cooperate in any MEC organization jointly agreed between U.S., UK and French Govts provided Turk Govt participates in that command on equal footing with those three powers."[90]

When the DP government gradually closed ranks behind the United States and Britain during the course of the early 1950s, the opposition began to criticize its policy using many of the same anti-imperialist arguments DP diplomats had privately made to Americans. Writing for

---

[88] American Embassy Damascus, October 7, 1952, ibid.
[89] Despatch No. 11, July 8, 1954. Visit of Libyan Prime Minister to Turkey, Classified General Records, U.S. Embassy, Ankara, Box 63, RG 84, NARA.
[90] September 18, No. 261 to Secstate, Washington, ibid.

a leading CHP paper in 1956, for example, Bülent Ecevit penned a series of columns articulating a foreign policy vision that was highly critical of Arab support for the Soviet Union, but also critical of the Turkish government's deference to Western interests. In fact, Ecevit suggested that in uncritically supporting Britain and America, the government was undermining Turkey's security by pushing the Arabs states into Moscow's arms. Instead, he suggested, Turkey could provide the Arab world a model of non-Communist resistance to colonialism, adding that if the Arabs could learn from Atatürk's example they could free themselves from Europe's grasp without falling into Soviet hands.

Ecevit's analysis, like that of Washington and Ankara, took for granted that the Soviet Union was trying to penetrate the Middle East by exploiting Arab hostility to Western imperialism and Israel. Noting that in recent years this hostility had been "revived in the Arab mind," Ecevit claimed the primary reason was surely Communist propaganda but that Turkish policy had helped lay the foundation for its success. To "erase" Arab "suspicion," Ecevit concluded, Republican Turkey should stay out of Arab affairs and "behave more independently [*müstakil hareket etme*] from our Western friends." He argued consistently that while Turkey could have engaged with the Middle East as a "regional power" or "not engaged at all" the DP government had instead chosen the worst option – of "engaging as a representative of western powers."[91]

As soon as Turkey became a NATO member, it took an interest in the internal affairs of the Arab world. Heedless of the future, it acted in the manner assumed to be of greatest benefit to its Western allies, especially England. In time it began to gain a reputation in the region as the representative of its Western allies who were regarded as "imperialists."[92]

Yet this approach had already begun to backfire:

Turkey became the nearest target of the negative feelings that the Arabs, rightly or wrongly, felt towards our Western allies. Above all, even when the Arabs struggled to secure their legitimate rights inspired by our own War of Independence, Turkey, for fear of offending our ally France, remained indifferent, and even openly opposed them. In doing so Turkey once again fanned

---

[91] "Türkiye'nin hatası," *Ulus*, December 1, 1956.   [92] Ibid.

the fears and suspicions directed against us. And all of this eased the Soviet's task in provoking the Arab world against us.[93]

It was a theme Ecevit returned to in successive articles, emphasizing that the DP's approach was harming not just Turkey but the Western alliance more broadly.[94] In line with this analysis, Ecevit went further in suggesting that by not siding with imperialist powers America too could gradually begin a profitable long-term strategy of winning Arab confidence and even friendship. But this critique did not necessarily imply full sympathy with Arab behavior. During the Suez crisis, he spelled out this view most explicitly:

We cannot praise Israel for its assault [*tecavuz*] against Egypt. But this does not mean we must be sorry for Egypt that it suffered an assault. We cannot excuse England and France for dismissing the United Nations and using force against Egypt. But this does not require us to see Egypt as a victim. England and France and Israel might be unjustified [*haksız*]. But this does not make Egypt justified.[95]

The problem, he explained in another article, was that every Arab leader wanted to be an Atatürk but they failed to truly understand Atatürk's example.[96] Men like Nasser only "saw what Atatürk had accomplished" but not the "behavior through which he accomplished it." In the case of Suez, for example, Ecevit explained that Nasser's aims were eminently justified but his methods were problematic. He did not follow Atatürk's "realist" [*realist*] and "honest" [*dürüst*] behavior. Atatürk, for example, sought full Turkish sovereignty over the Bosporus, but he "waited patiently for many long years ... and after that not with a unilateral and dramatic decision but by persuading all the interested states at an international conference claimed sovereignty over the straits." In this manner, Ecevit concluded, he secured "a legitimacy for Turkish sovereignty about which no friend or enemy could have the least doubt."

In essence, Ecevit's critique of DP foreign policy was that in allying too closely with the West, the government made it harder for the Arabs to find their inner Atatürk. And of course, in doing so the DP also

---

[93] Ibid.　[94] "Tutulacak Yol" *Ulus*, December 4, 1956.
[95] "Suçlu Kim?" *Ulus*, November 4, 1956.
[96] "Atatürk ve Atatürkler," *Ulus*, November 10, 1956.

betrayed the spirit of the Turkish nation as embodied by Fatih Sultan
Mehmet and Suleiman the Magnificent as well:

In the era lasting from Fatih Sultan Mehmet's coronation to Suleiman the
Lawgiver's death ... the Turkish nation struggled to unite East and West and
bring all nations into a state of being able to live together ... In that era if you
had asked the Turkish nation "why are we here" it would have been in
a better position to answer than any other nation ... Today, the elements
giving meaning and value to our existence as a nation are opening the road to
uniting the two separate realms of East and West by removing the East-West
divide in our own national life, being an example for the whole Middle East
by strengthening the concept of individual freedom on our own territory, and
defending the rights of nations who are fighting for independence.[97]

Concluding Cartoons

Both DP leaders and their opponents shared a complex and sometimes
contradictory set of anti-imperial instincts, anti-Soviet fears, and anti-
Arab prejudice. Alongside the debates discussed earlier, political cartoons from the era provide a remarkable record of the way prejudices
could be adapted to help reconcile anti-imperialism with Turkey's
newfound need to cooperate with European imperial powers against
the Soviet Union. Indeed, these cartoons illustrate the way Turkish
perceptions of the Arab world changed in response to changing geopolitical circumstances. In a cruel and colorful way, cartoons are ideally
suited to showing the ugliness of prejudice alongside its surprisingly
supple character. The pages of *Akbaba*, Turkey's most popular and
widely read satirical magazine from the 1930s through the 1950s, offer
a visual record of Turkish anti-imperialism, as well as the sympathy
Arabs received when they appeared as victims of imperial powers. Yet
Akbaba's cartoons also show how, in the 1950s, this sympathy turned
into hostility and how effectively the reserve of anti-Arab prejudice
could then be mobilized as Arab governments grew increasingly pro-
Soviet. When viewed as Russia's accomplices rather than Britain's
victims, downtrodden Arabs quickly turned into camels, caged birds,
and drunken women.

Many *Akbaba* covers from the 1930s and 1940s display the magazine's resolute anti-imperialism. In one, from 1935, an outsized Italian

[97] "Niçin varız," *Ulus*, August 26, 1955.

soldier in a gas mask carrying a host of modern weaponry bears down on a crudely caricatured Ethiopian with a spear declaring, "We are bringing civilization to Africa."[98] Another showed a similar scene with the caption: "Savage – 'Look Out! The savages are coming.'"[99] Following news of a revolt in Egypt the same year, one cover featured a pipe-smoking, slightly porcine Britain, sitting uncomfortably on the point of a pyramid and saying, "[The sun] is beginning to set here too?"[100]

Yet though these cartoons target European imperial powers, the victims are either elided or treated dismissively. Some cartoons about Palestine, for example, target British hypocrisy, while many are viciously anti-Semitic. Few, however, offered much direct sympathy for the Palestinians.[101] In one of the more sophisticated examples, a British soldier spots a Jew and an Arab arguing over a camel. He chases them both off, then calmly steals the camel. In a more typical example, a Jewish merchant implores an Arab, "Hajji Efendi, if you are going to burn Jewish villages at least buy the matches from us."[102] Moving into the 1950s, cartoons dealing with French rule in North Africans continued this approach. France is condemned, but the region's residents are often absent: one cartoon shows France urinating on "human rights," another shows a gun-toting French soldier posing for a "souvenir" photograph over the body of a dead Moroccan.[103]

Yet this attitude still stands in dramatic contrast to treatment directed at Arab states and leaders who drew closer to the Soviet Union in the mid- to late-1950s. In 1954, news that Egypt would seek greater cooperation with Russia prompted a cartoon of a bear leading a scantily clad woman labeled "modern Cleopatra" into his lair.[104] In 1955, Nasser's call for an Arab union was met with an *Akbaba* cover showing Arab leaders gathered together inside a giant red sickle.[105] Reports, in 1955, that Egypt, Syria, and Saudi Arabia would seek to form a joint Arab army were followed by a cartoon showing the three countries riding a camel with a Russian military cap and the face of a Russian soldier.[106]

[98] *Akbaba*, Issue 62, Cover, March 7, 1935.
[99] *Akbaba*, Issue 78, Cover, June 29, 1935.
[100] *Akbaba*, Issue 98, Cover, October 23, 1935.
[101] *Akbaba*, Issue 244, page 10, September 8, 1938.
[102] *Akbaba*, Issue 121, page 3, May 2, 1936.
[103] *Akbaba*, Issue 298, page 4, November 28, 1957.
[104] *Akbaba*, Issue 103, page 2, March 4, 1954
[105] *Akbaba*, Issue 160, Cover, April 7, 1955.
[106] *Akbaba*, Issue 159, Cover, March 3, 1955.

Throughout this period, gradually intensifying prejudice was still deployed according to the political events of the day. In October 1956, for example, amidst sympathetic Turkish coverage of the Suez crisis, Nasser appeared as a triumphant acrobat astride two gape-mouthed lions marked Russia and the United Kingdom.[107] By January 1957, however, Egypt appeared as a much darker-skinned beggar sitting under a palm tree holding his hands out for US and Russian aid. As Nasser became more pro-Soviet and more successful in his promotion of Arab unity, the Turkish satirical press became consistently the harsher in its caricatures. A cover (see Figure 6.1) from December 1956 showing Khrushchev leading prayers in Cairo's Al Azhar mosque is relatively tame.[108] Others from the following years depicted Russia leading Egypt and Syria in the form of a caravan of camels or a file of chador-wearing wives.[109] A cartoon from 1958 featured the Egyptian-Syrian Union as a windup dancing doll being ogled by Russia.[110] When Egypt and Syria invited other states to join, a cartoon showed the two inside a birdcage, with Russia calling out, "[H]ere little bird."[111]

Not surprisingly, amidst all this, the most vicious cartoons were reserved for Syria when Turkish-Syrian relations reached the brink of war in 1957. An *Akbaba* cover from November of that year shows Syria as a small dog barking at the Turkish moon as Khrushchev orders him to fetch.[112] Another cartoon from the same issue shows Russia riding a bridled man with distinctly African features labeled "Syria." Yet another shows Syria as a woman, partially naked, in the arms of a drunk Russian soldier pointing off toward a distant Turkey and saying, "[H]elp me friends, Turkey is going to molest me."

Taken together with diplomatic records, these cartoons help make the case that popular anti-Arab sentiments were as much a product of Turkey's foreign policy as they were a driver of it. As historical and geographical realities pushed Turkey and its Arab neighbors into different geopolitical camps, Turks invoked well-established but previously dormant prejudices accordingly. By the end of the 1950s,

---

[107] *Akbaba*, Issue 241, Cover, October 25, 1956.
[108] *Akbaba*, Issue 249, Cover, December 19, 1956.
[109] *Akbaba*, Issue 259, page 7, February 28, 1957. Issue 513, page 9, March 13, 1958.
[110] *Akbaba*, Issue 310, page 7, February 20, 1958.
[111] *Akbaba*, Issue 312, page 5, March 6, 1958.
[112] *Akbaba*, Issue 296, Cover, November 14, 1957.

anti-Arab prejudice had replaced anti-imperialist sympathy as Arabs found themselves on the wrong side of Turkey's Cold War.[113]

The strength of Turkish anti-imperialism during the 1950s, as manifested in ambassadorial meetings and popular cartoons, deserves attention in part because of the lingering impression that Turkish policy during this decade reflected an excessively pro-Western instinct that constantly prioritized the interest of European colonial powers over those of colonized Middle Easterners. In the context of both popular anti-imperial sentiment and privately expressed views however, Turkey's policies must be understood as the result of conscious decisions to prioritize interests over instinct. In this there was a clear parallel to US statesmen from the same period who, as has been amply documented, often found their own anti-imperial inclinations in conflict with the policies seemingly forced on them by their Cold War alignment of interests with Britain and France.

In Turkish foreign policy during the 1950s, history and geography played a contradictory role. Ankara could capitalize on the nostalgia even Hashemite rulers felt for Istanbul but, as Köprülü discovered, being able to speak Turkish with Arab leaders who were once his students hardly guaranteed any diplomatic breakthroughs. More than anything, it seems to have been a shared experience with Western colonialism that gave Turkish diplomats their most relevant, if seldom heeded, insights into Arab political sensibilities. Yet when these same diplomats found themselves forced to choose between anti-imperialism and their immediate interests, they consistently sided with the imperial powers.

The paradoxes that emerge in Turkey's relations with Middle Eastern states help reveal how ambiguity can give ideas their diplomatic relevance. In the case of NATO, as the alliance lost its geographic character to become a collection of those countries that the United States was genuinely committed to defend, this made non-Atlantic Turkey's membership suddenly appear imperative. Likewise,

---

[113] In 1961, amidst renewed Turkish-Syrian tensions over Hatay, *Women's Newspaper* editor İffet Oruz recalled her 1951 trip to Aleppo in very different terms than she reported it then. In 1951, she had reflected on the deep cultural and familial ties between Turkey and Syria and called for greater cooperation against imperial powers. Her glowing 1951 account discussed the warm welcome she received and had made no mention of the Hatay dispute. But in 1961, her recollections were focused entirely on how rude and aggressive her hosts had been on the subject.

Figure 6.1 "Imam and Congregation in Egypt's Al Azhar Mosque." *Akbaba*, 1956.

speculation about Turkish psychology served to bolster or challenge the case for Turkey's NATO membership in unexpected, seemingly contradictory ways. The Turks' commitment to fighting the Russians could be used to build an argument against including them in the alliance, while Ankara's evasive performance in the World War II could be used to conclude that Turkish membership was all the more necessary.

The claim, in 1950, that Turkey was a Middle Eastern power would have had a different meaning from the syntactically identical claim that Great Britain was a Middle Eastern power. The first could be taken to imply Turkey was, in some fundamental sense, Middle Eastern, while the second implied that Great Britain exercised power in the Middle East. Though often unsuccessful, Turkish diplomats did their best to treat this ambiguity as an asset rather than an obstacle in dealing with their partners in the West and their neighbors to the South and East. In discussions with Middle Eastern states, Turkish rhetoric emphasized their shared history – without, of course, mentioning who exactly had been ruling over whom while this history was being shared. At the same time, Turkish leaders also worked hard to ensure that in diplomatic dealings involving Western powers and Middle Eastern states, Turkey was acting as a full partner in the Western alliance.

Finally, on the subject of Turkey's geographic and historic identity, Turkish and American statesmen derived maximum benefit from exploiting the possibilities inherent in ambiguity. Diplomats from both countries could promote Turkey as a bridge between East and West in contradictory ways, just as US diplomats could push Turkey to be more Middle Eastern in order to better serve Western interests. And as the political logic of the Cold War eventually forced Turkey to pick sides, the malleable nature of prejudice helped reconcile Turkey's anti-imperialist instincts with its support for Western imperial powers.

7 | *The Path to Progress and to God*
Islamic Modernism for the Cold War

After a century of Westernization, Turkey has undergone immense changes – greater than any outside observer had thought possible. But the deepest Islamic roots of Turkish life and culture are still alive, and the ultimate identity of Turk and Muslim in Turkey is still unchallenged. The resurgence of Islam after a long interval responds to a profound national need. The occasional outburst of the *tarikas*, far more than the limited restoration of official Islam, show how powerful are the forces stirring beneath the surface. The path that the revival will take is still not clear. If simple reaction has its way, much of the work of the last century will be undone, and Turkey will slip back into the darkness from which she so painfully emerged. But that is not the only way, nor the most probable. In Turkey, as in other Muslim countries, there are those who talk hopefully of achieving 'a synthesis of the best elements of West and East.' This is a vain hope – the clash of civilizations in history does not usually culminate in a marriage of selected best elements, rather in a promiscuous co-habitation of good, bad, and indifferent alike. But a true revival of a religious faith on the level of modern thought and life is within the bounds of possibility. The Turkish people, by the exercise of their practical common sense and powers of improvisation, may yet find a workable compromise between Islam and modernism that will enable them, without conflict, to follow both their fathers' path to freedom and progress and their grand-fathers' path to God.

– Bernard Lewis, 1952[1]

So wrote historian Bernard Lewis, evaluating the state of religion in Turkey after the country's first full year as a multiparty democracy. In what appears to be his first published reference to the "clash of civilizations," he seemed to be suggesting that Turkey might be on track to resolving it. Through an extended marital metaphor, Lewis argued that

---

[1] Bernard Lewis, "Islamic Revival in Turkey," *International Affairs* Vol. 28, No. 1 (January 1952), p. 48. Reprinted in *The Emergence of Modern Turkey*, p. 424.

while the "clash" of Eastern and Western civilization, and by extension faith and modern thought, would not result in a "synthesis" of their "best elements," the "promiscuous cohabitation" that could stand in for this implausible "marriage" might at least be a "workable compromise" and, crucially, one "without conflict." In short, on a continuum between "clash" and "synthesis," Lewis thought it entirely possible that the outcome of Turkey's attempted mediation between Islam and modernism would be something much closer to the latter.

Lewis's cautious optimism reflected the belief of many at the time that Turkey was on the verge of transcending a long-standing but ultimately false division between religion and modernity. Thinkers from across the political spectrum disagreed on what this would mean in practice, but they shared a belief that reconciling Islamic piety and Western modernity was eminently achievable. Following the contours of their mid-century debate over faith and secularism – seeing where rival thinkers agreed and disagreed, as well as the rhetorical strategies they used – can help us better understand similar debates today.

Recent scholarship has often implied that the Islamism of the Justice and Development Party (AKP) represents the contemporary manifestation of a popular religiosity suppressed by the authoritarian modernization of the Kemalist regime.[2] In doing so, it explicitly contrasts an "alternative modernity" emerging from the late Ottoman period with the deterministic narrative of Western modernization implicit in Kemalist historiography. This approach to Turkish politics and history relies on the idea of a "popular" Islamic sentiment or practice in Turkey that Kemalist modernizers sought to extinguish, but that subsequently found expression in grassroots resistance to Kemalism. Thus the triumph of the Democratic Party (DP) in 1950 was a first step toward the contemporary emergence of this repressed religious consensus.

Yet this argument is itself dangerously deterministic and also misrepresents the extent to which Kemalists or Western historians ever believed in the vision of modernity they are now said to embody. Taking the religious debates of the 1950s on their own terms forces us to confront the fact that many people writing at the time thought society had already moved past simplistic binaries pitting religion,

---

[2] See, for example, Gavin Brockett's *How Happy to Call Oneself a Turk* (Austin: University of Texas Press, 2011), as well as the historiographical discussion in the Introduction.

particularly Islam, against modernity. If some of Turkey's early Westernizers truly believed that "Islam and modern life could not be reconciled," this was a minority view in postwar Turkey.[3] Today, when we contrast "alternative," "Islamic," or "non-Western" visions of modernity with a crude form of outdated high-modernism, we are merely rediscovering an insight that already seemed obvious to many self-proclaimed modernizers more than half a century ago. Reading postwar scholars wax optimistic about Turkey's emerging form of authentic religious modernity, it is hard not to look back with discouraged humility and ask what went wrong.

This chapter explores the religious transformations that occurred in mid-century Turkey by examining the efforts of Turkish thinkers at the time to present their country's ongoing or hoped-for religious revival in a global context. The majority of those advocating a greater role for religion in society at the time positioned themselves not only as part of a domestic response to several decades of official secularism, but also as part of a much broader trend, specifically a newfound sense of world-wide spirituality that could also be clearly seen in the Christian West. Religious thinkers – including those condemned as "reactionaries" – attributed this spiritual rebirth to a range of modern factors, including World War II, the Cold War, the Atomic Age, and recent scientific breakthroughs. In claiming they were responding to a widespread global disillusionment with positivism, these thinkers insisted, either explicitly or implicitly, that Turkish society was sufficiently modern to experience the same crises of modernity as Europe and America.

In this context, religious writers claimed that their promotion of faith was not "reactionary" but rather a move toward an even more contemporary appreciation for the role of spirituality in the world. While often explicitly rejecting a model of religious reform rooted in the Protestant reformation, they remained open to finding spiritual insights in the writing of postwar Christian thinkers, insisting that Turkey could emulate their recommendations in developing a more harmonious and modern relationship with the Islamic faith. That is, one of the aspects of Western or Christian modernity these thinkers took the most interest in was its spiritual response to the limits of traditional modernity itself.

---

[3] M. Şükrü Hanioğlu, "Garbcılar: Their Attitudes toward Religion and Their Impact on the Official Ideology of the Turkish Republic." *Studia Islamica*, No. 86 (1997). 141.

In short, by the 1950s, a wide range of Turkish thinkers believed that their country had become modern enough to participate in a global crisis of modernity. They believed that Turkey needed to harmonize religion and modernity, which were already fundamentally in harmony. This required secularists to stop hiding behind the mask of secularism in order to better understand the true nature of Western modernity and Islamists to stop hiding behind the mask of religion to better understand the true nature of Islam. This, in turn, would help Turkey become more Islamic and therefore more like the West, which was rapidly becoming more Christian.

Secularism, Religion, and the Communist Threat

Both in the 1950s and today, many have assumed that religiosity was either a natural or politically calculated response to the threat posed by "Godless Communism." Yet this was far from obvious to committed secularists at the time. To the contrary, at the outset of the Cold War, some Turkish politicians were quick to make the opposite case, claiming that the Soviet threat necessitated extra vigilance against religious reaction lest "communism enter Turkey under the banner of Mohammad."[4] In parliamentary debates and the popular press, particularly during the late 1940s, many individuals expressed the fear that Communism and religious fundamentalism were working hand in hand to destroy Turkey. At the same time, the Cold War conflict with Communism led some Kemalists to try to rearticulate their vision of secularism in terms of religious freedom rather than positivism and increasingly try to spell out what a sincere version of "secular Islam" would look like in practice. This was an alternative to both those who thought the Communist threat required Turkey to double down on traditional secularism and those who thought it called for a more conservative form of religiosity. In other words, understanding Turkey's 1950s religious revival in its Cold War context requires us to first recognize that the Cold War potentially provided the rationale for diverse religious responses, of which some proved more popular than others.

---

[4] Interior Minister Şükrü Saraçoğlu, quoted in Eşref Edip "Hükümetin Programı ve Ezan Meselesi," *Sebilürreşad*, May 1950, Volume IV, no. 80.

Recep Peker, the preeminent representative of the Republican People's Party (CHP) old guard, led the way in rejecting any Cold War concessions to religiosity. Delivering a speech before the Turkish parliament in 1945, Peker came out emphatically against a proposal for "teaching religion as an antidote to Communism." Religion, he claimed, was "too dangerous" and the "risk of exploitation" too high to take such a gamble.[5] Peker argued that relying on religion as a means of "protecting our structure from this social poison [Communism], is more or less similar to believing that a deadly poison can be cured by another poison at least as deadly."[6]

Peker did not, however, restrict his arguments about religion to Islam. Like many others arguing about the role of Islam in mid-century Turkey, he freely invoked examples of Christianity in the West as relevant to the broader question of religion in society.

It is entirely incompatible with the facts of the present day to claim that a Moslem who is pious, and loyal to all spiritual principles, cannot be a Communist, or that any religious creed can assure resistance to communism. Are not the Greeks of today pious orthodox Catholics? Yet look at the effect of communist movements in Greece today. Was not Spain, which only yesterday was the scene of great bloody adventures, a country influenced by the Church? Did this creed carry any definite worth as regards preventing Communism ruining the country in many parts?[7]

Peker then concluded by saying that Turkey stood on a plateau: "This plateau has precipices in front, behind, on its right and on its left. The one on our left is red, while the one on our right is the precipice of black and dark retrogression."

As discussed in this chapter, the coming decade would prove that the majority of Turkish voters, and even the majority of those in the CHP, disagreed with Peker. Many were in fact troubled by the lack of religious feeling and thought that the time to address it had already come. But if, in hindsight, Peker's argument appears as a rear-guard action against changing public opinion, at the time it nevertheless represented an important strain of Kemalist thinking. Alongside Peker's insistence on the continued need for strict secularism, one of the best indications of how deeply entrenched this view was in the

[5] *Ulus*, December 25, 1945. U.S. Embassy Press Reports, Unclassified General Records, U.S. Embassy, Ankara, Box 92, RG 84, NARA.
[6] Ibid.   [7] Ibid.

traditional Kemalist establishment comes from a secret report on the Communist menace conducted by Turkish security services and provided to the American Office of Strategic Services in 1945.[8] The report begins by arguing that "Soviet activity in the Near East presents a special problem because these nations are Moslem, and the Moslem religion is like that of the Jews in that it has somewhat of a socialist basis." The only thing mitigating this concern, the report suggests, is the fact that "[u]ntil recently there have not been many people who have had an understanding of Mohammedanism and Communism at the same time."[9] After laying out this fundamental resonance between Islam and Communism, the report then goes on to discuss specific aspects of the Communist threat in terms echoing the Kemalist language about religious reaction. Explaining the totalitarian ambitions of the Soviet government, for example, the report states, "Those who have lived in Turkey during the period of the Red Sultan, Abdul Hamit, know this form of government very well." More explicitly, youthful recruits to the Communist cause are compared to dervishes, "monks of a Moslem Monastery" in the translator's term.

The presumed link between Islam and Communism was reflected in newspaper and academic debates as well. A full-page cartoon from the magazine *Diken* shows an individual dressed in the stereotypical costume of a religious reactionary but labeled "Communism" standing outside the gates of a heavily guarded fortress labeled "Turkish Republic."[10] In the caption, he says, "I wonder if I can get in without revealing myself." Foreign observers also commented on the link between Communism and excess religiosity as well. Lewis, for example, wrote in 1951:

How far the religious revival is in fact an insurance against Communism is a subject of some discussion. The accusation is often made, in secularist quarters, that the revival, at least on the level of popular, dervish religion, is inspired by Communist agitators.[11]

---

[8]　John Megaw to Richard Gnade, October 9, 1945. Ankara Embassy, General Records, 1943–1949, Box 92, RG 84, NARA.

[9]　What's more, "in the Arabic countries with their low standard of culture and in countries with a Persian tongue Soviet Russia has always been regarded as a European Nation."

[10]　*Diken*, November 20, 1947.

[11]　Bernard Lewis, "Islamic Revival in Turkey."

Moreover, these same observers found such accusations credible. Lewis continues:

The Anatolian brotherhoods have in the past been no strangers to a form of primitive religious communism which clever propagandists might exploit for political ends. Developments in other Muslim countries show that Communism is not averse to collaborating with movements of mass fanaticism.[12]

In the early 1950s, it soon became clear that the majority of the Turkish people, as well as the Turkish government and many Americans, felt that religion, of the right sort at least, should be mobilized as an antidote to Communism. But this was not a universally and immediately apparent response to the outbreak of the Cold War. Rather, it likely reflected their own views and preferences about the role of religion in society.

Modern Islam for a Modern Turkey

In writing about religion in postwar Turkey, Turkish and foreign observers alike consistently identified a trend toward religious revival. While noting fears about the danger of "religious reaction," the majority agreed that, completely independent of concerns about Communism, this revival was a healthy and timely corrective to the perhaps necessary but nonetheless extreme strictness of early Kemalist secularism. Western scholars viewed Turkey's religious revival as natural and implicitly assumed that modernity was perfectly compatible with religious piety. As in US assessments of Turkish modernization seen earlier, the fundamentally sound judgment of the Turkish people revealed itself in their desire for modernity and in this case a modern version of their faith.

Noting that with the passage of time many of the religious leaders who had been trained in the late Ottoman era were dying, Western scholars like Lewis, Richard Robinson, and Howard Reed concurred

---

[12] Ibid. Similarly, Richard Robinson noted: "Charges have been made that the Soviet Union is using reactionary Islam as a political weapon to create social unrest. The charge has yet to be documented publicly, but coincidental religious activity of this nature in Turkey, Iran and Pakistan – all apparently aimed at upsetting the status quo – at least arouses suspicion." Richard D. Robinson. "The Lesson of Turkey," *Middle East Journal*, Vol. 5, No. 4 (Autumn, 1951). 424–438.

with their Turkish counterparts that a new emphasis on religious instruction would prevent reactionary forces from filling the void left by two decades of official neglect.[13] In the words of Howard Reed:

For the time being, and probably for all time, conservative, reactionary Islam has not been able to assert itself decisively in Turkish politics. Most Turks want it this way. In the long run, this clear separation between the Turkish state and Islamic religion may encourage the evolution of more mature democratic government and a more profound spiritual development among secularized Turkish Muslims. In dealing with this problem of Islam in its new political and social life, Turkey is answering a crucial question of its modern history. In doing so, it may point a way for other Islamic countries and may contribute toward the creation of a new, vital Islam which can add substantially to its already great heritage and contributions to world culture.[14]

Describing his hope for a "profound spiritual development" that would be fully consistent with secularism, Reed invoked the language of modernity in contrast to reaction and of a "new" faith in contrast to a "conservative one." Yet he identified modernization not with the victory of existing Kemalist secularism, but with the success of the religious revival underway. Reed believed this would happen in tandem with Turkey's evolution into a mature democracy, reinforcing the idea that the culmination of Kemalist reforms would come when they transcended their authoritarian origins. And in his insistence that "[m]ost Turks" oppose "conservative, reactionary Islam" Reed justified his belief that Turkey's innate "popular Islam" was compatible with a fully democratic form of secularism.

Reed articulated this vision of synthesis with specific reference to the way Turkey's new schools for training imams could help overcome the threat of religious reaction. Teachers he spoke to were "confident" in their ability to produce "a new type of rational, scientifically minded, informed imam who can provide intelligent and devout leadership in the villages and towns of Turkey."[15] Reed believed they were off to a "creditable start." The "devout, credulous yet ignorant majority of Turkish citizens" may be tempted by both "fanaticism" or "reaction" on one hand and "disdain, or neglect of religion on the other," he thought. But "most Turks still trust in Allah and are eager to know

[13] Howard A. Reed, "Revival of Islam in Secular Turkey," *Middle East Journal*, Vol. 8, No. 3 (Summer, 1954). 267–282.
[14] Ibid. [15] Ibid.

more about Islam in new ways that the graduates of the Imam-Hatip Okullari may find to tell them." Here too, the neglect of religion is presented as a problem on par with reaction, and the solution is to be found in a specifically modern form of religion taught by men who are both "intelligent" and "devout." Reed worried that the peasant's traditional nature made him susceptible to religious reaction, but he saw the solution not just in modernity but in a modern form of religiosity.[16] Moreover, Reed saw economic prosperity, and even free-market principles, as important elements in this modernization:

In the villages the agricultural boom is revolutionizing rural economy and village life. Many villages which had no hoca or imam, or else acquiesced in an ignorant, frequently fanatical, and slothful imam usually emanating from the Eastern Black Sea region renowned for such Oflu imams, are now able to pay for better qualified religious leaders. The villagers are often aware of the pious frauds which have been inflicted upon them at times and are now demanding and getting better service of new, better educated, and more sincere imams. Many have told me that Islam will flourish now that people have a little economic margin and can live somewhat better than their erstwhile day-to-day struggle for survival.

The conflation of "new," "better educated," and "more sincere" as desired qualities in imams captured a modernist vision that combined piety and rationality.

Western scholars from this period were also eager to challenge Turks and Americans alike whose views on modernization and secularization were too rigid. British historian and noted Turcophile Arnold Toynbee, for example, declared after a 1949 visit to Turkey that he feared the country was "in danger of losing contact with its rich culture of the past." Finding a way to "maintain contact and still move ahead" was one of Turkey's most important challenges.[17] Many argued that if Turkish society had temporarily lost its faith in an initial flurry of positivist over-exuberance, the new faith that reemerged would be a much-improved one, forged on democratic terms. Thus Reed concluded his report on the reasons behind Turkey's religious revival by citing "the frank, general recognition that too much time has gone by without enough attention to these matters," leading to the conclusion that "it behooves individuals and the community to re-evaluate their

---

[16] Ibid.   [17] Quoted in Robinson, "The Lesson of Turkey," 434.

spiritual heritage and rededicate themselves to an Islam which can and should properly demand more of their wholehearted allegiance."

While Western observers supported Turkey's Islamic revival on modernist terms, many Turkish thinkers were eager to engage with the work of Western counterparts who had critiqued the excesses of positivism. Like Christian writers from the same period, they sought to invoke the intellectual founders of Western modernity on behalf of their appeal to faith. In doing so, they presented Turkey's Islamic revival as part of a global trend toward greater religiosity in response to the excesses, or limits, of secularism.

Skimming the Ministry of Religious Affairs' list of 1954 radio broadcasts gives some indication of what religious discussions looked like during this period.[18] Appearing in alphabetical order between C and D, for example, were Cebrail, Celalü'd - Din-i Devvani, Con Devenport, Dr. Conson, Cüm'a Suresi, Darvin, Darüs - Selam, Davud, Dekart, and Duvmetü'l - Cendel. And what did listeners learn about Darwin? He was a man who believed in God and believed that the cosmos was created by him. Just further evidence of the fact that "the Cosmos itself testifies to God's existence."[19]

In fact, many of the Ministry's radio addresses from this period cited Western scholars speaking on the harmony of modernity and faith. They then sought to apply what had been said in a Christian context to the subject of Islam in Turkey. It was an approach that found its most energetic articulation in the official writing of Ahmet Hamdi Akseki, who served as Minister of Religious Affairs under both the CHP government and the DP (he held the post from 1947 until his death in 1951). Akseki provides one of the most concrete examples of the continuity in religious thought between these supposedly contrasting eras and thus serves as a starting point for investigating how the Turkish state, in an official capacity, invoked American scientists, Christian theologians, and Western critiques of materialism to promote the revival of Islamic piety in the postwar era as part of a global phenomenon.

In December 1950, for example, Akseki submitted a report on "Religious Instruction and Institutions" to the new DP prime minister's office. He began by explaining that "[f]rom now on, I assume that the

---

[18] *Radyoda Dini ve Ahlaki Konuşmalar* (Ankara: Örnek Matbaası, 1954).
[19] Ibid., 17.

need for religion will make itself more fully felt and every nation will occupy itself with this more seriously."[20] Before going on to deal with the question of training imams and opening a religious faculty in Turkey, he provided evidence for this assumption: "Here let's take America as an example .... It can be said that in America this attachment to the church grows a little stronger each day." Citing *Time Magazine*, he detailed the rapid growth in the number of Protestant and Catholic churches and churchgoers over the previous decade and a half, as well as the amount of money appropriated for building more. "All of this is clear proof," he concluded, "of how America's religious life is advancing with dazzling speed."[21]

Lest it seem that American examples were invoked simply to protect religious revival in Turkey from accusations of fundamentalism, Akseki's engagement with other Western thinkers shows a deeper desire to integrate Turkey's social and religious experience into a wider understanding of twentieth-century history. Perhaps the most systematic evidence of this appears in the Ministry of Religion's 1950 *Knowledge, Wisdom and Faith according to Scholars and Scientists of the Past Century*.[22] The book is a collection of essays, translated into Turkish, in which Western scientists, historians, sociologists, and psychologists argue for religion's importance in human affairs. In prefacing the work in his introduction, Akseki took the opportunity to present a history of Western thought in which the proponents of Godless materialism had always been challenged by intellectuals who recognized the value of spirituality.[23] Akseki began with the claim that "God and the religious idea" are among the "foundational ideas" that are "born alongside man himself."[24] His essay then wove together the work of thinkers from the Islamic and Christian traditions alike in support of this argument with a particular emphasis on the contemporary geopolitical moment:

As a great Western philosopher said, everything that we love, all of life's sweetness and blessings, could disappear in an instant. The uncontrolled

---

[20] Veli Ertan, *A. Hamdi Akseki: Hayatı, Eserleri ve Tesiri* (Istanbul: Üç Dal, 1966), 76.

[21] Ibid.

[22] M. Rahmi Balaban, editor. *Son Asrın İlim ve Fen Adamlarına Göre İlim, Ahlak, İman* (Ankara: Ministry of Religious Affairs Publications No. 26. New Press, 1950).

[23] Introduction, pages 3–15.   [24] Ibid., page 1.

application of science, intelligence and industrial strength could bring ruin. Such things are possible. There is only one thing in this world that is not possible: to fully destroy the idea of devotion [*tedeyyün*], to remove faith from the heart and discard it. This cannot happen; faith, in spite of everything, will be eternal. This will constitute the clearest proof belying the shocking and perverse ideas of those blind and deaf materialists who cannot see beyond the tips of their own noses, who want to force the force human thought and belief into the realm of living mud.

Following this dramatic preface, Akseki moved on to discuss the "reasons for religion's necessity." After quoting "the French philosopher and famous theologian" Auguste Sabatier, Akseki concluded that "religious feeling is eternal, natural and God-given." He then shifted reference points, quoting the Quran to show that "from the day mankind understood himself" he turned to the prophets to "give meaning to this primitive religious feeling."

Next, Akseki launched an attack on eighteenth- and nineteenth-century atheism: "Wrapping itself in a veneer of science, godlessness increased in severity, spreading in all directions and infecting the enlightened classes like the Spanish flue." Amidst repeated references to the plague-like spread of radical French atheism, Akseki highlighted a number of philosophers who bravely challenged this false belief. In citing European critiques of secularism, Akseki emphasized that in time, materialism actually strengthened religious feeling when it became clear to people that science could not solve everything. "William James expressed this well," he claimed: while science gave us the telegraph, lighting, electricity, and the cure for many diseases, religion brings people "tranquility of mind [*sükunet-i ruh*] and moral balance [*muvazene-i ahlakiye*]," which "for some people are a greater balm than science." Thus in defiance of those who would pit them against each other, "religion and science are two equally important keys for unlocking the secrets of the universe." And if the reader was left in any doubt, Akseki added, "These are the words of Europe's greatest philosophers and scientists. They prove the emptiness of propaganda like 'there is no room for religion in a scientific age.'"

Akseki also addressed the way such claims played out in modern life. Europeans, he wrote, with their long experience of godlessness, worried about the effects of atheism on family life and society: "The tragedies that began with the First and Second World War still continue. Today, every person of sound mind does not hesitate to accept that the root cause of the destruction, of the black nightmare that has descended upon the world, is our loss of spirituality." After discussing the revival of spirituality in America, as well as the appearance of similar movements in France and England, he finished with Soviet Russia as his final example. Communists, like the French revolutionaries before them, tried to destroy God but ultimately realized the error of their ways. Thus after World War II even the Soviet Union "once again sought to preserve its very existence by wrapping itself in religion." In light of the consequences of Godlessness, Akseki concluded, it would be obvious to all open-minded people that a return to religion was necessary to restore international peace and brotherhood.

The content of the diverse pieces that follow Akseki's introduction reflects a mid-century optimism about the compatibility, indeed the mutually reinforcing character, of religion and modern science: "Religious Feeling through the Lens of Experimental Psychology," a five-page summary of William James's *The Varieties of Religious Experience*, Dr. Alexis Carrel's views on the psycho-physiological aspects of prayer, "Religion through the Eyes of a Biologist" by Princeton University Professor Edward Grant Conklin, "Life after Death through the Lens of Physics," Einstein on "The Intersection of Science and Religion," and "A Religious Approach That Will Ensure the Decency of Character" by a professor at the University of Cluj, Romania.

Prefacing any potential sectarian concerns, Akseki explained at the outset that "[n]aturally some of these authors approach the subject of faith with a certain 'bias,' measuring it according to their own sometimes faulty or superstitious beliefs. If this is felt, it is important not to forget these writings pertain to Christianity and the superstitious shape Christianity has taken on." With this in mind, a second section was added to the book with the works of famous Islamic philosophers, of whom Akseki wrote, "[I]n time as mankind considers their arguments with a clear mind, it will adopt Islam." Throughout the text, the translator also offered a running commentary, reinforcing, elaborating, or critiquing the authors' claims from an Islamic perspective. In many cases he simply provided a Hadith or Quranic verse to support an author's argument. The statement "All civilized nations' religions are moral religions," for example, was followed by a footnote quoting a hadith in which Mohammad states, "I was but sent to bring the completion of morality."[25] "Today

---

[25] Ibid., 128.

religious matters cannot be solved with medieval theology" was followed by a note beginning, "In Islam the fruit of knowledge and science is great."[26] In other cases the translator acknowledged points of difference in a conciliatory manner. For example when the same author went on to state that "intelligence is part of the unity of existence ... part of God" the translator pointed out that "[w]hile Islam gives great importance to intelligence, it cannot accept that it is a part of the divine."[27] In another case, an author's unduly dismissive reference to angels prompted the translator to note, "Islam's views on angels are not of the sort that would be rejected by science."[28] Taken together, these frequent annotations suggest the translator's belief that while the differences between Islam and Christianity were real, and should be acknowledged, they are secondary to the shared aspects of human religious experience. Without any obvious change in tone, the translator moved from a footnote reminding readers that "according to the Quran, Allah taught bees their skills through revelation,"[29] to one noting that "[a]ccording to the Quran, Jesus was neither killed nor crucified."[30]

Akseki's thought is of interest for his unique position as the representative of official state Islam under both the İnönü and Menderes governments. But Akseki's eagerness to invoke the West's return to faith and cite Western scholars on the compatibility of science and religion also mirrors that of many privately published religious magazines, both purely devotional and more explicitly political. Alongside the official publications of the Turkish Ministry of Religion, magazines and books put out by privately run presses for popular audiences also contributed to positioning Turkey's religious revival as part of a global and modern trend.

The Light of Islam [İslam'ın Nuru] was one of the magazines to most enthusiastically embrace a self-consciously scientific approach to Islam. Published beginning in 1951 by Ali Kemal Belviranlı, it claimed to be a "religious, scientific, moral and literary magazine" appearing monthly at an affordable price. While it addressed political topics, its main focus was inspirational and devotional writing, as well as meditations on faith and poetry, all intended for an educated audience but not necessarily one with extensive religious training. In laying out the magazine's agenda in one of its first issues, the editors explained that "for every living thing, from mushrooms to people, adaptation [uyuma] is

---

[26] Ibid., 154.   [27] Ibid., 164.   [28] Ibid., 109.   [29] Ibid., 114.   [30] Ibid., 205.

a necessity." In this light, the magazine itself represented an attempt to adapt to the conditions of modern life as laid out by sociology and biology. The *Light of Islam*, the editors explained, "will work within the confines of science and promote Islam in accordance with science and in keeping with our national endeavor."

As promised, scientific motifs and metaphors appeared inside regular devotional features. An article on moral degeneration and regeneration[31] began by explaining that just as "microbes created in a laboratory can lose their ability to infect with the passage of time" people and animals can degenerate morally and physically if they don't live in a "hygienic" and "natural" way. Alongside such passing references were features that, like Akseki's work, enlisted Western intellectuals in defense not of Islam per se but faith more generally. For example, a piece titled "The Century's Men of Science Are Religious," ran alongside another called "Awareness among Enlightened Westerners" [*Uyanmış Garblilerde Dikkat*], which quoted arguments that men like Kepler had used to demonstrate the existence of God.[32] Other articles stressed the compatibility of Islam and scientific knowledge more explicitly. An article titled "Islam and Scientific Knowledge," for example, began by stating that "[t]he Islamic faith was undeniably founded on scientific knowledge [*ilim*]. Its first command begins [with the word] 'read!'" As the article explained, Islam "gives value and importance to all branches of knowledge" and "[i]n the era when Muslims stayed true to this principle and valued knowledge and learning they spread the light of Islam throughout the world."[33]

Writers in *The Light of Islam* also shared Akseki's desire to position the religious revival they were supporting as part of a global response to the shortcomings of modernity. An article titled "Global Issues and Islam," for example, claimed:

We are living in the Atomic Age. Today the world's present accomplishments and tools have reached such a remarkable degree that humanity, the pinnacle of creation, is worthy of being called the conqueror of nature .... Natural forces, created by God in a holy manner, are daily yielding to man's wit and will. Distances have shrunk and continents drawn near one another. Physics' and chemistry's positive discoveries have been given to man's command. .... But in the face of such material wealth and monuments to wealth we do not find ourselves or our world living in peace.[34]

---

[31] *İslam'in Nuru*, Year 1, Issue 4, page 36.   [32] Ibid.   [33] Ibid.
[34] *İslam'in Nuru*, Year 1, Issue 17, September 1952, pp. 28–29.

The solution to this situation, needless to say, could be found in a return to faith.

[Today] humanity is not on the right path. It has fallen into a dangerous state where all those technical and material accomplishments could be erased in a single action .... There are many who seek the cause of this. But we see the cause in two basic factors: lack of faith [*imansızlık*] and social injustice.[35]

Another mainstream reflection of this same discourse came in the magazine *Selamet* or *Salvation*. In discussing the relationship between Islam and science, for example, several articles in the magazine focused on the golden age of Turkish and Muslim scientific achievement. Alongside pieces such as "Scientific Currents in the Umayyad and Abbasid Eras" and "One of the First Independent Universities in the World Was Founded in Istanbul in 1470," other features argued that if after a promising start the "positive sciences" had not been abandoned, "Ottoman-Turkish" scientific life would not stand so diminished alongside that of contemporary nations."[36]

Salvation's coverage also highlighted the global religious context in which Turkish Muslims sought to locate themselves. An article published after Gandhi's death in 1948, for example, and subtitled "the Eastern World's Great Loss," began by describing Gandhi as one of "our century's greatest and most distinctive figures":

He was both a saint and a man of politics, and one of his life's most noteworthy features was his combining and unifying religious life with political struggle. The source of his ideas for seeking personal perfection were diverse, not singular. Just as he took inspiration from within Hinduism, he also took from Islam, Christianity, and European authors like Tolstoy.[37]

That is, in addition to positioning Turkey's experience in a global context, they went one step further in identifying with other non-Western figures, from non-Muslim religious traditions, who had themselves drawn on other traditions to manifest a non-sectarian awareness of global religious currents. Conveniently, in Gandhi's case, this fit nicely with the author's own domestic agenda of integrating religion into politics.

[35] Ibid. [36] Ibid., Issue 10, 1957. [37] *Selamet*, 1948.

A more direct comparison to the Ministry of Religion translation series discussed above comes from a book prepared by *Salvation*'s editor, Ömer Rıza Doğrul. As the son-in-law of the famous poet Mehmet Akif Ersoy and a graduate of Al Azhar University, Doğrul had earned both praise and condemnation for his earlier involvement with translating the Quran into Turkish. In the early 1950s, he set out to translate, less controversially, Henry Link's 1936 work *A Return to Religion* [*Dine Dönüş*].[38] In his introduction, Doğrul praised the book for explaining the lifelong importance of teaching children religion. As a caveat, he added that "of course the writer's focus was on Christianity," but the book was not by any means "Christian propaganda." Rather it would "awaken religious spirit and religious desire" in the presumably Muslim reader. Still, Doğrul included footnotes to "explain the superiority of our own principles." The book would have been even better, he noted, if it had been written about Islam but "we hope psychology will take hold in this country, and people will see Islam accords even better with modern psychology." Doğrul's footnotes indeed served as a running commentary on the superiority of Islam on modernist terms. When Link mentioned historic tensions between science and Christianity, for example, Doğrul added that while this applied to Christianity, it was necessary to distinguish Islam because Islam "encouraged scientific discoveries in all fields ... and commands Muslims to serve science."[39] When Link offered tips for living a successful life based on the psychological traits Jesus exhibited, Doğrul noted, "For us the best example in this regard is our Prophet Mohammad. We encourage our readers to learn about his life."[40]

It is impossible, absent more detailed evidence about circulation statistics, to evaluate which of these magazines were the most popular or, absent written responses from readers, truly understand how their

---

[38] Henry Link, *Dine Dönüş* (Istanbul: Ahmet Halit Kitabevi, 1949).

[39] Ibid., 2. Taking this argument one step further, an article for *Religious History World* [*Din Tarihi Dünyası*] suggested Christian intellectuals fell into "profanity" and "error" because they were smart enough to reject their own irrational faith but not courageous enough to embrace Islam: "A literate Westerner would have his faith shaken encountering the discrepancies and irrational contradictions in his sacred books with this belief ... If he had not feared learning about Islam, he could have achieved a scientific and investigative faith." Issue 2, page 14.

[40] Ibid., 83.

treatment of faith and modernity was received. But the appearance of a similar discourse across a range of the best-known publications from the period (see Figure 7.1) nonetheless remains indicative of the fact that, to whatever extent "mainstream Islam" can be identified or discussed in this period, this appears to be the approach that it took in positioning itself with regard to Western modernity. In the eyes of its promoters, Turkish Islam was not rejecting secularism but, like Western Christianity, experiencing a revival prompted by its society's belated recognition of secularism's limits.

Many elements of this Western-oriented post-positivist approach can be found in publications that both then and today would have been seen as "reactionary." For example, *Serdengeçti*, an Islamist publication whose editor was repeatedly arrested during the 1950s, employed a similar modernist discourse.[41] It is precisely because *Serdengeçti* – the name refers to the designation of Ottoman soldiers resigned to martyrdom – existed beyond the scope of mainstream religiosity that these points of convergence stand out. Tellingly, even those who positioned themselves at the more radical end of the anti-Kemalist spectrum remained discursively committed to a thoroughly "modern" form of their faith compatible with Western secularism as they understood it.

In an early issue, *Serdengeçti* editor Osman Yüksel Serdengeçti identified modernization in the abstract as one of the redeeming elements of Kemalism.

One of the most important successes of the Turkish revolution was to bring an affirmative, dynamic understanding of life to replace the East's static, fatalist worldview ... Asia was the land of a thousand and one nights, Europe the land of Robinson Crusoe. According to one view well-being [*saadet*] comes from chance and the whims of mysterious forces, according to the other men seize it with their own effort. After defeating the nation's enemies,

---

[41] Another striking example comes from İbrahim Kafesoğlu, a conservative thinker famous as a founder of the Turkish-Islamic synthesis: "With Pascal, Einstein and other geniuses we can see their rationality coexisting perfectly well with religion and mysticism [*mistiklik*] .... Has religion disappeared or been eliminated in America or Europe, which have reached the highest point of science and technology? Only Communist Russia has made religion an enemy in the name of science and technology ... The examples of Europe and America show that, along with the development of civilization, religious thought and feeling also develop. This does not hinder scientific and technological progress. If anything, they fill the void these things leave in the human heart with a sublime feeling." Editorial, "Medeniyet Meselesi," *İstanbul*, Volume 1, Issue 10, August 1954.

Figure 7.1 Covers of *True Path, Light of Islam, Serdengeçti,* and *Kemalism, the Reform of Our Religion.*

Mustafa Kemal began a relentless war against the Asian mentality and ideas behind this kind of mysterious chance and fatalism.[42]

In his subsequent critique, he went on to attack contemporary secular Turkish culture for having failed to live up to the modernist promise of the Kemalist revolution.

Everything changed. Just one thing didn't. The mentality. Before long the old eastern laziness and impassivity [*vurdum duymazlığı*] showed itself again. Cafes replaced dervish lodges. Hızır Aleyhisselam's spot was taken by lotteries, horse races and poker tables. Green tombs, closed; blue ticket offices, opened .... To be contemporary or reactionary is a matter of choice ... haven't you seen the mother lifting her child from the cradle then rushing off to buy a lottery ticket for him saying "maybe something will come of it?"[43]

---

[42] "Değişmeyen Zihniyet," *Serdengeçti*, Year 1, Issue 1, April 27, 1947, p. 5.
[43] Ibid.

Figure 7.1 (continued)

"Only the words changed," he concluded, as "old fashioned" terms for fate and destiny like *"Mukadderat," "alın yazısı"* and *"kader"* gave way to new ones like *şans* [chance] and *sürpriz* [surprise].[44]

Serdengeçti built on this critique in much of its commentary, suggesting that in their hyper-Westernization contemporary secularists had failed to grasp the true meaning of West:

The West is not only a world where every misdeed is permitted during carnival, where Mambo maniacs stop passers-by on the streets and youth frothing at the mouth with rock and roll epilepsy stomp about. In the West at the same time Wagner, Mozart, Beethoven and Schumann's kingdom of sound, Goethe, Hugo, and Schiller's literary kingdom command millions . . . . The West is also a land of universities, museums, books, working factories, thinking minds and sweat-covered brows . . . As long as our

[44] Ibid.

understanding of the West remains flawed, we will never get one step closer to it.[45]

Like other religious magazines of the period, *Serdengeçti* positioned itself as supporting a fundamental compatibility between modernity and faith that was rooted in a more accurate understanding of the Western experience. In this effort, *Serdengeçti* relied heavily on the example of the United States. In an article entitled "Americans Are More Muslim than We Are," for example, the author claimed that when Turkey failed to send imams to accompany its soldiers in Korea, "the Americans asked us 'Do you not have a religion? Where are your men of God. We are here in Korea fighting against the Godless.'"[46] Another article discusses the complete freedom and overwhelming respect enjoyed by leaders of all faiths in America, as well as examples of them taking firm stands against social immorality:

Teachers in secular America work together to explain Christianity and Jesus's life … . In America, considered the cradle of religious freedom, everyone expects from others a compulsory respect for their faith, and on holy days would even intervene if someone from another faith took the opportunity to play the piano in their own private apartment.[47]

The article continued in a similar vein, explaining that in America parents begin religious instruction for their children at age four or five, priests give sermons on the television and radio, and every family baptizes their babies without even thinking about the matter of germs.

The essence of *Serdengeçti*'s critique, then, revolved around the fact that instead of appreciating and appropriating the essence of European and American modernity, Turkey had instead fallen victim to the worst sort of cultural imperialism. In this way, it critiqued Kemalist Westernization on both religious and nationalist grounds:

'We lagged behind,' 'we have to become more European,' for these reasons we were going to take science, technology and procedures from Europe.

---

[45] "Garp Nedir, Ne Değildir," *Serdengeçti*, Issue 11, March 27, 1948, p. 1.
[46] "Amerikalılar Bizden Müslümanmış!" *Serdengeçti*, Issue 12, November 1950.
[47] Hikmet Tanyu, "Amerikada Rahipler Bizde Din Adamları," *Serdengeçti*, June 12, 1950. pp. 6–7.

Because these had no nation or nationality. They were the property of all mankind. The doors we closed tightly against political occupiers we opened wide to spiritual imperialists [*manevi emperyalistler*] and cultural colonialists [*kültür istismarcıları*] ... Just as in the past we bowed before Arabs from the desert today we bow in the same way before every plain thing that comes from Europe.[48]

Focusing on America, he went on to complain that when Wendel Wilkie visited Turkey he reported spending a wonderful evening at a reception in Ankara "dancing to American music, drinking English whiskey and eating Russian Caviar." "Why don't we honor a guest the way we would a Turk with Turkish food?" Yüksel asked.[49] In terms that sounded strikingly similar to CHP attacks on Menderes's policies,[50] *Serdengeçti* ultimately critiqued Turkey's relationship with America on nationalist rather than religious grounds:

We have never been against Turkish-American political friendship. We understand the present state of the world. Turkish-American friendship and military cooperation are necessary for our freedom and survival in these circumstances. But this friendship should remain in the political and military, even economic realm. Our criticism is not of guns but of tricks, not of dollars but of bridles. [*silaha değil, külahadir. Dolara değil yularadır.*] Our relations must be pursued with equal rights and equal conditions. We Turks are strange people. We become friends with someone and suddenly we curse, deny and abandon ourselves. We disappear.

[48] "Manevi Emperyalizm," *Serdengeçti*, year 1, Issue 3, September 1947, p. 3. Making the link between religion and nationalism even clearer, Yüksel insisted: "We aren't a nation living in Africa or the Pacific islands who see their first white men in the form of some Christian missionaries."

[49] Ibid.

[50] In a 1955 column titled "How an 'Economic Colony' Happens" but focused as much on culture as economics, Bülent Ecevit argued that the DP's relations with the United States had gone too far toward subservience. The column began with a friend's observation that the staff at the newly opened Hilton Hotel would not take orders in Turkish. In fact, they treated Turkish speakers like "colonial natives [*bir sömürgenin yerlileri*]." Adding that there were storekeepers and drivers who would not take Turkish money, Ecevit recalled the city's Allied occupation after World War I and demanded to know what steps the government was taking to prevent Turkey from becoming an economic colony: "Precautions must be taken against those who want to replace the Turkish language and the Turkish currency in Istanbul, a city that has been ours for 502 years." Bülent Ecevit, "How an 'Economic Colony' Happens," *Ulus*, July 21, 1955.

We allow our friends into our most private places and surrender everything to them.[51]

Turkey's mistake, in essence, had been in appropriating Western materialism rather than Western spirituality.[52]

In Search of a Secular Faith

In this same period, there was also a striking convergence
between supporters of a more conservative religious revival and
a group of thinkers who were seeking a form of faith that was at
once Kemalist and genuinely pious. There was nothing new about
Turkey's most zealous secular reformers claiming to be advocates
of a true or purified Islam, but the 1950s saw a renewed enthusiasm among those who embraced this position in their own
eccentric way.[53]

---

[51] Ibid.
[52] In addition to explicitly embracing a reconciliation of religion and
      modernity, the religious press also embraced stylistic and rhetorical elements
      from the popular press. *Religious History World*, for example, shared the
      sensationalism of *History World*, with pieces on inquisition tortures or "the
      pirate priest" serving to denigrate Christianity and maintain reader interest
      at the same time (*Din Tarihi Dünyası*, Volume 2, page 16). *Light of Islam*, in
      turn, offered cover photos of Istanbul's mosques surrounded by colorful
      floral décor which could be "hung in a home or office, set under glass in
      a frame whose light color would offset the blues of the image" (*İslam'in Nuru*,
      Issue 1, page 43). As the editors noted, "the houses and museums of wealthy
      Americans and Europeans were full" of this style of Islamic design. There was "no
      equal to our national artistic talent anywhere in the world." *Serdengeçti*, like some
      political magazines, had a feature called "Our Humor Page" with brief,
      paragraph-long jokes and anecdotes making fun of rival publications, editors, and
      politicians. In one, a man tells his friend that Hasan Ali Yücel, the Minister of
      Education under İsmet İnönü, had once been a member of the Mevlevi order.
      Implicitly comparing Yücel's perceived lack of integrity and susceptibility to
      political pressure with the Mevlevi whirling dervish tradition, the friend responds,
      "Yes and he still really knows how to turn" (*Serdengeçti*, Year 1, Issue 2,
      May 1947).
[53] Reed, for example, cited a 1925 quote from Inönü in which the Pasha explained,
      "Ten years hence, the whole world, and those who are now hostile to us or who,
      in the name of religion, are anxious because of our policy, will observe that the
      cleanest, purest and truest form of Islam will flourish in our midst. (Prolonged
      applause)." Reed, "Revival of Islam," 270.

In the late 1940s and early 1950s, some Turkish officials remained sufficiently confident in their brand of religiosity that they felt comfortable lecturing the Saudi ambassador on the similarities between Kemalist reforms and Wahabbism:

Parallel with Turkey's social decline, religious scholars descended into indifference and ignorance, truth gave way to superstition, and a set of ignorant individuals inserted themselves between the individual and god. As a result, *tarikats* and a coterie of saints [*evliya*] were popular, and so Atatürk, just like Saudi Arabia, felt the need to eliminate their lodges and tombs. Atatürk in one move separated religion from worldly affairs. After a generation passed religious classes were instituted in primary schools and a Theology Faculty was opened that would provide training suitable to true faith.[54]

Moreover, in this case the speaker reported the ambassador was "remarkably pleased" with his explanations. Similarly, in 1946, Recep Peker voiced his enthusiastic belief in the sublimity of contemporary Kemalist faith:

For one thing it is a self-evident fact that the conception of religion in Turkey has reached the highest peak of sublimity, so much so as to leave no room to look with envy upon the conditions in any other place on earth. Religion has assumed its noblest meaning in Turkey. Religion in Turkey has been cleaned of its character destructive to society, as is still the situation in many places; it has been rendered harmless to society; it is no longer an instrument for low worldly interests, and it has taken its sublime and heavenly place. A citizen's own conscience, his faith and his creed have reached a most sacred stage in unblemished freedom.[55]

In defending this view, Peker went on to offer a telling statement: "In my work in the Council of Ministers or in the Assembly, I do not oppose my colleague sitting next to me who is a pious worshipper" and in turn "my indifference to worship does not bother my colleague."

To date, discussion of such Kemalist religious claims has, understandably, been defined by the fact that at the end of the day men like

---

[54] "Pakistan Gezisi," *Ankara University Faculty of Language, History and Geography Journal*, Volume 8, Issue 3, September 1950. 92/387.
[55] *Ulus*, December 25, U.S. Embassy Press Reports, Unclassified General Records, U.S. Embassy, Ankara, Box 92, RG 84, NARA.

Recep Peker were not interested in praying and, whatever the official quoted above claimed, the Saudi ambassador was most likely not actually impressed by his description of Kemalist Islam. Yet in over-looking the work of those who did take their Kemalist faith more seriously, we ignore the resonance between their efforts and the broader, enduring religious trends of the period.

For a typically atypical and entirely personal version of Kemalist religiosity, consider Ahmet Yaşner's 1949 book *God's Commands and the Creation of Mankind.*[56] The book is resolutely Republican in its framing, published by Inkılap or Revolution press and dedicated to Atatürk's "esteemed spirit." Yet the contents of the book quickly reveal an unexpected synthesis of piety and Kemalist themes. Among other arguments, the author presented a spirited defense of translating the Quran. Claiming that the prophet himself would have praised Atatürk for beginning this effort, Yaşnar argued that expect-ing moral advice from someone who cannot read the Quran is like expecting treatment from a doctor who does not know how to mix medicines. Medicine, he pointed out, does not lose its power when its formula is translated.[57]

Yaşnar was more expansive on the relation between true Kemalist faith, nationalism, and the challenge of maintaining independence in the Cold War era. Arguing that "success in this world is only possible through spiritual purity," a claim for which he later cites Gandhi's success against the English as an example, Yaşnar wrote that the Ottoman Empire was destroyed by "spiri-tual corruption" and "fanaticism," after the "Sultans betrayed Islam." Atatürk, by contrast, was a defender of true Islamic faith, which he restored through his reforms. Thus, he claimed, "Atatürk was an example for all Muslims," as well as "the teacher of revolution and development to all colonized nations." In fact, if not for him "Turkey would have become a slave like other Eastern nations." Now, by preserving a unity rooted in faith and democracy (and Islamic values displayed by Fatih Sultan Mehmet and the prophet himself), "Turkish soldiers and

---

[56] Ahmet Yaşnar, *Tanrı/Allah Buyrukları ve İnsan Alemi* (Istanbul: İnkılap, 1949).

[57] Ironically, while the title of the book printed on the cover refers to god as "*Tanrı*," the title on the interior page refers to "*Allah*," the term that is used throughout the book.

future Mustafa Kemals" have thwarted Russia by making the Bosporus into "a Fortress of the East [Şark Kalesi]."

Despite his wholehearted embrace of Kemalist modernism, Yaşnar also shared the ambivalence about certain aspects of modernity manifest in many other religious publications from the period. In a subsequent chapter, he went on to condemn the possibility of a manned moon-landing, suggesting that having already "ruined earth" mankind should not now "stretch his dirty hand toward the moon" in order to ruin it too. Flying to the moon, he argued, would replicate the folly of the Babylonian King Nimrod, who tried to travel to space in a chariot drawn by ravenous vultures and was punished by God for his arrogance.

A more prominent, though still in its own way eccentric, example of Kemalist piety came from Osman Nuri Çerman's 1957 *Dinimizde Reform Kemalizm*, or *Kemalism, the Reform of Our Religion*. Çerman had been known from 1928 on as an outspoken advocate of religious reform. As a parliamentarian he introduced resolutions on the subject in the early 1950s and in 1956 wrote a book prefiguring much of what would appear in his magazine. And just as his ideas had been largely dismissed in the one-party era, he repeatedly faced prosecution in the 1950s for the suspect nature of his beliefs. Yet despite this, the era of relatively free press, and religious debates flourishing in the 1950s gave him a chance to publicize his ideas in a way that would not have been possible earlier. Indeed, his praise of Menderes and the DP is striking, specifically in that he credits them with giving him the freedom to promote his ideas. For the purposes of this chapter, it is also telling that his fixation with translating the Quran, as well as other elements of his approach, fit so neatly with prevailing religious trends, even as other aspects would prove to be beyond the pale of what anyone at the time would accept as mainstream.

From the beginning when he outlined "Kemalist Islam's Sacred Principles," Çerman insisted what he advocated was "neither a new religion nor the lack of religion."[58] "Whatever is in Atatürk's words is also in the Quran. Without a doubt the sacred principles of Kemalism are a work of divine inspiration." "If Atatürk had not had divine inspiration," he went on, "could Turkey have once again been

[58] Issue 1, December 1957.

a proud presence on the world's stage again after Sevres?"[59] In his defense of the Turkish Quran, for example, Çerman offered many of the same modernist and nationalist arguments as his more traditionally religious contemporaries. In the first two principles for his Kemalist faith, Çerman explained that "worshipping God in the national tongue" will "save and protect the word religion from being a tool or mask for the enemies of Turkish civilization, as well as for treason, hypocrisy, and slavery."[60] At other points he argued that for someone who only speaks Turkish, an Arabic Quran is little more than an idol or totem.[61] If the people wanted to go to San Francisco or London, he asked, and only the theological faculty or our imams knew the route, should they simply tell the people how to get there – that is, preach to them about the Quran – or just give them the map – in this metaphor the Quran itself?

In other aspects, his commitment to a Kemalist faith clearly went beyond mainstream limits, such as conflating the Anıtkabir, Atatürk's burial place, and the Kaaba. In going outside these confines, Çerman perhaps deserves comparison with no one more than his long-time rival Osman Yüksel, the editor of *Serdengeçti*. With the subsequent rise of Turkish Islamism, scholars have often, and understandably, treated explicitly Islamist works like *Büyük Doğu* and *Serdengeçti* as the defining examples of Turkey's 1950s religious revival. Yet at the time it would have been more difficult to identify these publications as harbingers of things to come. These authors represented the Islamist end of a spectrum which also included a range of less politicized devotional magazines and, on the other extreme, more marginal works of Kemalist religiosity. That many of the Islamist papers from the period faced official censorship, of course, makes it difficult to determine how popular their message might have been in a truly free marketplace of ideas. But while we cannot rule out the possibility they would have enjoyed much greater followings, we should not automatically assume this either.

Manifest in the pages of *Serdengeçti*, as well as other religious publications with a more explicitly political line, is evidence of both the editors' financial trouble and their continued frustration with the popularity of mainstream, "immoral" publications. *The Struggle against Communism* [*Komünizme Karşı Mücadele*], a paper that

[59] Ibid.   [60] Ibid.   [61] Ibid., page 13.

combined religious themes with anti-Communist tirades and ads for both *Serdengeçti* and the *Light of Islam*, regularly published plaintive announcements begging readers for support. "Friends," one read, "our magazine is published amidst a thousand indignities," and "in order to continue our mission we need money." Another read, "if you would like us to continue, please pay your debts."[62] Similarly, while *Serdengeçti*'s financial difficulties may well have been connected with its editor's legal troubles, there were also elements of its editorial line that might have rendered it distinctly unpopular. One article, for example, condemned "Ahmets, Mehmets, Ayşes and Fatmas" for their love of cinema. Another denounced Turkish youth for wasting their energy shouting "goal" at a Galatasaray-Fenerbahçe match instead of devoting it to a more noble cause.[63]

In this light, the heated, often personal debate that occurred in the later part of this decade between the editors of *Serdengeçti* and *Kemalism, the Reform of Our Religion*, could be seen as highlighting the degree of common consensus on faith in this period by tracing its outer boundaries. In keeping with the profoundly nationalist tone of both publications, each consistently sought to portray the other as, intentionally or not, aiding Soviet Communism at the expense of the country. Thus *Serdengeçti's* Yüksel suggested that Çerman's secularism was tantamount to Communist atheism, while Çerman, in turn, cited examples from Ottoman history to demonstrate how religious reaction had always helped facilitate Russian expansion. But a more subtle, though ultimately more telling, rhetorical similarity between the two publications appears in the specific language with which they both attacked one another. Consistently, Çerman and Yüksel accuse each other of operating "behind the screen" [*perde arkası*] of their nominal values to ultimately promote a more sinister agenda.[64] Thus Çerman regularly accused Yüksel of operating "behind the screen" of religion to promote a reactionary agenda while Yüksel accused Çerman of operating "behind the screen" of science and modernization to sabotage religion. Each end of the ideological spectrum, in other

---

[62] See for example February 1, 1952 or May 1, 1952.
[63] Year 2, Issue 5, 1948, page 3.
[64] Eşref Edip, the editor of *Sebilürreşad*, would also refer to his opponents as hiding behind the "niqab of secularism." Eşref Edip, "hakka arka çevirenlerin akıbeti," Volume 4, Issue 78, May 1950.

words, nominally supported the same set of values, including both piety and modernity. Ideologues on both sides wanted readers to know that they were not opposed to faith or to science, but rather feared that their opponents were perverting or exploiting one of the two.

Republican feminist rhetoric during this period was also remarkably consistent in presenting authentic Islam as both compatible with and indeed prefiguring their contemporary understanding of women's rights. The writers at the *Women's Newspaper* repeatedly stressed the importance accorded to women in early Islam. One article, for example, announced that at the time of the prophet, "protecting women was seen as a guarantee of social stability" and, "such an elegant social doctrine cannot be found in any other religion or set of beliefs.[65] Another article, on motherhood in Islam, claimed that "Islam recognized women's power as the source of mankind's propagation."[66] As a result, "if its teachings had been followed in past centuries, the Islamic community would be the most advanced, most dazzling in the world."

In accordance with this narrative, writers regularly explained how Islam had departed from this ideal state. One piece argued that political rulers, to escape from the requirements of religion, imposed a number of dictates that had no place in the teachings of Mohammad.[67] Another argued that the persecution of women came from the reaction and superstition that the Ottoman sultanate used as a source of political support.[68] This narrative was evoked most forcefully in reference to women's veiling: "No faith expresses the fact that virtue is found in morality, in the spirit, as well as Islam. Despite this, fundamentalists did not hesitate to draw a dark curtain over these clean souls. And this thing called covering descended like a dark cloud over the Islamic world."[69] The paper presented a number of potential explanations for the initial origins of veiling. One article claimed that in the time of Murat Han, when women walked around uncovered and men would be fined for looking at them, a Turkish tribe entered Ottoman territory

[65] Ziya Çalıkoğlu, "Din Kadını Daima Korumuştur," *Kadın Gazetesi*, June 23, 1952.
[66] Ziya Çalıkoğlu, "İslamlıkta ana ve Kadın Telakkisi," *Kadın Gazetesi*, May 28, 1952.
[67] Aziz Haydar Omur, "Diyanet İşleri Reisi Sayın Hamdi Akseki'den bir Dilek," *Kadın Gazetesi*, August 24, 1947.
[68] "Cumhuriyet Devrinde Türk Kadını," *Kadın Gazetesi*, November 14, 1949.
[69] "Baş Örtüsü ve Boya Meselesi," *Kadın Gazetesi*, March 26, 1955.

whose women were so beautiful local judges made them cover their faces. As a result, covering one's face became a symbol of beauty and "[i]n this way, wearing the veil became a tradition in Turkish lands."[70] Or perhaps veiling, and the separation of men and women, was actually a Byzantine tradition, first encountered by Arabs in the palaces of Damascus. "If it hadn't been for this, the Turks would not have followed this Greek tradition."[71]

In defending women's rights on religious terms, mid-century feminist thinkers reflected many of the core assumptions of Kemalist religious discourse. Not only did they highlight the fundamental compatibility of religion and modernity and stress the superiority of Islam from this perspective, they also invoked nationalism to discredit those whose views on the subject they disagreed with.

Alongside women's role in society, the question of what a modern faith would look like took concrete form in the debate over translating the Quran. As discussed in the first chapter, the Turkish translation of the call to prayer is now widely seen as an example of Kemalist overreach. And yet the idea of translating the Quran into Turkish, which was also considered controversial at one time, has now become widely accepted. While distinguishing between a "translation of the meaning of the Quran" and a translation of the book itself, even the most conservative Turkish Islamists do not object to the existence of translated texts or their use by those who have not had the opportunity to learn Arabic. As discussed in Brett Wilson's "Translating the Quran in the Age of Nationalism," the achievement of this consensus "is remarkable given that, at the dawn of the twentieth century, the vast majority of Muslim scholars considered Qur'an translations to be impossible, impermissible and even impious."[72] In supporting the translation of the Quran for private use while rejecting the use of Turkish translations for public ceremonial purposes, Turkey's mid-century religious press helped solidify this enduring shift.

As Wilson explains, the controversy over producing a state-sponsored Turkish Quran stemmed largely from fears that Atatürk

---

[70] "Türk İslam Kadınları Yüzlerini ne Zaman Örttüler," *Kadın Gazetesi*, May 24, 1947.

[71] Kazım Nami Duru, "Türk Kadını Bilsen," *Kadın Gazetesi*, February 7, 1949.

[72] Brett Wilson, "The First Translation of the Quran in Modern Turkey," *International Journal of Middle Eastern Studies*, Vol. 41, No. 3 (2009), p. 420.

would use this translation to replace the Arabic original in oral readings in the country's mosques. While many supported the idea of a translation that could be read by literate believers, few wanted Turkish to assume a dominant role in religious ritual. As a result, while the idea of a translated Quran had already been accepted, the implementation of this idea remained mired in controversy throughout the Republican period. The debates of the 1950s, by contrast, were shaped by the fact that the Quran was already being translated, and these translations were already selling. At the same time, following the return of the Arabic call to prayer, there was less concern over the government forcing citizens to use the Turkish translation, making its existence less controversial.

In fact, during the course of the 1950s, many publications were already printing translated passages as a regular feature in their pages. The *Light of Islam*, for example, in addition to promising Arabic lessons for children, offered two pages of Quranic verses, translated and explained, at the beginning of every issue. *Salvation* also included a regular feature called "Inspiration from the Quran" with translated Quranic passages, and, in response to a reader's enquiry, recommended a translation entitled *God's Command*. Where decades earlier the Kemalist state had failed in its effort to produce an official Turkish version of the Quran, in the late 1950s subscribers could write to the editor of an independent religious magazine to receive advice on which privately printed translation they should buy.

In this context, many religious publications began calling for the state to take a more active role in policing the spread of unlicensed translations. One of the most striking calls came from *True Path*, which lambasted the government for failing to ensure that new translations were printed with sufficient accuracy and care. The editors argued that "to go along explaining it is impermissible to print the Quran with Turkish letters is to refuse to recognize the legitimate rights of those millions of people deprived of the blessing and opportunity to read the Quran in Arabic."[73] But rather than debate whether the Quran should be translated, the editors of *True Path* were more concerned with ensuring that it was translated properly. Pointing out that in the past the government checked Qurans for accuracy, they called on the Ministry of Education and the Ministry of Religious Affairs to do the

[73] Ibid.

same for Qurans printed in Turkish letters. Specifically, the editors took great offense to the "made up letters and orthographic marks" appearing in unsupervised translations on sale: "Printing the Quran cannot be left to the whims of nature like an ordinary book" [*tabiinin keyfine bırakılmaz*]. Describing the current flood of freely printed Turkish Qurans, the editors declared, "Are they wrong? Right? Are there missing letters? Words? Or entire verses? No one stops to ask."[74]

Not surprisingly, 1950s opponents of translation could also make their case by invoking emerging Western critiques of positivist modernity. Where Republican translation efforts were motivated by the belief that "translation does not involve interpretation and that [the translator's] task is to seamlessly transfer information from one language to another," critics, by contrast, cited the "contemporary axiom that every translation is an interpretation."[75] Writing in *Turkish Thought*, for example, İbnutayyar Semahaddin Cem claimed that the Quran's contemporary translators displayed an even greater arrogance than those who translated Western literature.[76]

When a poem or piece of literature is translated into a foreign language it always loses, either partially or completely, its essential meaning and feeling. For this reason many individuals, in order to read the original of a great work, learn the language.

If even the best translation could not even capture the genius of Goethe or Baudelaire, he suggested, how could it do justice to a book that was written in the language of God?

Conclusion

When Ahmet Hamdi Akseki died in 1951, Ömer Rıza Doğrul's obituary in *Zafer* praised him for his decades-long struggle to steward the essence of faith through the storms of revolution. Akseki, he wrote, ensured that the people were not left bereft of religion before a purer faith could emerge from the necessary destruction of the Kemalist era. At a time when the confusion of secularism with irreligion reigned, Akseki worked "in a spirit appropriate to the revolution" to provide

---

[74] Ibid.   [75] Wilson, "The First Translations," 427.
[76] "Kuranın Tam Tercümesi Meselesi," *Turkish Thought*, April 15, Issue 25. For good measure, Cem also added that the whole idea of translating holy books started with Martin Luther, who was a Jew.

Turkish citizens with the "spiritual nourishment" they needed. Now, with the advent of democracy, Doğrul went on, Islam had achieved true freedom for the first time since the arrival of the Umayyads – neither subject to oppression nor a tool of oppression. If Akseki could see the subject to which he devoted his entire professional life solved in such a satisfactory manner, Doğrul concluded, he would surely be pleased.[77]

So what happened to the modern, democratic Islam that both Ahmet Hamdi Akseki and Bernard Lewis envisioned? In 1999, Turkish Prime Minister Bülent Ecevit told an audience in Washington, DC, that his country was an exemplar of it. Turkey, he claimed, could serve as an example for the Islamic world because "the Turkish experiment has proven that Islam can be compatible with modernity."[78] Two years later, amidst widespread talk of a renewed "clash of civilizations" following September 11, Ecevit returned to Washington with an Ottoman Quran for President George Bush. Accepting the gift, Bush in turn stressed the importance of Turkey's model as a secular, democratic, and Islamic country.[79]

Yet shortly thereafter, many Western academics would conclude that Erdoğan, not Ecevit, was the one who would finally realize Lewis's vision.[80] Secular leaders like Ecevit, they suspected, had misunderstood the essence of Western modernity by embracing a no-longer-sufficiently modern version of it. As a result, it fell to Erdoğan to reconcile Islam

[77] Ömer Rıza Doğrul, "Merhum Üstad Ahmet Hamdi Akseki," *Zafer*, November 1, 1951.

[78] Bülent Ecevit, "An Address by the Turkish Prime Minister," *The Washington Institute*, September 28, 1999. www.washingtoninstitute.org/policy-analysis/address-turkish-prime-minister-full-transcript.

[79] Yasemin Çongar, "Bush'tan Ecevit'e: YANINIZDAYIZ," *Milliyet*, January 17, 2002.

[80] For some American evangelicals, the AKP also initially appeared as an ally in a common fight against an oppressively secular understanding of modernity. In 2007, former Bush speechwriter Michael Gerson described Kemalist Turkey as an "ACLU utopia" with "restrictions that would drive religious Americans frantic with resentment." As Gerson explained, a "series of political parties have called for the Turkish state to be more tolerant of public religious expression – and been serially disbanded by the secular establishment." He therefore sympathized with the AKP's base, "educated, entrepreneurial, pious and resentful of the secular elite," as they took on the dubious assumption, grounded in the Enlightenment and the "sociological theories of the 20th century," that "religion was in decline." Michael Gerson, "An Islamic Test for Turkey," *Washington Post*, June 6, 2007.

with modernity and, in doing so, move Turkey past the oppressive model of secular modernity identified with scholars like Lewis himself.

Now, a decade and a half later, many Turkish citizens would claim that Erdoğan has indeed helped their country reconcile Islam and modernity. Many, of course, are equally insistent that he has set them against each other by pursing a fundamentalist version of religion at the expense of modernity. And some are still demanding he go further in the direction of religion. If Turkish politics become even more religious, scholars can continue to attack the false determinism of secular modernization. If key elements of Turkish secularism reemerge, however, scholars may perhaps conclude that their dismissal of secular modernity contained a dubious determinism of its own. In either case, Turkey's next government will likely claim to offer a recalibrated compromise between religion and modernity with a renewed promise of resolving this long-standing conflict in keeping with Turkey's long-standing tradition. Perhaps if they succeed, the 1950s can take its place in a newly deterministic account of how this compromise was reached.

Conclusion

In late 2008, the *New York Times'* Turkey correspondent took a boat tour along the Bosporus with historian Murat Belge. "History can be slippery in Turkey," the *Times* told its readers.[1] Over fish and rakı, Belge elaborated, "We have a very unhealthy relationship with our history ... It's basically a collection of lies."

Indeed, the ensuing years proved just how slippery history could be. Historians kept correcting lie after lie and yet somehow the truth kept getting away. In the 1950s, many thinkers initially assumed modernity would bring democratic freedom. But they quickly realized the relationship between the two was far more complicated. Over the past decade, a new generation of thinkers was equally optimistic that dismantling the oppressive intellectual and political architecture of twentieth-century high modernism would finally be liberating. But things once again proved complicated.[2] It turned out that our well-meaning critiques of early and mid-century modernizers could be just as malleable, misleading, and malignant as their old ideas about modernity. We need not forgive our predecessors' errors or return to their ideas. But recognizing the sophisticated ways they were wrong, rather than reducing them to clichés, can lead us to be more cautious about the politics of our own work. At the very least, it should make us question our faith that sophistication, objectivity, or good intentions will protect our scholarship from being misused.

---

[1] Sabrina Tavernise, "On the Bosporus, a Scholar Tells of Sultans, Washerwomen and Snakes," *New York Times*, October 24, 2008.

[2] Ironically, many critics of high modernism in the 2000s remained just as convinced as their predecessors in the 1950s that democracy was the natural end point of social and political development. Thus they saw their task as identifying the specific factors that had prevented Turkey from emerging as a liberal democracy and assumed that addressing these factors – the traumas of the early Republic or the tension between Islam and modernity – would be sufficient to facilitate democratization.

As concerns over what were then called Erdoğan's "authoritarian tendencies" began to mount, the *New York Times* provided readers its own version of Turkish history in which Kemalist high modernism remained the real threat. "A look to Turkey's past," the *Times* wrote in 2008, "is useful to understand its complicated present."[3] Turkey was "still suffering the consequences" of its "painful birth" when Atatürk "disassembled the structure of the Ottoman state, which had been in place for 600 years."[4] Because Atatürk concluded that religion "was a major hindrance to becoming modern," he made "religious Turks" into "second-class citizens," who were "always on the periphery."[5] "From this point on ... a powerful elite of military officers, judges and senior bureaucrats ... steered the country from behind the scenes" and "imposed Western values onto the conservative Anatolian heartland below."[6] Then, in the second half of the twentieth century, "Europe redefined its ideas of modernity in ways that emphasized democracy, tolerance and human rights."[7] But "Turkey's leaders continued down a path of rigid, corrupt and sometimes harshly repressive rule."[8] The ironic result, according to the *Times*, was finally playing out in the early twenty-first century: "[T]he secularists who founded the state out of the Ottoman Empire's remains are now lagging behind religious Turks in efforts to modernize it."[9]

---

[3] Sabrina Tavernise, "Turkey's Power Struggle an Old Feud," *New York Times*, June 22, 2008.

[4] Tavernise, "On the Bosporus ... "; Sabrina Tavernise, "In Turkey, A Rumble Is Heard in Atatürk's Grave," *New York Times*, May 19, 2007.

[5] Ibid; Sabrina Tavernise, "Hard Liners Make Gains in Turkey Election," *New York Times*, July 23, 2007.

[6] Sabrina Tavernise, "86 Accused in Coup Plot Go on Trial in Turkey," *New York Times*, October 20, 2008; Sabrina Tavernise, "Presidential Candidate in Turkey, Once Doomed as an Islamist, Is Ascendant," *New York Times*, August 28, 2007.

[7] Tavernise, "In Turkey, A Rumble is Heard ... " [8] Ibid.

[9] Sabrina Tavernise, "In Turkey's Religious Heartland, Secularism Thrives," *New York Times*, May 29, 2007.

The *Times* certainly stood out in its embrace of this narrative, and the late 2000s were certainly its heyday. But as late as 2015 it continued to appear, even in articles critical of the AKP. *Der Spiegel*, for example, offered this version: "Before the AKP came to power, Turkey's political and economic realms were controlled by a secular elite of generals, judges and bureaucrats. They saw themselves as the guardians of the legacy of Turkey's founder, Kemal Atatürk, a man who cared little for the pious, conservative majority of the population." Kazim, Popp et al, "The Rise and Fall of Erdoğan's Turkey," *Der Spiegel*, September 24, 2015.

Subsequently, with the 2013 Gezi Park protests, even once supportive Western media outlets like the *New York Times* concluded that
Erdoğan would not be the one to democratically modernize Turkey.
However, some academics continued to push back against Erdoğan's
critics using the same language the *Times* had. For example, when a
2014 *New York Times* editorial declared that Erdoğan's authoritarian
behavior was distancing Turkey from the West, historian Şükrü
Hanioğlu responded that the problem was less with Turkey's "deviation"
than with the Western model itself.[10] Turkey was not a "disobedient
child" for rejecting a flawed and impossible vision of Westernization.
Rather, it was seeking "new syntheses" that "could more harmoniously
accommodate social realities and values." In another column, Hanioğlu
argued that Western observers failed to understand societies like
Turkey and Egypt because they confused the imitation of Western
modernity with liberalism. As a result, they embraced "elitist," "coup-
supporting," "pseudo-liberals" whose opponents they condemned as
"anti-democratic conservatives."[11] About the Gezi park protests, he
lamented that the movement's emancipatory seed had been subsumed
by those "voicing the 'controlling' desires of a Weberian status group
that seeks to impose its own lifestyle on society through a monopoly on
modernity."[12]

At the same time, some contemporary critics of authoritarian modernization continue to see it as the culprit behind the AKP's rise to
power. Most recently, the book *Hotels and Highways*, a critical study
of mid-century US development experts in Turkey, condemns their
modern-day successors as the AKP's key champions. After drawing
parallels between Turkey's US-built highway system and the Dersim
massacre, as well as between the Hilton Hotel and Iraq's Green Zone,
the work concludes:

Prime Minister Erdoğan's less-than-tolerant response to the [Gezi Park]
protests apparently came as a surprise to "experts" who had so recently
been extolling his model of neoliberal democracy.... This should come as no
surprise. During the Cold War, upholding the replicability of the Turkish
model required the erasure of its authoritarian, hierarchical elements.

---

[10] Şükrü Hanioğlu, "Batı 'model'inden 'sapmak,'" *Sabah*, November 30, 2014.
[11] Şükrü Hanioğlu, "'Liberal' seçkinciler, demokrat muhafazakârlar," *Sabah*,
     October 20, 2013.
[12] Şükrü Hanioğlu, "Bir sene sonra 'Gezi,'" *Sabah*, July 8, 2014.

Experts and policy makers relied on this model to promote the developmental and capitalistic vision of American foreign policy and its core ideological offering, modernization theory.[13]

Of course, the *New York Times*' critique of Kemalism, Hanioğlu's critique of the Western model, and *Hotels and Highways*' critique of neoliberal development experts are all in very important ways true. And yet somehow these truths come together to form a contradictory cycle: first the *New York Times* supported Erdoğan in challenging an oppressive Western model of modernization. Then Hanioğlu condemned the *Times* for using this same oppressive model to criticize Erdoğan. Finally, *Hotels and Highways* claimed it was this model that had driven Western support for Erdoğan all along.

The problem appears to be that the complexity of the world will accommodate a range of different political uses, without ever fully justifying any of them. Ideas prove useful only in so much as they have political resonance. Thus, scholars strip some of the nuance and caveats from their analysis as they try to condense a 200-plus-page monograph into a concise conclusion which speaks directly to the ideological questions that inspired it. Diplomats and journalists, or at times scholars themselves, then condense these ideas further as they work to make them explicitly relevant for the public or policymakers. The process by which academic arguments are mobilized for political purposes then sets the stage for the next round of academic critiques, as scholars go back and condemn the ideologically motivated scholarship of their predecessors. Crucially, this criticism often involves ignoring the caveats and ambiguity in earlier scholars' work in order to focus on its explicitly political implications. Similarly, the qualifications and contradictions used by diplomats and journalists in making their arguments are often ignored as well in order to more clearly characterize their intellectual misdeeds. In other words, by overlooking the complex way others' work became simplified and politicized, it becomes easier for us to simplify the relationship between their work and their politics. The result is that we can more easily present our own politicized work as an objective correction to the politicized work of others.

---

[13] Begüm Adalet, *Hotels and Highways: The Construction of Modernization Theory in Cold War Turkey* (Stanford University Press: Stanford, 2018), 200–201.

Indeed, the *Times*, Hanioğlu, and *Hotels and Highways* all offered important nuances that have been overlooked in the preceding characterizations. Even as it was defending the AKP in the late 2000s, the *Times* raised concerns over press freedom and minority rights for which it seldom gets credit. Hanioğlu, for his part, often used discussions of early Republican-era authoritarianism in his columns to subtly critique the AKP's contemporary version. And *Hotels and Highways* itself features a particularly insightful exploration of the tensions between the personal views of mid-century American modernization theorists and the political ends their work served.

So where does this leave us, and where does it leave Turkey in relation to its past and its future?

Erdoğan's turn toward right-wing nationalism, starting in late 2014 and exemplified by his political alliance with the Nationalist Action Party, gives new life to long-standing scholarly critiques of racist, state-sponsored nationalism going back to the early Republic. Where the unique circumstances of Turkey's founding sometimes led observers to treat nationalism and religion in Turkey as opposing ideologies, their symbiosis, not surprising in a global context, may now become more evident. If Erdoğan's Ottoman nostalgia once appeared antithetical to traditional Turkish nationalism, it is now beginning to seem like a typical act of nationalist appropriation. Similarly, where contemporary scholarship has emphasized the top-down and elite nature of Kemalism, the enduring appeal of nationalist rhetoric today may draw greater attention to its popular resonance in the early Republic.

Scholars looking for new themes in twentieth-century Turkish history, or seeking to explain the successes and failures of Turkish democratization, might take a newfound interest in the endurance of conservative religious nationalism, particularly as a unifying force in the face of perceived internal and external threats. While much recent work has focused on the founding of the Republic as the starting point for grand narratives, the Cold War also played a formative role in shaping contemporary Turkish politics. Understanding both the political tradition represented by Adnan Menderes and Süleyman Demirel, as well as the coups that toppled them, requires a renewed exploration of the different flavors of right-wing nationalism in the period between the 1950 election and the 1980 military takeover. This focus, if taken to an extreme, can also carry risks of its own. But a growing body of research from historians such as Behlül Özkan, Nazım İrem, Halil

Karaveli, James Ryan, and İlker Aytürk has also demonstrated the insights it can provide.[14]

Alongside condemning conservative nationalism, academics and their colleagues in the cultural sphere will undoubtedly seek positive examples of liberal modernity, untainted by authoritarianism of either the high-modernist or religious variety. Sarah-Neel Smith has advanced this argument with reference to the newfound interest in an earlier generation of female artists like Mihri Rasim and Sabiha Bozcalı, both recently featured at the SALT Gallery in Beyoğlu.[15] We may also see further reappraisal of Republican-era feminists, once cast as complicit in the hegemonic Kemalist modernization project, which recognizes their efforts to co-opt this discourse for their own ends.[16] At the same time, the AKP's intense criticism of the early Republic will almost certainly drive a growing backlash in which scholarly revisionism blends with nostalgia for the early Republican era.[17] Those searching for exemplars of liberal modernity may come into conflict with others trying to rehabilitate the entire Kemalist political tradition, leaving figures like Bülent Ecevit caught in the middle.

In the realm of foreign policy, Turkey's deepening tensions with its erstwhile Western allies will likely inspire a growing interest in the history of anti-Western and anti-imperialist thinking in twentieth-century Turkey. Works by scholars like Onur İşçi and Samuel Hirst

---

[14] Behlül Özkan, "Cold War Era Relations between West Germany and Turkish Political Islam: From an Anti-Communist Alliance to a Domestic Security Issue," *Southeast European and Black Sea Studies*, Volume 19, 2019; Nazım İrem, "Turkish Conservative Modernism: Birth of a Nationalist Quest for Cultural Renewal," *International Journal of Middle East Studies*, Vol. 34, No. 1 (February 2002); Halil Karaveli, *Why Turkey Is Authoritarian: Right-Wing Rule from Atatürk to Erdoğan*, Pluto Press: London, 2018; James Ryan, "Ideology on Trial: The Prosecution of Pan-Turkists and Leftists at the Dawn of the Cold War in Turkey, 1944–1947" Prisms: Perspectives on Southeast European History, forthcoming; İlker Aytürk, "Nationalism and Islam in Cold War Turkey, 1944–1969," *Middle Eastern Studies*, Vol. 50, No. 5, 2014.

[15] Sarah-Neel Smith, *Metrics of Modernity: Art and Development in Postwar Turkey*. University of California Press, forthcoming. Sabiha Bozcalı is perhaps most famous as one of the illustrators for Koçu's *Istanbul Encyclopedia*. Her brother, Ali Nur, was an employee of the US consulate who frequently penned memos on the Turkey's history and politics.

[16] For an early example of this reassessment, see İpek Yosmaoğlu, "Our Women Treasures: Early Republican Turkish Women and Their Public Identity," in Baki Tezcan and Karl K. Barbir, eds. *Identity and Identity Formation in the Ottoman World*. (Madison: University of Wisconsin Press, 2007), 213.

[17] Esra Özyürek, *Nostalgia for the Modern: State Secularism and Everyday Politics in Turkey*, Duke University Press: Durham, 2006.

have begun painting a more nuanced picture of Turkey's relationship with Russia that emphasizes both the practical and ideological nature of the two countries' historic ties.[18] In a similar vein, we will likely see a reassessment of Turkey's past relations with the Middle East, which moves beyond the clichés of Kemalist alienation. Amit Bein's work on Turkish policy in the region during the early Republic represents an important step in this direction.[19]

Global trends will inevitably shape the history of Turkey in the coming decades as well. Growing alarm about the rise of illiberal populism around the world will be reflected in the way scholars view Turkey's experience with democracy and the nature of modernization more broadly. Few people now envision modernization as an inexorable process whereby diverse societies eventually converge on a common model of Western liberal democracy. But we may see renewed interest in the idea of modernization leading to a less positive form of convergence, perhaps closer to the reality of 1950s Turkey than its liberal aspirations. If more countries, Western and non-Western alike, embrace a political system based on aggressive nationalism, crass consumerism, popular piety, and media-driven majoritarianism, a darker mid-century Turkish model might finally have its moment. And if things turn out differently, we can revise the era's history accordingly.

---

[18] Onur İşçi, *Turkey and the Soviet Union during WWII: Diplomacy, Discord and International Relations*, I. B. Tauris: London, 2019; Samuel Hirst, "Anti-Westernism on the European Periphery: The Meaning of Soviet-Turkish Convergence in the 1930s," *Slavic Review*, March 2013.
[19] Amit Bein, *Kemalist Turkey and the Middle East: International Relations in the Interwar Period*, Cambridge University Press: London, 2017.

Bibliography

Archives, Libraries, and Collections

African & Middle Eastern Reading Room, Library of Congress, Washington.
İ.B.B. Atatürk Kitaplığı, Istanbul.
Başbakanlık Cumhuriyet Arşivi, Ankara.
Beyazıt Devlet Kütüphanesi, Istanbul.
Personal Papers of Bülent and Rahşan Ecevit, Bülent Ecevit Bilim Kültür ve Sanat Vakfı, Ankara.
İbrahim Hakkı Konyalı Kütüphanesi ve Arşivi, Istanbul.
Kadın Eserleri Kütüphanesi ve Bilgi Merkezi Vakfı, Istanbul.
George McGhee Papers, Georgetown University Library, Washington DC.
National Archives and Records Administration. College Park, Maryland (NARA).
Record Group 59, Central Decimal Files of the Department of State.
Record Group 84, Records of the Foreign Service Posts of the Department of State.
Record Group 306, United States Information Service Decimal Files.
Record Group 334, Records of Interservice Agencies.
Sahaflar Çarşısı, Aslıhan Pasajı, Istanbul.
Türkiye Büyük Milli Meclis (T.B.M.M.) Tutanak Dergisi, Ankara. www.tbmm.gov.tr/

Selected Newspapers and Periodicals

Akbaba, Ankara Üniversitesi Dil ve Tarih-Coğrafya Fakültesi Dergisi, Coğrafya Dünyası, Cumhuriyet, Dinimizde Reform Kemalizm, Doğru Yol, Doğu, İslam'in Nuru, İstanbul Ekspres, Kadın Gazetesi, New York Times, Resimli Tarihi, Sebilürreşad, Selamet, Serdengeçti, Son Çağ, Tarihten Sesler, Tarih Dünyası, Tarih Hazinesi, Türk Düşüncesi, Türk Yurdu, Ulus, Vatan, Winston-Salem Journal, and *Zafer.*

Published Works

Abadan, Nermin. *Yeşil Göller Diyarı*. Istanbul: Hilmi Kitabevi, 1950.

Adalet, Begüm. *Hotels and Highways: The Construction of Modernization Theory in Cold War Turkey*. Stanford: Stanford University Press, 2018.

Adams, Walter and Garraty, John. *Is the World Our Campus?* East Lansing, MI: Michigan State University Press, 1960.

Adas, Michael. *Machines as Measures of Men*. New York: Cornell University Press, 1989.

Afinoguénova, Eugenia. *Spain Is (Still) Different*. New York: Lexington Books, 2008.

Ağaoğlu, Samet. *Arkadaşım Menderes*. Istanbul: Yapı Kredi Yayınları, 2011.

Ahmad, Feroz. *Turkey: The Quest for Identity*. Oxford: Oneworld Publications, 2003.

Akcan, Esra. *Architecture in Translation: Germany, Turkey, and the Modern House*. Durham, NC: Duke University Press, 2012.

"Critical Practice in the Global Era: The Question Concerning 'Other' Geographies." *Architectural Theory Review* Vol. 7 (2009), 37–57.

Akseki, Ahmet Hamdi, *Radyoda Dini ve Ahlaki Konuşmalar*. Ankara: Örnek Matbaası, 1954.

Albayrak, Mustafa. *Türk Siyasi Tarihinde Demokrat Parti (1946–1960)*. Ankara: Phoenix, 2004.

Altınay, Ayşe Gül. *The Myth of the Military-Nation: Militarism, Gender, and Education in Turkey*. New York: Palgrave Macmillan, 2004.

Altınyıldız, Nur. "The Architectural Heritage of Istanbul and the Ideology of Preservation." *Muqarnas* Vol. 24 (2007), 281–303.

Alvarez, David J. *Bureaucracy and Cold War Diplomacy: The United States and Turkey 1943–1946*. Thessaloniki: Institute for Balkan Studies, 1980.

Anderson, Benedict. *Imagined Communities: Reflections on the Origin and Spread of Nationalism*. London: Verso, 2006.

Appadurai, Arjun. *Modernity at Large*. Minneapolis: University of Minnesota, 1993.

Apter, Emily. "Global Translation: The 'Invention' of Comparative Literature, Istanbul, 1933." *Critical Inquiry* Vol. 29, No. 2 (January 1, 2003), 253–281.

Arat, Zehra (ed.). *Deconstructing Images of "The Turkish Woman."* New York: St. Martin's Press, 1998.

Atatürk, Mustafa Kemal. *Atatürk'ün Söylev ve Demeçleri: Volume 2*. Istanbul: Maarif Matbaası, 1945.

A Speech by Gazi Mustafa Kemal, 1929 Leipzig translation, 586.

Athanassopoulou, Ekavi. *Turkey-Anglo-American Security Interests 1945–1952: The First Enlargement of NATO.* London: Frank Cass, 1999.

Aydemir, Şevket Süreyya. *İkinci Adam.* Istanbul: Yükselen Matbaası, 1967. *Menderes'in Dramı.* Istanbul: Yükselen Matbaası, 1969.

Aydın, Cemil. *The Politics of Anti-Westernism in Asia.* New York: Columbia University Press, 2007.

Aydın, Mustafa and Erhan, Cağrı (eds.). *Turkish-American Relations: Past, Present and Future.* New York: Routledge, 2004.

Aytürk, İlker. "Nationalism and Islam in Cold War Turkey, 1944–1969." *Middle Eastern Studies* Vol. 50, No. 5 (2014), 693–719.

"Post-Post-Kemalizm: Yeni Bir Paradigmayı Beklerken." *Birikim* Vol. 319, (2015), 34–48.

Azak, Umut. *Islam and Secularism in Turkey: Kemalism, Religion and the Nation State.* Cambridge: Cambridge University Press, 2010.

Balaban, M. Rahmi (ed.). *Son Asrın İlim ve Fen Adamlarına Göre İlim, Ahlak, İman.* Ankara: New Press, 1950.

Bayar, Celal. *Ben De Yazdım.* Istanbul: Sabah Kitapları, 1997.

Bayar, Yeşim. *Formation of the Turkish Nation-State, 1920–1938.* New York: Palgrave MacMillan, 2014.

Bein, Amit, *Kemalist Turkey and the Middle East: International Relations in the Interwar Period.* Cambridge: Cambridge University Press, 2017.

Bektaş, Cengiz. *Türk Evi.* Istanbul: Yapı Endüstri Merkezi Yayınları, 2013.

Berger, Mark. "Decolonization, Modernization and Nation Building: Political Development Theory and the Appeal of Communism in Southeast Asia, 1945–1975." *Journal of Southeastern Asian Studies* Vol. 34, No. 2 (2003), 421–447.

Bienen, Henry (ed.). *The Military Intervenes: Case Studies in Political Development.* New York: Russel Sage Foundation, 1968.

Bilsel, S. M. Can. "'Our Anatolia': Organicism and the Making of Humanist Culture in Turkey." *Muqarnas* Vol. 24 (2007), 223–241.

Birand, Mehmet Ali, Dündar, Can, et al. *Demirkırat: Bir Demokrasinin Doğuşu.* Istanbul: Milliyet, 1993.

Bozdoğan, Sibel. *Modernism and Nation Building: Turkish Architectural Culture in the Early Republic.* Seattle, WA: University of Washington Press, 2001.

Building: Turkish Architectural Culture in the Early Republic. Seattle, WA: University of Washington Press, 2001.

Bozdoğan, Sibel and Esra Akcan. *Turkey: Modern Architectures in History.* London: Reaktion Books, 2012.

Bozdoğan, Sibel and Kasaba, Reşat (eds.). *Rethinking Modernity and National Identity in Turkey.* Seattle: Washington University Press, 1997.

Brazinsky, Gregg. *Nation Building in South Korea: Koreans, Americans, and the Making of a Democracy*. Chapel Hill, NC: University of North Carolina Press, 2007.

Brockett, Gavin. *Towards a Social History of Modern Turkey: Essays in Theory and Practice*. Istanbul: Libra Kitapçılık ve Yayıncılık, 2011.

How Happy to Call Oneself a Turk: Provincial Newspapers and the Negotiation of a Muslim National Identity. Austin: University of Texas Press, 2012.

Burwell, Francis (ed.). *The Evolution of U.S. Turkish Relations in a Transatlantic Context*. Carlisle, PA: Strategic Studies Institute, 2008.

Çağaptay, Soner. *Islam, Secularism and Nationalism in Modern Turkey: Who is a Turk?* London: Routledge, 2006.

Çarkoğlu, Ali and Kalaycıoğlu, Ersin. *The Rising Tide of Conservatism in Turkey*. New York: Palgrave Macmillan, 2009.

Celaloğlu, Mustafa (Sadettin Tokdemir, translator), *Osmanlı İmparatorluğunun Yükselme Devrinde Türk Ordusunun Savaşları ve Devletin Kurumu, İç ve Dış Siyasası*. Istanbul: Askeri Matbaası, 1937.

Çınar, Alev. *Modernity, Islam and Secularism in Turkey: Bodies Places and Time*. Minneapolis: University of Minnesota Press, 2005.

Citino, Nathan J. "The Ottoman Legacy in Cold War Authoritarianism." *International Journal of Middle East Studies* Vol. 49 (2008), 579–597.

Envisioning the Arab Future: Modernization in U.S.-Arab Relations, 1945–1967. Cambridge: Cambridge University Press, 2017.

Chatterjee, Partha. *Nationalist Thought and the Colonial World: A Derivative Discourse*. Minneapolis: University of Minnesota Press, 1986.

Clifford, James. *Routes: Travel and Translation in the Late Twentieth Century*. Cambridge, MA: Harvard University Press, 1997.

Crinson, Mark. *Empire Building: Orientalism and Victorian Architecture*. London: Psychology Press, 1996.

Çolak, Yılmaz. "Ottomanism vs. Kemalism: Collective Memory and Cultural Pluralism in 1990s Turkey," *Middle Eastern Studies* Vol. 42, No. 4 (July 2006), 587–602.

Copeaux, Etienne. *Espaces et temps de la nation turque: analyse d'une historiographie nationaliste, 1931–1993*. Paris: CNRS éditions, 1997.

Coşar, Ömer and İpekci, Abdi. *İhtilalin İç Yüzü*. Istanbul: Uygun, 1965.

Danişmend, İsmail Hamdi. *İstanbul Fethinin İnsani ve Medeni Kıymeti*. İstanbul: İstanbul Halk Basımevi, 1953.

Dankwart, Rustow and Ward, Robert (eds.). *Political Modernization in Japan and Turkey*. Princeton: Princeton University Press, 1968.

De Luca, Anthony. "Soviet American Politics and the Turkish Straits," in *Political Science Quarterly* Vol. 92, No. 3 (Autumn 1977), 503–524.

Deringil, Selim. *Turkish Foreign Policy during the Second World War.* Cambridge: Cambridge University Press, 1989.

"'They Live in a State of Nomadism and Savagery': The Late Ottoman Empire and the Post-Colonial Debate." *Comparative Studies in Society and History* Vol. 45, No. 2 (April 2003), 311–342.

Dibek, Esma Ceyda, "Bülent Ecevit: Continuity and change in his political views." PhD Dissertation, Bilkent Üniversitesi, 2002.

Döşemeci, Mehmet. *Debating Turkish Modernity: Civilization, Nationalism, and the EEC.* Cambridge: Cambridge University Press, 2013.

Duffy, Sean Patrick. "The Construction of Inequality: U.S. Foreign Policy, Development Discourse, and the Postwar Expansion of the International System." PhD Dissertation, Yale University, 1997.

Durgun, Şenol. "Left-Wing Politics in Turkey: Its Development and Problems." *Arab Studies Quarterly* Vol. 37, No. 1 (2015), 9–32.

Eissenstat, Howard. "The Limits of Imagination: Debating the Nation and Constructing the State in Early Turkish Nationalism." PhD Dissertation, UCLA, 2007.

Engerman, David and Gilman, Nils, et al (eds.). *Staging Growth: Modernization, Development and the Global Cold War.* Boston: University of Massachusetts Press, 2003.

Enginün, İnci, and Zeynep Kerman (eds.). *Günlüklerin Işığında: Tanpınar'la Başbaşa.* Istanbul: Dergâh Yayınları, 2007.

Erimtan, Can. *Ottomans Looking West? The Origins of the Tulip Age and Its Development in Modern Turkey.* London: I. B. Tauris, 2008.

Eroğul, Cem. *Demokrat Parti.* Ankara: İmge Yayınları, 2003.

Ertan, Veli. *A Hamdi Akseki: Hayatı, Eserleri ve Tesiri.* Istanbul: Üc Dal, 1966.

Ersanlı, Büşra, "The Ottoman Empire in the Historiography of the Kemalist Era: A Theory of Fatal Decline," in Fikret Adanir and Suraiya Faroqhi, eds. *The Ottomans and the Balkans: A Discussion of Historiography.* Boston: Brill, 2002.

Fleming, Ian. *From Russia with Love.* London: Signet, 1957.

Gaddis, John Lewis. *We Know Now: Rethinking Cold War History.* Oxford: Clarendon Press, 1997.

Gedik, Fuad. *Amerika.* Cumhuriyet Maatbası, Istanbul: 1946.

Geertz, Clifford. "Ideology as a Cultural System," in *Ideology and Discontent.* David Apter, ed. New York: Free Press, 1964.

Gilman, Nils. *Mandarins of the Future: Modernization Theory in Cold War America.* Baltimore: Johns Hopkins University Press, 2003.

Gingeras, Ryan. *Mustafa Kemal Atatürk: Heir to an Empire*. Oxford: Oxford University Press, 2014.

Heroin, Organized Crime, and the Making of Modern Turkey. Oxford: Oxford University Press, 2017.

Eternal Dawn: Turkey in the Age of Atatürk. Oxford: Oxford University Press, 2020.

Göktepe, Cihat. *British Foreign Policy toward Turkey*. London: Routledge, 2003.

Göle, Nilüfer. "Snapshots of Islamic Modernities." *Daedalus* Vol. 129, (2000), 91–119.

Gövsa, Alaettin. *Meşhur Adamlar*. Istanbul: Yedigün, 1935.

50 Türk Büyüğü. İstanbul: Yedigün, 1939.

Türk Meşhurları Ansiklopedisi. Istanbul: Yedigün, 1945.

Gregory, Derek. "Colonial Nostalgia and Cultures of Travel" in Nezar Al Sayyad, (ed.) *Consuming Tradition, Manufacturing Heritage*. London: Routledge Press, 2001, 111–151.

Gül, Murat. *The Emergence of Modern Istanbul: Transformation and Modernization of a City*. London: I. B. Tauris, 2009.

Gürağlar, Şehnaz Tahir. *The Politics and Poetics of Translation in Turkey, 1923–1960*. Amsterdam: Rodopi, 2008.

Gürbüz, Mehmet V. "An Overview of Turkish-American Relations and Impact on Turkish Military, Economy and Democracy, 1945–52." PhD Dissertation. University of Wisconsin – Madison, 2002.

Gürel, Perin, *The Limits of Westernization: A Cultural History of America in Turkey*. New York: Columbia University Press, 2017.

Gürkan, Nilgün. *Türkiye'de Demokrasiye Geçişte Basın (1945–1950)*. Istanbul: İletisim, 1998.

Gürpınar, Doğan. *Ottoman/Turkish Visions of the Nation, 1860–1950*. London: Palgrave Macmillan, 2013.

Gürtunca, M. Faruk. *Bu Arslan Dokunmayın*. Istanbul: Ülkü Kitap Yurdu, 1939.

Haines, Gerald. *The Americanization of Brazil: A Study of U.S. Cold War Diplomacy in the Third World, 1945–1954*. Wilmington, DE: Scholarly Resources Inc., 1989.

Hale, William. *Turkish Politics and the Military*. London: Routledge, 1993.

Turkish Foreign Policy Since 1774. London: Routledge, 2012.

Hale, William and Özbudun, Ergun. *Islamism, Democracy and Liberalism in Turkey: The Case of the AKP*. London: Routledge, 2010.

Hanioğlu, M. Şükrü. "Garbcılar: Their Attitudes toward Religion and Their Impact on the Official Ideology of the Turkish Republic." *Studia Islamica* Vol. 86, 1997, 133–158.

A Brief History of the Late Ottoman Empire. Princeton: Princeton University Press, 2003.

Atatürk: an Intellectual Biography. Princeton: Princeton University Press, 2013.

Hansen, Bent. *The Political Economy of Poverty, Equity, and Growth: Egypt and Turkey*. Oxford: Oxford University Press, 1991.

Harris, George. *Trouble Alliance: Turkish-American Problems in Historical Perspective, 1945–1971*. Washington: American Enterprise Institute, 1972.

Harris, George, (ed.) *The Middle East in Turkish-American Relations*. Washington: The Heritage Foundation, 1984.

Harris, George and Criss, Nur Bilgi (eds.). *Studies in Atatürk's Turkey: The American Dimension*. Boston: Brill, 2009.

Hart, Parker. *Two NATO Allies on the Threshold of War: Cyprus: A Firsthand Account of Crisis Management, 1965–1968*. Durham: Duke University Press, 1990.

Heper, Metin. *İsmet İnönü: The Making of a Turkish Statesmen*. Leiden: EJ Brill, 1998.

Heper, Metin and Sayarı, Sabri. *Political Leaders and Democracy in Turkey*. Lanham, MD: Lexington Books, 2002.

Herzog, Christoph and Motika, Raoul. "Orientalism 'Alla Turca': Late 19th / Early 20th Century Ottoman Voyages into the Muslim 'Outback.'" *Die Welt Des Islams* Vol. 40, No. 2 (July 2000), 139–195.

Hirst, Samuel. "Anti-Westernism on the European Periphery: The Meaning of Soviet-Turkish Convergence in the 1930s," *Slavic Review* Vol. 72, No. 1 (March 2013), 32–53.

Hobsbawm, Eric and Terence Ranger (eds.). *The Invention of Tradition*. Cambridge: Cambridge University Press, 1992.

Hock, Stefan. "This Subject Concerns the Mass Rather Than a Group": Debating Kemalism, Labor, and State Feminism during the Transition to a Multi-Party Republic in Turkey," *Journal of the Ottoman and Turkish Studies Association* Vol. 1, No. 1–2 (2014), 187–206.

Howard, Harry. *Turkey, The Straights and U.S. Policy*. Baltimore: The John Hopkins University Press, 1975.

Humbaraci, Arslan. *The Middle East Indictment: From the Truman Doctrine, the Soviet Penetration and Britain's Downfall to the Eisenhower Doctrine*. London: Robert Hale Limited, 1958.

Hunt, Michael. *Ideology and U.S. Foreign Policy*. New Haven, CT: Yale University Press, 2009.

Huyssen, Andreas. "Geographies of Modernism in a Globalizing World." *New German Critique* Vol. 34, No. 100 (Winter 2007), 189–207.

Hüsnü, Kılkışlı Hüseyin. *Manzum Türk Tarihi*. Izmir: Yeni Matbaa, 1933.

Ihrig, Stefan. *Atatürk in the Nazi Imagination*. Cambridge, MA: Harvard University Press, 2014.

İnan, Afet. "Bir Türk Amirali," *Belleten* Vol. 1, (1937), 317–349.

"Türk-Osmanlı Tarihinin Karakteristik Noktalarına bir Bakış," *Belleten* Vol. 2, No. 5/6, (1937–April 1938), 123–132.

İnönü, İsmet. *Defterler 1919–1973*. Istanbul: Yapı Kredi Yayınları, 2016.

Inboden, William. *Religion and American Foreign Policy, 1945–1960: The Soul of Containment*. Cambridge: Cambridge University Press, 2008.

İrem, Nazım. "Turkish Conservative Modernism: Birth of a Nationalist Quest for Cultural Renewal," *International Journal of Middle East Studies* Vol. 34, No. 1 (February 2002), 87–112.

İsen, Can Kaya. *22 Şubat – 21 Mayıs Geliyorum Diyen İhtilal*. Istanbul: Kaknüs Yayınları, 2010.

İşci, Onur. *Turkey and the Soviet Union during WWII: Diplomacy, Discord and International Relations*. I. B. Tauris: London, 2019.

Işın, Ekrem. *Mindful Seed Speaking Soil: Village Institutes of the Republic 1940–1954*. Istanbul: Istanbul Araştırmaları Enstitüsü, 2012.

Kacıroğlu, Murat. "'Cehennemden Selam' Romanı Örneğinde İlk Dönem (1927–1940) Tarihi Macera Romanlarda Kanonik Söylem Yahut Angaje Eğilim," *Turkish Studies* Vol. 5/2 Spring 2010.

Kaçmazoğlu, Bayram H. 1997. *Demokrat Parti Dönemi Toplumsal Tartışmaları*. Istanbul: Birey Yayincilik.

Kaplan, Sam. *The Pedagogical State: Education and the Politics of National Culture in Post-1980 Turkey*. Stanford: Stanford University Press, 2006.

Kapur, Geeta. *When Was Modernism: Essays on Contemporary Cultural Practice in India*. New Delhi: Tulika, 2000.

Karal, Enver Ziya. *Osmanlı Tarihi*. Ankara: Türk Tarih Kurumu, 1947.

Karaveli, Halil. *Why Turkey is Authoritarian: Right-Wing Rule from Atatürk to Erdoğan*. London: Pluto Press, 2018.

Karpat, Kemal. *Turkey's Politics: The Transition to a Multi-Party System*. Princeton: Princeton University Press, 1959.

"The Republican People's Party, 1923–1945," in M. Heper and J. M. Landau eds. *Political Parties and Democracy in Turkey*. London: I. B. Tauris, 1991.

(ed.). *Ottoman Past and Today's Turkey*. Boston: Brill, 2000.

Politicization of Islam. Oxford: Oxford University Press, 2000.

"Actors and Issues in Turkish Politics, 1950–1960." *International Journal of Turkish Studies* Vol. 17, No. 1/2 (2011), 115–157.

Kayaoğlu, Barın. "Strategic Imperatives, Democratic Rhetoric: The United States and Turkey, 1945–52," *Cold War History* Vol. 9, No. 3, 2009, 321–345.

Kemal, Yahya. Şinasi, Abdülhak and Hamdi, Ahmet. *İstanbul*. Istanbul: Doğan Kardeş Yayınları, 1953.

Keyder, Çağlar. "The Political Economy of Turkish Democracy." *New Left Review*, No. 115 (June 1979), 24–47.

Kezer, Zeynep. *Building Modern Turkey: State, Space, and Ideology in the Early Republic*. Pittsburgh: University of Pittsburgh Press, 2016.

Kieser, Hans Lukas (ed.). *Turkey Beyond Nationalism: Towards Post-Nationalist Identities*. London: I. B. Tauris, 2006.

Kınıklıoğlu, Suat. "Bülent Ecevit: The Transformation of a Politician." *Turkish Studies* Vol. 1, No. 2, 2000, 1–20.

Koçak, Cemil. *Türkiye'de Milli Şef Dönemi (1938–1945)*. Istanbul: İletişim Yayınları, 2018.

Koçak, Orhan. "Westernization Against the West: Cultural Politics in the Early Turkish Republic" in Celia Kerslake, Kerem Öktem and Philip Robins, (eds.) *Turkey's Engagement with Modernity: Conflict and Change in the Twentieth Century*. London: Palgrave Macmillan, 2010, 305–322.

"1920'lerden 1970'lere Kültür Politikaları," in Ahmet İnsel's, ed. *Modern Türkiye'de Siyasal Düsünce vol. 2, Kemalizm*. İstanbul: İletişim, 2004, 370–418.

Koçu, Reşat Ekrem. *Fatih Sultan Mehmed*. İstanbul: Kervan Yayınları, 1973.

Koloğlu, Orhan. *Ecevit ile CHP: bir aşk ve nefret öyküsü*. İstanbul: Büke Yayınları, 2000.

Köprülü, Fuat, (Gary Leiser Translator). *The Origins of the Ottoman Empire*. Albany, NY: State University of New York Press, 1992.

Kuniholm, Bruce R. *The Origins of the Cold War in the Near East: Great Power Conflict and Diplomacy in Iran. Turkey, & Greece*. Princeton: Princeton University Press, 1980.

The Near East Connection: Greece and Turkey in the Reconstruction and Security of Europe, 1946–1952. Brookline, MA: Hellenic College Press, 1984.

Kunter, H. Baki and Ülgen, A. Saim. *Fatih Camii ve Bizans Sarnıcı*. Istanbul: Cumhuriyet Matbaası, 1939.

Lamprou, Alexandros. *Nation-Building in Modern Turkey: The "People's Houses", the State and the Citizen*. London: I. B. Tauris, 2015.

Latham, Michael. *Modernization as Ideology in American Social Science and Nation Building in the Kennedy Era*. Chapel Hill: University of North Carolina Press, 2000.

Leffler, Melvyn. *A Preponderance of Power: National Security, the Truman Administration, and the Cold War*. Stanford: Stanford University Press, 1992.

"Strategy, Diplomacy, and the Cold War: The United States, Turkey, and NATO, 1945–1952," in *The Journal of American History* Vol. 71, No. 4 (March 1985), 807–825.

Lewis, Bernard. "Islamic Revival in Turkey," *International Affairs* Vol. 28, No.1 (January 1952), 38–48.

The Emergence of Modern Turkey. Oxford: Oxford University Press, 1961.

Lerner, Daniel. *The Passing of Traditional Society: Modernizing the Middle East*. Glencoe, IL: Free Press, 1958.

Lewis, Geoffrey. *Turkey*. London: Ernest Benn Ltd., 1966.

Libal, Kathryn. "From Face Veil to Cloche Hat: The Backward Ottoman Versus New Turkish Woman in Urban Public Discourse," in Stephanie Cronin, ed. *Anti-Veiling Campaigns in the Muslim World: Gender, Modernism and the Politics of Dress*. London: Routledge, 2014.

Little, Douglas. *American Orientalism: The United States and the Middle East since 1945*. Chapel Hill: University of North Carolina Press, 2008.

Livingstone, Craig. "'One Thousand Wings': The United States Air Force Group and the American Mission for Aid to Turkey, 1947–50." *Middle Eastern Studies* Vol. 30, No. 4 (October 1994), 778–825.

McGhee, George. *The U.S.-Turkish-NATO Middle East Connection: How the Truman Doctrine Contained the Soviets in the Middle East*. New York: St. Martin's Press, 1990.

Makal, Mahmut (Wyndham Deedes Translator). *A Village in Anatolia*. London: Valentine, Mitchell & Co., 1954.

Makdisi, Ussama. "Ottoman Orientalism." *The American Historical Review* Vol. 107, No. 3 (June 2002), 768–796.

Meeker, Michael. *A Nation of Empire: The Ottoman Legacy of Turkish Modernity*. Berkeley: University of California Press, 2001.

Mercer, Kobena (ed.). *Cosmopolitan Modernisms*. Cambridge, MA: MIT Press, 2005.

Mitchell, Timothy. *Rule of Experts: Egypt, Techno-Politics, Modernity*. Berkeley: University of California Press, 2002.

Mufti, Aamir R. "Auerbach in Istanbul: Edward Said, Secular Criticism, and the Question of Minority Culture." *Critical Inquiry* Vol. 25, No. 1 (October 1, 1998), 95–125.

Nüzhet, Selim. *Türk Temaşası: Meddah – Karagöz Ortaoyunu*. Istanbul: Matbaa-ı Ebüzziya, 1930.

Öndin, Nilüfer. *Cumhuriyet'in Kültür Politikası ve Sanat 1923–1950*. Istanbul: İnsancıl Yayınları, 2003.

Önsal, Başak. "Emergence of Art Galleries in Ankara: A Case Study of Three Pioneering Galleries in the 1950s." MA Thesis, Middle East Technical University, 2006.

Özavcı, Hilmi. *Intellectual Origins of the Republic: Ahmet Ağaoğlu and the Geneology of Liberalism in Turkey.* Leiden: EJ Brill, 2015.

Özkan, Behlül. "Cold War Era Relations between West Germany and Turkish Political Islam: From an Anti-Communist Alliance to a Domestic Security Issue," *Southeast European and Black Sea Studies* Vol. 19, 2019, 31–54.

Özyürek, Esra. *Nostalgia for the Modern: State Secularism and Everyday Politics in Turkey.* Durham: Duke University Press, 2006.

Pamuk, Orhan. *İstanbul: Hatıralar ve Şehir.* İstanbul: İletişim. 2002.

Parla, Taha and Andrew Davison. *Corporatist Ideology in Kemalist Turkey: Progress or Order?* Syracuse: Syracuse University Press, 2004.

The Social and Political Thoughts of Ziya Gökalp. Leiden: EJ Brill, 1985.

Pearce, Kimber Charles. *Rostow, Kennedy and the Rhetoric of Foreign Aid.* East Lansing, MI: Michigan State University Press, 2001.

Polar, A. Zeki. *Osmanlı İmparatorluğunun Çüküş Sebepleri.* Istanbul: Ak Kitabevi, 1962.

Poulton, Hugh, *Top Hat Grey Wolf and Crescent: Turkish Nationalism and the Turkish Republic.* London: Hurst, 1997.

Provence, Michael. *The Last Ottoman Generation and the Making of the Modern Middle East.* Cambridge: Cambridge University Press, 2017.

Reed, Howard A. "Revival of Islam in Secular Turkey," *Middle East Journal* Vol. 8, No. 3 (Summer, 1954), 267–282.

Roberts, Mary. *Intimate Outsiders: The Harem in Ottoman and Orientalist Art and Travel Literature.* Durham: Duke University Press, 2007.

Istanbul Exchanges: Ottomans, Orientalists, and Nineteenth-Century Visual Culture. Berkeley: University of California Press, 2014.

Robinson, Richard D. "The Lesson of Turkey," *Middle East Journal* Vol. 5, No. 4 (Autumn 1951), 424–438.

The First Turkish Republic: A Case Study in National Development. Cambridge: Harvard University Press, 1965.

Romeran, Gabriel. (Ali Kemali Aksut, Translator). *Tepedenli Ali Paşa.* Istanbul: Ikbal Kitabevi, 1939.

Rostow, W. W. *The Stages of Economic Growth: A Non-Communist Manifesto.* New York: Cambridge University Press, 1960.

Rubin, Andrew N. *Archives of Authority: Empire, Culture, and the Cold War.* Princeton: Princeton University Press, 2012.

Şakir, Ziya. *Türkler Karşısında Napolyon.* Istanbul: Anadolu Türk Kitap Deposu, 1943.

Şarman, Kansu. *Türk Promethe'ler: Cumhuriyet'in Öğrencileri Avrupa'da, 1925–1945.* Istanbul: Türkiye İş Bankası, 2005.

Sayarı, Sabri. and Yılmaz, Esmer (eds.). *Politics, Parties and Elections in Turkey.* Boulder: Lynne Rienner Publishers, 2002.

Scott, James C. *Seeing Like a State: How Certain Schemes to Improve the Human Condition Have Failed.* New Haven: Yale University Press, 1998.

Sertoğlu, Midhat. *Resimli Osmanlı Tarihi Ansiklopedisi.* İstanbul: İstanbul Matbaası, 1958.

Shaffer, Marguerite. *See America First: Tourism and National Identity 1880–1940.* Washington: Smithsonian Books, 2001.

Shaw, Wendy M. K. *Ottoman Painting: Reflections of Western Art from The Ottoman Empire to the Turkish Republic.* London: I. B. Tauris, 2011.

Shaw, Stanford and Shaw, Ezel. *History of the Ottoman Empire and Modern Turkey*, Cambridge: Cambridge University Press, 1977.

Shissler, Holly. "Beauty Is Nothing to Be Ashamed Of: Beauty Contests as Tools of Women's Liberation in Early Republican Turkey," *Comparative Studies of South Asia, Africa and the Middle East* Vol. 23. No. 1 (2004), 107–122.

Simpson, Bradley. *Economists With Guns: Authoritarian Development and U.S.-Indonesian Relations, 1960–68.* Palo Alto: Stanford University Press, 2008.

Sofos, Spyros and Özkırımlı, Umut. *Tormented by History: Nationalism in Greece and Turkey.* New York: Columbia University Press, 2008.

Sünnetçioğlu, Kemal. *1939 Nevyork Dünya Sergisi Seyahat Hatıraları.* Istanbul: Güven Basımevi, 1944.

Swartz, Avonna Deanne. "Textbooks and national ideology: A content analysis of the secondary Turkish history textbooks used in the Republic of Turkey since 1929." PhD Dissertation, The University of Texas at Austin, 1997.

Tamkoç, Metin. *Warrior Diplomats: Guardians of the National Security and Modernization of Turkey.* Salt Lake City: University of Utah Press, 1976.

Tanışık, İbrahim Hilmi. *İstanbul Çeşmeleri I.* Istanbul: Maarif Matbaası, 1943.

Tansel, Selahattin. *Osmanlı Kaynaklarına Göre Fatih Sultan Mehmed'in Siyasi ve Askeri Faaliyeti.* Ankara: Türk Tarih Kurumu Basımevi, 1953.

Tansu, Samih Nafiz. *Osmanlı Tarihi Özü.* Istanbul: Nümune Matbaası, 1944.

Taştan, Zeki. "Türk Edebiyatında Tarihî Romanlar," PhD Dissertation, İstanbul Üniversitesi, 2000.

Tarih: *Yeni ve Yakın Zamanlarda Osmanlı – Türk Tarihi* Vol. III. Istanbul: Devlet Matbaası, 1931.

Tekeli, Şirin (ed.), *Women in Modern Turkish Society*. London: Zed Books, 1995.

Toker, Metin. *Demokrat Parti Yokuş Aşağı, 1954–1957*. Ankara: Bilgi, 1990.

Demokrat Partinin Altın Yılları, 1950–1954. Ankara: Bilgi, 1990.

Toprak, Zafer. *Türkiye'de Kadın Özgürlüğü ve Feminizm (1908–1935)*. Istanbul: Tarih Vakfı Yurt Yayınları, 2014.

Trask, Robert R. "The Terrible Turk and Turkish-American Relations in the Interwar Era," *Historian* Vol. XXXIII (November 1970), 40–53.

The United States Response to Turkish Nationalism and Reform, 1914–1939. Minneapolis: University of Minnesota Press, 1971.

Topuzoğlu, Ali. *Halk Adamı Ecevit*. İstanbul: Tok Yayınları, 1975.

Turan, İlter. "Continuity and Change in Turkish Bureaucracy: The Kemalist Period and After," in Jacob Landau, (ed.) *Atatürk and the Modernization of Turkey*. Leiden: EJ Brill, 1984.

Tülbentçi, Feridun Fazıl. *Geçmişte Bugün*. Ankara: Akbaba, 1943.

Türk Büyükleri ve Türk Kahramanları. İstanbul: İnkılap ve Aka Kitabevleri, 1967.

Barbaros Hayrettin Geliyor: Istanbul: İnkılap Kitabevi, 2008.

Tünay, Bekir. *Menderes Devri Anıları*. Istanbul: Nilüfer Matbaası, 1968.

Üngör, Uğur Ümit. *The Making of Modern Turkey*. Oxford: Oxford University Press, 2011.

Uzunçarşılı, İsmail Hakkı. *Osmanlı Tarihi* Vol. 2, Ankara: Türk Tarihi Kurumu.

VanderLippe, John. *The Politics of Turkish Democracy: İsmet İnönü and the Formation of the Multi-Party System, 1938–1950*. Albany, NY: State University of New York Press, 2005.

Waldman, Simon. and Çalışkan, Emre. *The New Turkey and Its Discontents*. Oxford: Oxford University Press, 2017.

Weber, Frank. *The Evasive Neutral: Germany, Britain and the Quest for the Turkish Alliance in the Second World War*. Columbia: University of Missouri Press, 1979.

Weiker, Walter. *The Turkish Revolution 1960–1961*. Washington: Brookings Institution, 1963.

Political Tutelage and Democracy in Turkey: The Free Party and Its Aftermath in Turkey. Leiden: EJ Brill, 1973.

Weisband, Edward. *Turkish Foreign Policy, 1943–1945: Small State Diplomacy and Great Power Politics*. Princeton: Princeton University Press, 1973.

Westad, Odd Arne. *Global Cold War: Third World Interventions and the Making of Our Times*. Cambridge: Cambridge University Press, 2005.

Wilson, Brett. The First Translations of the Qur'an in Modern Turkey (1924–38)," *International Journal of Middle East Studies* Vol. 41, No. 3 (August 2009), 419–435.

Translating the Qur'an in an Age of Nationalism: Print Culture and Modern Islam in Turkey. Oxford: Oxford University Press, 2014.

White, Jenny. *Islamist Mobilization in Turkey: A Study in Vernacular Politics.* Seattle: University of Washington Press, 2002.

Yalman, Ahmet Emin. *Yakın Tarihte Gördüklerim ve Yaşadıklarım.* Istanbul: Yenilik, 1970.

Yaşnar, Ahmet. *Tanrı/Allah Buyrukları ve İnsan Alemi.* Istanbul: İnkılap, 1949.

Yaqub, Salim. *Containing Arab Nationalism: The Eisenhower Doctrine and the Middle East.* Chapel Hill: University of North Carolina Press, 2004.

Yıldız, Murat. "Strengthening Male Bodies and Building Robust Communities: Physical Culture in the Late Ottoman Empire." PhD Dissertation, UCLA, 2015.

Yılmaz, Hale. *Becoming Turkish: Nationalist Reforms and Cultural Negotiations in Early Republican Turkey, 1923–1945.* Syracuse, NY: Syracuse University Press, 2013.

Yosmaoğlu, İpek. "Our Women Treasures: Early Republican Turkish Women and Their Public Identity," in Baki Tezcan and Karl K. Barbir (eds.) *Identity and Identity Formation in the Ottoman World: A Volume of Essays in Honor of Norman Itzkowitz.* Madison: University of Wisconsin Press, 2007, 213.

Ziya and Rahmi. *Girit Sefer.* Istanbul: Askeri Matbaa, 1933.

Ziyaoğlu, Rakım. *İstanbul Albümü.* Istanbul: Milli Eğitim Basımevi, 1952.

Zorlu-Durukan, Şefika Akile. "The Ideological Pillars of Turkish Education: Emergent Kemalism and the Zenith of Single-Party Rule." PhD Dissertation. The University of Wisconsin – Madison, 2006.

Zürcher, Erik Jan. *The Unionist Factor: The Role of the Committee of Union and Progress in the Turkish Nationalist Movement, 1905–1926.* Leiden: EJ Brill, Press, 1984.

Turkey: A Modern History. London: I. B. Tauris, 2005.

Zürcher, Erik Jan and Atabaki, Taraj. *Men of Order: Authoritarian Modernization under Atatürk and Reza Shah.* London: I. B. Tauris, 2003.

Index

Page numbers in *italics* refer to illustrations.

243

9 781108 833240